NUMBER 352

THE ENGLISH
EXPERIENCE

ITS RECORD IN EARLY PRINTED BOOKS
PUBLISHED IN FACSIMILE

SIR DAVID LINDSAY

THE WARKIS OF
SCHIR DAVID LYNDESAY

EDINBURGH 1574

DA CAPO PRESS
THEATRVM ORBIS TERRARVM LTD.
AMSTERDAM 1971 NEW YORK

The publishers acknowledge their gratitude
to the Trustees of the National Library of Scotland
for their permission to reproduce
the Library's copy (Shelfmark: F5. b. 40)

S.T.C. No. 15660
Collation: A^6, B-Z^8, $\mathbf{2}$ ^{6}.

PR
2296
.L6
1574a

Published in 1971 by
Theatrum Orbis Terrarum Ltd.,
O.Z. Voorburgwal 85, Amsterdam

&

Da Capo Press
- a division of Plenum Publishing Corporation -
227 West 17th Street, New York, 10011
Printed in the Netherlands

ISBN 90 221 0352 8

The warkis of the famous and worthie Knicht Schir Dauid Lyndesay of the Mont Alias, Lyoun King of Armes. Newly correctit, and vindicate from the former Errouris quhairwith thay war befoir corruptit: And augmentit with sindry warkis quhilk was not befoir imprentit.

(***)

❡ The Contentis of the Buik, and quhat warkis ar augmentit the nixt syde sall schaw.

Viuet etiam post funera virtus.

❡ I O B V I I.

Militia est vita hominis super terram.

Imprentit at Edinburgh be Thomas Bassandyne, dwelland at the nether Bow.

M. D. LXXIIII.

Cum Priuilegio Regis.

THE CONTENTIS
of the First Buke.

The Contentis of the Secund Buke.

The Contentis of the Thrid Buke.

A ij   Of the

F I N I S.

ANE ADHORTATION

of all Eſtatis, to the reiding of
thir preſent warkis.

✼✼✼

SEn that it is maiſt worthie for to be
Lamentit, of euerie warldlie wicht:
To ſe the warkis of pleſant Poetrie
To ly ſa hid, and ſylit from the ſicht
Of thoſe in hart, quha dois reiois aricht
In Vulgar toung for to behald and heir
Vertew and vice diſcloſit, and brocht to licht.
In thair richt collouris planelie to appeir.

Thairfoir (gude Reider) haue I trauell tane,
Intill ane Volume now breiflie for to bring,
Of Dauid Lyndeſay the haill warkis Ilk ane,
Knicht of the Mont, Lyoun, of Armis King,
Quha in our day is now did laitlie ring.
Quhais pregnant practick, and quhais ornate ſtyle,
To be commendit be me, neidis na thing:
Lat warkis beir witnes, quhilkis he hes done compyle.

Thocht Gawine Dowglas Biſchop of Dunkell
In ornate meter ſurmount did euerilk man:
Thocht Kennedie, and Dunbar bure the bell,
For the large race of Rethorik thay ran.
Zit neuer Poet of our Scottiſche clan,
Sa cleirly ſchew that Monſtour with his markis,
The Romane God, in quhome all gyle began:
As dois gude Dauid Lyndeſay in his warkis.

A iij   Quhair

Ane Adhortatioun

Quhairin na ſtait he ſpairit, bot ſtoutlie ſchew them
How thay baith God and man had ſoir offendit,
VVith fleſchehukis of flatterie he neuer clew thame.
Of quhat degre ſa euer thay diſcendit,
Thair auld miſdeid he prayit thame ay to mend it
Empriour, nor King, Duke, Erle, Prince, nor Paip,
Gif thay to quell Chriſtis Flock zit ſtill pretendit:
Goddis Iuſt Iudgementis na way ſuld thay eſchaip.

VVith prettie Problemis, and Sentences maiſt ſage
VVith pleſant Prouerbis in his warkis all quhair,
VVith ſtaitlie Storyis aggreing to our age,
VVith Similitudis ſemelie he dois declair,
VVith weill waillit wordis, wyſe, and familiar,
Of queynt connoy, this Ioyous Gem Iocound,
Intill his Buikis to ſpeik, he did nocht ſpair,
Aganis all vice, ay quhair it did abound.

Princes approche, cum Rewlaris in ane Randoun:
Reid heir ze Lordis of the meyner menze,
The end of hicht, zour pryde leirne to abandoun,
Cum ſchameles ſchauelingis of Sathanis Senze,
Reynnant in vice, ay ſtill with oppin Renze,
Of proud Prelatis, reid heir the ſuddane fall:
Quha for to ſtoup zit, did neuer Denze,
Vnder the zock of him, that creat all.

Cum teynefull Tyrannis trimilling with zour trayne
Cum nouchtie Newtrallis With zour bailfull band:
Ze haue ane cloik now reddy for the rayne:
For fair wedder, ane vther ay at hand.
Idolateris draw neir to Burgh and Land,
Reid heir zour lyfe at large, baith mair and min,
VVith Hypocrites ay ſlyding as the ſand.
As Humloik how of wit, and Vertew thin.

Oppreſ.

To all Eſtatis.

Oppreſſouris of the pure, cum in till Pairis:
Flatteraris Flok fordwart, for I hard tell,
Ze had ane ſaw richt ſicker for all ſairis.
Lawieris, and Scrybis, quha hes zour Saulis to ſell:
Craftiſmen, and Merchandis, gif ze do mell
VVith fraud or falſet, than I zow deſyre,
Reid in this Buke, the ſpeiche gif ze can ſpell,
Quhat Iuſt reward ze ſall haue for zour hyre.

Amang the reſt, now Courteouris cum hidder,
Thocht ze be ſkeich, and ſkip abone the ſkyis,
Zit conſtantlie I pray zow to conſidder.
In to this Scrow, quhat Lyndeſay to zow cryis,
Cum all degreis, in Lurdanie quha lyis,
And fane wald ſe of ſin the feirfull fyne:
And leirne in Vertew how for to vpryis,
Reid heir this Buke, and ze ſall find it ſyne.

VVith Scripture, and with Storyis Naturall,
Richelie repleniſchit from end till end.
In till this Buke, quha liſt to reid, thay ſall
Find mony Leſſoun largelie to commend
The braid difference, quhairin weill may be kend,
Betwene verteous and vicious leuing.
Lat vs thairfoir our lyfe in Vertew ſpend,
Sen vice of mankynde is the haill miſcheuing.

Lat Lyndeſay now as he war zit on lyif,
Pas furth to licht, with all his ſentence hie:
Vnto all men thair dewtie to deſcryue,
Quhairin they may ane lyueiie Image ſe,
Of his expreſſit mynd in Poetrie,
Prentit, as he it publiſchit with his pen,
That him ſelf ſpeik: I think it beſt for me:
Gif gloir to God, quhilk gaif ſic giftis to men.

THE EPISTIL NVN-
cupatorie of Schir Dauid Lyn-
desay of the Mount Knicht, on his
Dialog of the miserabill Estait
of the warld.
(*⁎*)

How lytil quair, of matter miserabill
VVeill aucht thow, coucrit for to be
with Sabill,
Renunceand Grene, the Purpur, Reid,
and Quhyte,
To Delicate men, thow art not Delectabill:
Nor zit till Amourous folkis Amyabill,
To reid on the, thay will haue na delyte.
VVarldlie Pepill will haue at the dispyte,
Quhilk fixit hes thair hart, and haill Intentis
On sensuall Lust, on Dignitie, and Rentis.

VVe haue na King, the to present allace
Quhilk to this countrie bene ane cairfull cace.
And als our Quene of Scotland Heritour,
Scho dwellis in France, I pray God saue hir Grace,
It war to lang, for the to rin that race.
And far langer, or that zoung tender Flour
Bring haine till ws ane King and Gouernour,
Allace thairfoir, we may with sorrow sing,
Quhilk must sa lang remane without ane King.

I not quhome to thy simpilnes to send,
VVith cunning men, from tyme that thow be kend.
Thy vaniteis na way thay will auance,
Thinkand the proud sic thingis to pretend.
Notwithstanding the straucht way sall thow wend,
To thame quhilk hes the Realme in Gouernance.

Declais

The Epiſtill

Declair thy mynd to thame with circumſtance.
Ga firſt till Iames, our Prince, and Protectour,
And his brother, our Spirituall Gouernour.

And Prince of Preiſtis in his Natioun,
Efter reuerend recommendatioun
Vnder thair feit, thow lawlie the ſubmitt,
And mak thame humbill Supplicatioun,
Gif thay in the find wrang Narratioun,
That thay wald pleis, thy faultis to remitt.
And of thair grace, gif thay do the admitt,
Than ga thy way, quhair euer thow pleiſis beſt.
Be thay content, mak reuerence to the reſt.

To faithfull prudent Paſtouris Spirituall,
To Nobill Erlis, and Lordis Temporall,
Obedientlie till thame thow the addres,
Declairing thame this ſchort Memoriall,
How Mankynd bene to Miſerie maid thrall.
At lenth to thame the caus planelie confes.
Beſeikand thame all Lawis to ſuppres,
Inuentit be Mennis traditioun,
Contrair to Chriſtis Inſtitutioun.

And caus thame cleirlie for till vnderſtand,
That for the breking of the Lordis Command
His thrinfald wand of Flagellatioun,
Hes ſcurgit this pure Realme of Scotland,
Be mortall weiris, baith be ſey and land,
With mony terribill tribulatioun. 2. Reg. 24.
1. Cor. 2.
Thairfoir mak to thame trew Narratioun.
That all thir weiris, this derth, hunger, and peſt,
Was nocht, bot for our Sinnis manifeſt.

Declair

The Epiftill

G:nef.7.
Declair to thame, how in the tyme of Noy,
Alluterlie, God did the warld diftroy,
Genef.19.
As haly Scripture makis mencioun,
Sodom, Gomor, with their Regioun and Roy,
Matth.23
Luc.12.
God fpairit nouther man, Woman, nor boy,
Bot all war brint for their Offenfioun.
Ierufalem, that maift tryumphand Town
Deftroyit was, for thair Iniquitie.
As in the Scripture planelie thay may fe.

Ierem.15.
Declair to thame this mortall Miferie,
Be Sword and Fyre, Derth, Peft, and Pouertie
Proccidis of Sin, gif I can richt defcryue,
For laik of Faith, and for Idolatrie,
For Fornicatioun, and for Adulterie
Of Princes, Prelatis, with mony ane man and wyfe.
Expell the caus, than the effect belyue
Sall ceis quhen that the pepill dois repent,
Than God fall flak the Bow, quhilk zit is bent.

Mak thame requeift, quhilk hes the gouernance,
The finceir word of God for till auance,
Conforme to Chriftis Inftitutioun,
VVithout Hypocrifie or diffimulance,
Caufing Iuftice hald euinlie the Ballance,
On Publicanis, making punitioun.
Commending thame of gude Conditioun.
That being done, I doubt not, bot the Lord
Sall of his countrie haue Mifericord.

Thocht God with mony terribill effrayis,
Hes done this cuntrie fcurge be diuers wayis
Be Iuft Iudgement for our greuous offence,
Declair to thame, thay fall haue merie dayis
Efter this troubill, as the Propheit fayis.

Quhen

Nuncupatorie.

Quhen God fall fe our humbill Repentence,
Till ftrange pepil,thocht he hes geuin licence
To be our fcurge Induring his defyre,
Will quhen he lift,that fcurge caft in the fyre.

Pray thame that thay put not thair efperance
In mortall men, onlie thame till aduance,
Bot principallie in God Omnipotent.
Than neid thay not to charge the Realme of France,
VVith Gunnis,Galayis,nor vther Ordinance
Sa that thay be to God obedient.
In thir premiffis be thay nocht negligent,
Difplayand Chriftis Baner hie on hicht,
Thair enemeis of thame fall haue na micht.

Ga hence pure Buke,quhilk I haue done Indyte
In rurall Ryme, in maner of difpyte,
Contair the warldis Variatioun.
Of Rethorik heir I proclame the quyte.
Idolatouris, I feir, fall with the flyte,
Becaus of thame thow makis Narratioun.
Bot cure thow nocht the Indignatioun
Of Hypocritis, and fals Pharifience,
Howbeit on the thay cry ane loud vengeance

Requeift the Gentill Reidar,that the reidis,
Thocht ornate termes into thy Park not fpreidis,
As thay in the may haue Experience.
Thocht barrane feildis,beiris nocht bot weidis,
Zit brutall beiftis fweitlie on them feidis,
Defyre of thame nane vther Recompence,
Bot that thay wald reid the with Pacience.
And gif thay be in any way offendit,
Declair to them it fall be weill amendit.

FINIS.

The Prolog of the

Miferabill Eſtait of the warld, III.
Betuix Experience, and ane
Courteour.

Uſing and meruelling on the mi-
ſerie,
from day to day in eirth quhilk
dois incres:
And of ilk ſtait the inſtabilitie,
Proceiding of the reſtles beſynes,
Quhairō y moſt part dois thair mynd addres
Inordinatlie, on houngrie Couetyce,
Uane glorie, diſſait, and vther ſenſuall vyce.

Bot tumbling in my bed, I micht not ly,
Quhairfor I fuir furth, in ane May morning
Confort to get of my melancholie
Sum quhat afore freſche Phebus vpryſing,
Quhair I micht heir the birdis ſweitly ſing,
In till ane park I paſt for my pleſure,
Decorit weill, be craft of dame Nature.

How I reſauit confort Naturall,
for till deſcriue at lenth, it war to lang,
Smelling the holſum herbis medicinall,
Quhair on the dulce, & balmy dew doun dang
Lyke Orient Perlis on the twiſtis hang,
Or how that the Aromatik odouris
Did proceid from the tender fragrant flouris.

Or how Phebus that king Etheriall
B   Swyftly

Swyftly sprang vp into the Orient,
Ascending in his throne Imperiall:
Quhose bricht and buriall bemis resplendent,
Illuminat all vnto the Occident:
Confortand euery corporall Creature,
Quhilk formit war,in eirth,be Dame Nature.

Quhose donk impurpurit vestimēt nocturnal
With his embrowderit mantill matutyne:
He left in till his Regioun aurorall,
Quhilk on him waitit, quhen he did declyne,
Towart his Occident palice Vespertyne:
And rose in habite gay and glorious,
Brichter nor gold , or stonis precious.

Bot Cynthia the hornit nichtis Quene,
Scho lost hir licht, and led ane lawer saill:
Frō tyme hir souerane lord that scho had sene,
And in his presence waxit dirk and paill:
And ouer hir visage , kest ane mistie vaill.
So did Venus, the Goddes amorous,
With Juppiter,Mars, and Mercurius.

Richt so the auld Jntoxicat Saturne,
Persauing Phebus , powre his bemis bricht,
Abufe the eirth, than maid he no sudgeourne:
Bot suddandlie did lose his borrowit licht,
Quhilk he durst neuer schaw bot on the nicht
The Pole artick,Ursis,and sterris all,
Quhilk situat ar in the Septentrionall.

Till errand schippis,quhilkis ar wont al gyde
Connoyand thame vpon the stormie nicht:
Within

Within thair frostie circle did thame hyde:
Howbeit that sterris haue none vther licht,
Bot the reflex of Phebus bemis bricht:
That day durst none into the heuin appeir,
Till he had circuite all our Hemispheir.

We thocht it was ane sicht Celestiall,
To sene Phebus so Angellyke ascend,
In till his fyrie Chariot tryumphall·
Quhose bewtie bricht, I could not comprehend,
All warldlie cure did fro me wend.
Quhen fresche Flora spred furth hir tapestrie,
Wrocht be Dame Nature queynt & curiouslie.

Depaint wt mony hundreth heuinlie hewis,
Glaid of the ryfing of thair royall Roy,
With blomes brekand on the tender bewis:
Quhilk did prouoke myne hart to natural ioy
Neptune that day, and Eoll, held thame coy:
That men on far micht heir the birdis sound,
Quhose noyis did to ye sterrie heuin redound.

The plefand powne, prunzeand his federem fair
The mirthfull Maueis maid greit melodie,
The luftie Lark ascending in the air:
Numerand hir naturall notis craftelie,
The gay Goldspink, ye Merll richt merilie:
The noyis of the nobill Nychtingailis,
Redoundit throw ye morainis, meidis & vailis.

Contempling this melodious harmonie,
How euerilk bird, drest thame for till aduance
To salute Nature with thair melodie:

B ij   That I

That I ſtude gaiſing halfingis in ane trance
To ȝeir thame maß that naturall obſeruance
So royallie,that all the Roches rang,
Throuch repercuſſioun of ȝair ſuggurit ſang.

I loſe my tyme , allace for to rehers
Sic vnfrutefull and baine Deſcriptioun
Or wryt in to my raggit rurall Uers
Mater without Edificatioun,
Conſidering how that myne intentioun
Bene till deploze the moztall Miſereis,
With continuall cairfull Calamiteis.

Conſiſting in this wretchit baill of ſorrow:
Bot ſad Sentence,ſuld haue ane ſad Indyte.
So termes bricht, I liſt not for to bozrow,
Of murning mater , men hes no Delyte :
With rouſtie termes thairfoir will I wryte
With ſozrowfull ſichis, aſcēding frō the ſplene
And bitter teiris diſtelling from myne ene.

Without ony bane Inuocatioun
To Minerua , or to Melpomine,
Nor ȝit will I mak Supplicatioun
For help to Cleo , nor Calliope,
Sic marrit Muſis may mak me no ſupple.
Proſerpine I refuſe,and Apollo,
And richt ſo Euterpe, Juppiter and Juno.

Quhilkȝ bene to pleſand Poetis cōfozting:
Quhairfoir , becauſe I am nocht one of tho.
I do deſyze of thame no ſuppozting ,
For I did neuer ſleip on Pernaſo,

                                        As did

As did the Poetis of lang tyme ago,
And speciallie the ornate Ennius,
Nor drank I neuer with Hesiodus.

Of Grece the perfyte Poeit Souerane
Of Helicon the Sons of Eloquence,
Of that mellifluous famous fresche fontane,
Quhairfoir I aw to thame no reuerence:
I purpose nocht to mak Obedience,
To sic mischeant Musis no Mahumetrie,
Afoir tyme vsit in to Poetrie.

Rauand Rhamnusia, Goddes of despyte,
Micht be to me ane Muse richt conuenable:
Gif I desirit sic help for till indyte
This murning mater, mad, and miserable:
I mon go seik ane Muse more confortable,
And sic vane superstitioun to refuse,
Beseikand the greit God to be my Muse.

Be quhose wysedome all maner of thing bene Genes.1.
   wrocht,
The hie heuinnis, with all thair ornamentis:
And without mater maid all thing of nocht,
Hell in myd Center of the Elementis,
That heuinlie Muse, to seik, my haill intent is
The quhilk gaif Sapience to king Salomon Psal.89.
To Dauid grace, stréth to y strang Sampson. Reg.13.

And of pure Peter maid ane prudēt preichour
And be the power of his Deite Matth.4.
Of cruell Paule he maid ane cūning teichour. Act.9.
I mon beseik richt lawlie on my kne

       B iij   His hich

His hich superexcellent Maieste:
That with his heuinlie spreit he me inspyre,
To wryte na thing, contrarie his despre.

Luc. 1.   Beseikand als his souerane Sone Iesu,
Quhilk was consauit of the holy Spreit,
Incarnat of the purifyit Virgin tru:
And in quhome the Prophecy was compleit,
Matt. 27. That Prince of peice, most humill & mansweit:
Luc. 24.   Quhilk vnder Pylate sufferit passioun,
Ioan. 19. Upon the Croce, for our Saluatioun.

And be that cruell deith intolerabill,
Lowsit we war from bandis of Beliall,
And mairatouer, it was so proffitabill:
That to this hour, come neuer man, nor sall,
To the tryumphant Ioy Imperiall:
Heb. 9.   Of lyfe, howbeit that thay war neuer so gude,
Bot be the vertew of that precious blude.

Quhairfoir in steid, of the mont Pernaso,
Swyftlie, I sall go seik my Souerane,
To mot Caluarie, the straucht way mon I go:
To get ane taist of the most fresche Fontane,
That sors to seik, my hart may nocht refrane:
Of Helicon, quhilk wes boith deip and wyde,
Ioan. 19. That Longinus did graue in till his syde.

Fro ye fresche fontane sprag ane famous flude
Quhilk redolent riuer, throw ye warld rinnis,
As chrystall cleir, and mixit bene with blude:
Quhose sound abufe the hiest heuinnis dinnis,
All faithfull pepill, purging from thair sinnis:
                                                 Quhair

Quhairfoir I sall beseik his Excellence,
To grant me Grace, Wisedome , & Eloquence.

And bath me w̃ those dulce & balmy strandis
Quhilk on the Croce, did spedilie out spring,
From his most tender feit , and heuinlie hãdis:
And grãt me grace, to wryte nor dyte no thing
Bot till his hich honour, and loud louing:
but quhose support yair may ua gude be wrocht
Till his plesur, gude workis, word, nor thocht.

Thairfoir, O Lord, I pray thy Maieste,
As thow did schaw thy hich power Deuyne,
First planelie, in the Cane of Galile:
Quhair thow conuertit cald water in wyne,
Conuoy my mater till ane fructuous syne:
And saue my sayingis, baith from schame & sin,
Take tent, for now I purpose to begin.

Ioan. 2.

ANE DIALOG IIII.

Of the miserabill Estait of this
warld : Betuix Experience, and
ane Courteour.

Nto that Park I saw appeir,
One agit mã quhilk drew me neir
Quhose beird wes well thre quar
ter lang,   (hang:
His hair doun ouer his schulders

B iiij.   Quhome

The quhilk as ony ſnaw wes quhyte,
Quhome to behald, I thocht delyte:
His habit Angellyk of hew,
Of colour lyke the Sapheir blew:
Onder ane Holyne he repoſit,
Of quhoſe pꝛeſence I was reioſit.
I did him ſalute reuerentlie,
So did he me, richt courteſlie:
To ſit doun he requeiſtit me,
Onder the ſchaddow of that tre:
To ſaif me from the Sonnes heit,
Amangis the flouris ſoft and ſweit.
Foꝛ I wes weirie foꝛ walking,
Than we began to fall in talking:
C. I ſpeirit his name with reuerence?
E. I am (ſaid he) Experience.
C. Than Schir (ſaid I)ʒe can nocht faill,
To geue ane Deſolate man counſaill:
Ʒe do appeir ane man of fame,
And ſen Experience bene ʒour name:
I pꝛay ʒow Father Wenerabill,
Geue me ſum counſaill confoꝛtabill?
E. Quhat bene(quod he)thy vocatioun
Makand ſic Supplicatioun?
C. I haue (quod I)bene to this hour,
Sen I could ryde ane Courteour:
Bot now Father, I think it beſt,
With your counſaill to leif in reſt:
And from thyne furth to tak myne eiſ
And quyetlie my God to pleiſ,
And renunce Curioſite,

                              Leuing

Leuing the Court, and lerne to de.
Oft haue I sailit ouer the strandis,
And trauellit throuch diuers landis:
Boith South & North, Eist & West,
Zit can I neuer find quhair rest:
Doith mak his habitatioun,
Without zour supportatioun.
Quhen I beleue to be best eisit,
Most suddandlie I am displeisit:
From troubill quhen I fastest fle,
Than find I most aduersite.
Schaw me, I pray zow hartfullie,
How I may leue most plesandlie:
To serue my God, of kingis king:
Sen I am tyrit for trauelling.
And lerne me, for to be content,
Of quyet lyfe, and sober rent:
That I may thank the king of gloze,
As thocht I had ane Millioun moze:
Sen euerilk Court bene variant,
Full of Jnuy, and Jnconstant.
Micht I but troubill leif, in rest,
Now in my age, I think it best.
E. Thow art ane greit fule, Sone (said he,)
Thing to desyze, quhilk may nocht be:
Zarning to haue Prerogatyue,
Aboue all Creature on lyue:
Sen Father Adam creat bene,
Into the Campe of Damascene:
Mycht no man say, vnto this hour,
That euer he fand perfite plesour:

B v   Nor neuer

Nor neuer fall, till that he fe,
God in his Deuyne Maieste:
Quhairfoir prepare the for trauell,
Sen mennis lyfe bene bot battell.
All men begynnis for till De,
The day of thair Natiuite:
And Journellp thay do proceid,
Till Atropos cut the fatail threid.
And in the breue tyme that thay haue,
Betuir thair birth, vnto thair graue:
Thow feis quhat mutabiliteis,
Quhat miferabill Calamiteis:
Quhat troubill, trauell, and Debait,
Seis thow in euery mortall Stait.
Begin at pure law Creatouris,
Afcending fyne to Senatouris:
To greit Princis, and Poteftatis,
Thow fall nocht fynd in none eftatis:
Sen the begynning generallie,
Nor in our tyme, now fpeciallie:
Bot tedious reftles befynes,
But ony maner of fikkernes.
C. Prudent Father (quod I) allace,
Ze tell to me ane cairfull cace:
Ze fay that no man to this hour,
Hes found in eirth perfite plefour:
Without infortunate variance,
Sen we bene thrall to fic mifchance:
Quhy do we fet fo our Intentis,
On Ryches, Dignite, and Rentis:
Sen in the eirth bene no man fure

Iob. 8.

One Day,

One day, but troubill till indure?
And werst of all, quhen we leist wene,
The cruell deith, we mon sustene.
Gif I zour Fatherhede durst demand,
The cause I wald fane vnderstand?
And als Father, I zow imploze,
Schaw me sum troubill gone afoze:
That hering vtheris indigence,
I may the moze haue pacience:
Marrowis in tribulatioun,
Bene wzetchis Consolatioun.
E.(Quod he) efter my small cunnyng,
To the I sall make answeryng:
Bot ozdourlie foz to begin,
This Miserie pzoceidis of Sin:
Bot it war lang, to be defynit,
How all men ar to Sin inclynit:
Quhen Sin aboundantlie doith ring
Iustlie God makith punisching.
Quhairfoir greit God into his handis
To dant the warld, hes diuers wandis:
Efter our euill conditioun,
He makis on vs punitioun:
With Hounger, Deirth, and Indigence,
Sum tyme greit Plaigis, and Peltilence:
And sum tyme with his bludy wand,
Throw cruell Weir, be Sey, and Land:
Concluding all our miserie,
Pzoceidis of Sin alluterlie.
C. Father (quod I) declare to me,
The cause of this Fragillite:

                          That we

That we bene all to Sin inclynd,
In werk,in word,and in our mynd:
I wald the verite war schawin,
Quho hes this seid amang vs sawin:
And quhy we ar condampnit to dede,
And how that we may get remede.
E.(Quod he)the Scripture hes concludit,
Men from felicite wer denudit,
Genes.3. Be Adam our Progenitour,
Umquhyle of Paradyce possessour:
Be quhose most wilfull arrogance,
Wes Mankynd brocht to this mischance:
Quhen he wes Inobedient,
In breking Goddis Commandement:
Rom.5. Be Solistatioun of his Wyfe,
He lost that Heuinlie plesant Lyfe:
Eiting of the forbiddin trie,
Thare began all our Miserie.
So Adam wes cause Radicall,
That we bene fragill Sinnaris all.
Adam brocht in this Natioun,
Sin, Deith,and als Dampnacioun:
Quho will say,he is no Synnar,
Christ sayis,he is ane greit Lear.
Mankynd sprang furth of Adamis loynis,
1.Ioan.1. And tuke of him flesche,blude,and bonis:
And so efter his qualite,
All ar inclynit Synnaris to be.
   But zit, my Sone, dispare thow nocht,
For God, that all the warld hes wrocht:
Hes maid ane Souerane Remede,

                    To saif

To saif vs baith from Sin and Dede,
And from eterne Dampnatioun:
Thairfoir take Consolatioun,
For God, as Scripture doith recorde
Hauing of Man Misericorde,
Send doun his onely Sone Jesu,
Quhilk lichtit in ane Virgin tru,
And cled his hich Diuinitie
With our pure vyle Humanitie,
Syne from our sinnis to conclude,
He wesche vs with his precious blude   Apoc.2.
Howbeit throw Adam we mon de: Rom.5.
Throuch that Lord we sall raisit be,   Hebr. 10
And euerilk man he sall releue,
Quhilk in his blude doith firm beleue
And bring vs all vnto his glore,
The quhilk throw Adam bene forlore
Without that we throw laik of Faith
Of his Godheid incur the wraith:
Bot quho in Christ firmely beleuis,   Ioan.3.
Salbe releuit from all mischeuis.
C. Quhat faith is that, that ʒe call ferme:
Sir gar me vnderstand that terme?
E. Faith without Hope and Cheritie,   Hebr.11.
Auailith nocht, my Sone (said he.)
C. Quhat Cherite bene, that wald I knaw?
E. Quod he, my Sone, that sall I schaw:
First lufe thy God aboue all thing,
And thy Nichtbour : but fenʒeing   1.Cor.13
Do none iniure, nor velanie,
Bot as thow wald war done to the.?   Iac.2.

                        Quick

Quick Faith,but Cheritable werkis,
Can newer be,as wryttis Clerkis:
More than the fyre , in till his micht,
Can be but heit,nor Sunne but licht.
Geue Cheritie into the sailis,
Thy Faith nor Hope , na thing auailis:
The Deuill hes Faith,＆ trimmillis for dreid,
But he wantis hope , and lufe in deid.
Do all the gude,that may be wrocht,
But Cherite,all auailis nocht:
Quhairfoir pray to the Trinite,
For till support thy Cherite.

 Now haue I schawin the , as I can,
How father Adam the first man,
Brocht in the warld,boith Sin ＆ dede,
And how Christ Jesu maid remede:
Quhilk on the day of Judgement,
Sall vs delyuer from torment :
And bring vs to his lesting glore,
Quhilk fall indure for euer more.
But in this warld thow gettis no rest,
I mak it to the manifest:
Thairfoir, my Sone,be diligent,
And lerne for to be pacient:
And into God set all thy trest,
All thing fall than cum for the best.
C.Father I thank zow hartfullie,
Of zour confort and cumpanie:
And heuinlie Consolatioun,
Makand zow Supplicatioun:
Gif I durst put zow to sic pyne,

That

That ʒe wald pleis,foʒ to defyne:
And gar me cleirlie vnderſtand ,
How Adam bʒak the Loʒdis Command:
And how thʒow his tranſgreſſioun,
Wes puniſt his Succeſſioun?
E.My Sone (quod he) wald thow tak cure,
To luke on the Diuyne Scripture:
Into the Buke of Geneſis,　　　　Gene.25
That Hiſtoʒie thair thow ſall nocht mis:
And alſwa ſindʒie cunning Clerkis,
Hes done rehers into thair werkis:
Of Adamis fall, full oʒnatly,
Ane thouſand tymes better noʒ J:
Can wʒyte of that vnhappie man,
Bot J ſall do the beſt J can:
Schoʒtlie to ſchaw that cairfull cace,
With the ſuppoʒt of Goddis grace.

Ane Exclamation to the Redar, V.
Twiching the wrytting of Vulgar,
and Maternall language.
Entill Redar, haue at me none
diſpyte,
Thinkand that J pʒeſumpteouſly
pʒetend, 　　　　(wʒyte:
In vulgar toung ſo hie mater to
Bot quhair J mys, J pʒay the till amend,
Till vnlernit, J wald the cauſe wer kend,
Of our moſt miſerabill trauell and toʒment,
And how in eirth,no place bene permanent,
　　　　　　　　　Howbeit

Howbeit that diuers deuot cūning Clerkis,
In Latyne toung hes written sindrie buikis.
Our vnleirnit knawis lytle of thir werkis:
More than thay do, the rauing of the ruikis:
Quhairfoir to Colȝearis, Carteris, ⁊ to cuikis
To Jok and Thome, my Ryme salbe directit,
With cunning men, howbeit it wilbe lactit.

Thocht euerie cōmoun may not be ane clerk
Nor hes no Leid, except thair toūg maternall:
Quhy suld of God, ẏ maruello⁹ heuinlie werk,
Be hid frō thame, I think it nocht fraternall:
The Father of heuin, quhilk wes, ⁊ is eternall
Exod.20 To Moises gaue the Law, on Mont Sinay,
Nocht into Greik nor Latyne, I heir say.

He wrait the Law, in Tablis hard of stone,
In thair awin vulgare language of Hebrew,
That all the Barnis of Israell euery one
Micht knaw the Law, ⁊ so the same ensew.
Had he done wryt, in Latyne or in Grew,
It had to thame bene bot ane sauirles Jest.
Ze may weill wit, God wrocht all for ẏ best.

Aristotell, nor Plato, I heir sane,
Wrait nocht thair hie Philosophie naturall
In Duche, nor Dence, nor toung Italiane:
Bot in thair most ornate toung Maternall,
Quhose fame and name dois regne perpetuall,
Famous Virgill, the Prince of Poetrie:
Nor Cicero, the flour of Oratrie.

Wrait not in Caldie language, nor in Grew,
Nor

Nor zit into the language Saracene,
Nor in the naturall language of Hebrew:
Bot in the Romane toung, as may be sene,
Quhilk was thair proper láguage, as I wene:
Quhen Romanis rang Dominatoris in deid,
The ornate Latyne, wes thair proper Leid.

In the mein tyme, quhen þ thir bald Romance
Ouer all the warld had the Dominioun,
Maid Latyne sculis, thair gloze for till auance:
That thair language micht be ouer all cōmoun
To that intent, be my Opinioun:
Traisting that thair Impyre suld ay indure,
Bot of Fortune, alway thay wer nocht sure.

Of languagis, the first Diuersitie,
wes maid be Goddis maledictioun,
Quhen Babilon wes beildit in Caldie:
Those beildaris gat none vther afflictioun,
Afore the tyme of that punitioun:
was bot ane toung, quhilk Adam spak him self
Quhare now of toungis, thare bene thre scoze
    and twelf.

Nochtwithstanding, I think it greit plesour,
Quhair cunning men hes languagis anew,
That in thair zouth, be diligent laubour,
Hes leirnit Latyne, Greik, and auld Hebrew,
That I am nocht of that sort, sore I rew:
Quhairfoir I wald all buikis necessare,
For our Faith, wer in till our toung vulgare.

Christ efter his glorious Ascentioun,   Act.2.
        C   Till his

Till his Discipulis send the holy Spreit,
In toungis of fyre, to that intentioun:
Thay beand all of languagis repleit,
Throuch all ẏ warld with wordis fair & sweit:
Till every man the Faith, thay suld furth schaw
In thair awin leid, delyuerand thame ẏ Law.

Thairfoir I think ane greit derisioun,
To heir thir Nunnis, & sisteris, nicht and day,
Singand, and sayand Psalmes and Orisoun:
Nocht vnderstanding quhat thay sing or say,
Bot lyke ane Stirling, or ane Popingay:
Quhilk leirnit ar to speik, be lang vsage,
Thame I compair, to birdis in ane cage.

Richt so Chyldren, and Ladyis of honouris,
Prayis in Latyne, to thame ane vncouch leid,
Mumlād thair matynis, euinsāg & thair houris
Thair Pater noster, Aue, and thair Creid,
It wer als plesand to thair Spreit in deid:
God haue mercy on me, for to say thus,
As to say, Miserere mei Deus.

Sanct Jerome in his proper toung Romane,
The Law of God he trewly did translait,
Out of Hebrew, and Greik in Latyne plane:
Quhilk hes bene hid frō vs lāg tyme, God wait
Unto this tyme, bot efter myne consait:
Had sanct Jerome bene borne in till Argyle,
Into Irische toung his bukis had done cōpyle.

Prudent sanct Paull doith make narratioun,
Cor.14.   Twiching the diuers leid of euery land,
Sayand

Sayand thair bene mair edificatioun:
In fyue wordis that folk doith vnderstand,
Nor to pronunce of wordis ten thousand:
In strãge lãguage,syne wait not quhat it menß
I think sic pattring is not worth twa penis.

Unleirnit pepill on the holy day,
Solemnitlie thay heir the Euangell soung,
Not knawin quhat the preist dois sing nor say:
Bot as ane bell,quhen that thay heir it roung,
Zit wald the preistis in thair mother toung.
Pas to the Pulpite, and that doctrine declare,
Till lawid pepill,it wer mair necessare.

I wald Prelatis and Doctouris of the Law
With vs lawid pepill, wer nocht discontent,
Thocht we in our vulgare toung did knaw:
Of Christ Iesu,the lyfe and Testament,
And how that we suld keip commandement:
Bot in our language, lat vs pray and reid,
Our Pater noster,Aue,and our Creid.

I wald sum Prince,of greit Discretioun,
In vulgar language,planelie gart translait,
The neidfull Lawis,of this Regioun:
Than wald thair not be half so greit debait,
Amang vs pepill of the law Estait:
Gif euery man, the verite did knaw,
We neidit nocht,to treit thir men of Law.

Till do our nychtbour wrãg, we wald be war
Gif we did feir,the Lawis punischement,
Thair wald nocht be, sic brawlyng at the bar:
Nor men

Nor men of Law, lope to sic Royall rent,
To keip the Law, gif all men wer content:
And ilk man do, as he wald be done to,
The Iugis wald get lytle thing ado.

The Propheit Dauid king of Israell,
Compyld the plesand Psalmes of the Psaltair,
In his awin proper toung, as I heir tell:
And Salomon, quhilk wes his Sone & Air,
Did make his buke, in till his toung vulgair:
Quhy suld not thair sayng be till vs schawin,
In our láguage, I wald the cause wer knawin

Lat Doctouris wryte thair curious questions
And argumentis, sawin full of Sophistrie:
Thair Logick, and thair hich Opinions,
Thair dirk Iugementis of Astronomie,
Thair Medecine, and thair Philosophie:
Lat Poetis schaw thair glorious Ingyne,
As euer thay pleis, in Greik, or in Latyne,

Bot lat vs haue the buikis necessare,
To commoun weill and our Saluatioun,
Iustlie translatit in our toung vulgare:
And als I make the Supplicatioun,
O gentill Redar, haue none Indignatioun:
Thinkand I mell me with so hie matair,
Now to my purpose fordwart will I fair.

The Crea-

The Creatioun of Adam and Eue.

VI.

When God had maid the heuinnis bricht,
The Sun, & Mone, foꝛ to gif licht:
The ſterry heuin, and chꝛyſtalline,
And be his Sapience Diuine:
The Planeitis in thair circles round,
Quhirlyng about, with merie ſound:
Of quhome Phebus was pꝛincipall,
Juſt in his lyne Eclipticall.
And gaue be Diuyne Sapience,
Till euery Ster thair Influence:
With motioun continuall,
Quhilk doith indure perpetuall:
And farreſt from the Heuin Empyꝛe,
The Eirth, the Watter, Air, and Fyꝛe.
He cled the Eirth with Herbis and Treis,
All kynd of Fiſchis in the Seis:
All kynd of Beiſt, he did pꝛepair,
With Foulis, fleing in the Air.
Thus be his woꝛd, all thing was wꝛocht,
Without materiall, maid of nocht:
So by his wiſedome infinite,
All was maid pleſand, and perfite.
　Quhen Heuin and Eirth, and thair contentis
Wer endit with thair Oꝛnamentis:
Than laſte of all, the Loꝛd began,

C iij　　　　Of moſte

Of moſt vyle eirth to make the man.
Nocht of the Lillie, noz of the Roſe,
Noz Cyper tre, as I ſuppoſe:
Nother of Gold, noz pzecious ſtonis,
Of eirth he maid Fleſche, Blude, and Bonis.
To that intent, God maid hym thus,
That man ſuld nocht be glozious:
Noz in him ſelf na thing ſuld ſe,
Bot mater of humilite.
Quhen man wes maid, as I haue tauld,

Geneſ. 2.　God in his face, did hym behauld:
Bzeithand in hym ane lyflie Spzeit,
Quhen all thir werkis wer compleit:
He maid man to his ſimilitude,
Pzecelland into pulchzitude.
Dotit with giſtis of Nature,
Abuſe all eirthlie Creature:
Syne pleſandlie, did hym connoy,
To ane Regioun repleit with Joy:
Of all pleſour, quhilk beir the pzyce
And callit eirthlie Paradyce.
And bzocht be Diuyne Pzouidence,
All beiſtis, and birdis till his pzeſence:
Adam did craftelie impone,
Ane ſpeciall name till euery one.
And to all thingis materiall,
He namit thame in ſpeciall:
How he thame namit, zit bene kend,
And ſalbe to the warldis end.
Into that gardyng of pleſance,
Twa treis grew, moſt till auance:

Abuſe all

Abufe all vther , quhilk bair the pryce,
In middis of that Paradyce.
The ane wes callit the tre of lyfe,
The vther tre began our ſtryfe:
The tre to knaw baith gude and euill,
Quhilk be perſwaſioun of the Deuill,
Began our miſerie and wo,
Bot lat vs to our purpoſe go.
How God gaif Adam ſtrait command
That tre to twiche nocht with his hand
All vther fructis of Paradyce,
He bad hym eit at his deuyce.
Sayand, gif thow eit of this tre,
With dowbill deith, than ſall thow de:
Thairfoir I the command be war,
And from this tre, thow ſtand a far.
Zit Father Adam wes allone,
But companie of ony one:
Than thocht the Lord it neceſſar,
Till hym to create ane helpar.
God pat in Adam ſic Sapour,
That for to ſleip, he tuke pleſoure:
And laid hym doun vpon the ground,
And quhen Adam wes ſleipand ſound:
He tuke ane Rib, furth of his ſyde,
Syne fillit vp, with fleſche and hyde.
And maid ane woman of that bone,
Fairar of forme, wes neuer none.
Than till Adam incontinent,
That fair Lady, he did preſent:
Quhilk ſchortlie ſaid, for to conclude,

C iiij   Thow art

Thow art my Flesche, my Bonis, and Blude:
And Uirago, he callit hir than,
Quhilk is interpreit, maid of Man:
Quhilk Eua efterwart was namit,
Quhen for hir falt, scho wes defamit.
Than did the Lord them Sanctifie,
Saying, Incres and multiplie:
Be this, men suld leif all thair kinne,
And with thair wyffis mak dwellinne:
And for thair saik leif Father and Mother
And lufe thame best, abufe all vther:
For God hes ordanit them trewlie,
To be twa Saulis, in one bodie.
    My wit is waik for till indyte,
Thair heuinlie plesouris infinyte:
Wes neuer none eirthlie Creature,
Sen syne had sic perfyte plesure.
Thay had puissance Imperiall,
Abufe all thing materiall:
Als cunnyng Clerkis dois conclude,
Adam precellit in pulchritude:
Most naturall, and the fairest man,
That euer was, sen the warld began:
Except Christ Jesu, Goddis Sone,
To quhome wes no comparisone.
And Eua the fairest Creature,
That euer wes formit be Nature:
Thocht thay war naikit, as thay wer maid,
No schame ather of vther haid.
Quhat plesour mycht ane man haue more,
Nor haue his Lady hym before:

                                So lustie,

So luſtie, pleſand, and perfyte,
Reddy to ſerue his appetyte.
Thay had none vther cure, I wis,
Bot paſt thare tyme, with joy and blis:
Wyld Beiſtis did to thame repair,
So did the Fowlis of the air:
With noyis moſt Angelicall,
Makand thame mirthis Muſicall.
The Fiſchis ſwemand in the ſtrandis,
Wer holelie at thair commandis.
All Creaturis with ane accord,
Obeyit hym, as thair ſouerane Lord:
Thay ſufferit nother heit nor cald,
With euery pleſour that thay wald.
Als to the Deith, they wer nocht thrall,
And richt ſo ſuld we haue bene all:
For he and all his Succeſſouris,
Suld haue poſſedit thoſe pleſouris:
Syne from that Joy materiall,
Gone to the glore Imperiall.
Thay had geue, I can richt deſcryue,
Greit Joy in all their wittis fyue:
In Heiring, Seing, Guſting, Smelling
Induring thair delyteſum dwelling.
Heiring the birdis Harmoneis,
Taiſting the fructis of diuers treis:
Smelling the balmy dulce odouris,
Quhilk did proceid from fragrät flouris.
Seing ſo mony heuinlie hewis,
Of blomes breking on the bewis:
Of twicheing, als thay had delyte,

                    C v   Of vtheris

Of vtheris bodyis soft and quhyte:
But dout , Induring that plesour,
Thay luffit vther Paramour:
Na maruell,thocht swa suld be,
Considering thair greit bewte:
Als God gaif thame command expres,
To multiplie,and till incres
That thair seid,and successioun,
Micht pleneis euery Natioun.

I list nocht tarie,til declair,
All properteis of that place preclair:
How herbis,& treis, grew ay grene,
Nor of the temperat air serene.
How fructis Indeficient,
Ay alyke rype and redolent:
Nor of the Fontane,nor the fludis,
Nor of the flouris pulchritudis.
That mater Clerkis dois declair,
Onhairfoir, I speik of thame na mair:
The Scripture makis no mentioun,
How lang thay rang in that Regioun:
Bot I beleif, the tyme wes schort,
As diuers doctouris dois report.

Of the

Of the miferabill Tranfgref-
fioun of Adam.

VII.

Ather, how happinit ỹ mifchance?
(Quod I) fchaw me the circum-
ftance:
Declare me that cairfull cace,
How Adam loft that plefand place
From him, and his fucceffioun,
How did proceid that tranfgreffioun?
E. (Quod he) efter my rude Ingyne,
I fall rehers the that rewyne:
Quhen God the Plafmatour of all,
Into the Heuin Emperiall:
Did creat all the Angellis bricht,
He maid ane Angell moft of micht.
To quhome he gaif preeminence,
Abufe thame all in Sapience:
Becaufe all vther he did prefer,
Namit he wes bricht Lucifer.
He was fo plefand and fo fair,
He thoucht hym felf without compair:
And grew fo gay, and glorious,
He gan to be prefumpteous.
And thoucht that he wald fet his fait,
Into the North, and mak debait:
Agane the Maiefte Deuyne,

Quhilk

Quhilk wes the cause of his rewyne:
For he incurrit Goddis Ire,
And banyst from the heuin Empire:
With Angellis mony one Legioun,
Quhilkis wer of his opinioun.
Innumerabill with him thair fell,
Sum lichtit in the lawest hell:
Sum in the sey did mak repair,
Sum in the Eirth, sum in the Air,
That most vnhappie Companye,
At Father Adam had Inuye:
Persauing Adam and his seid,
Into their placis to succeid.
Genes. 3 The Serpent wes the subtellest,
Abone all beistis, and craftiest:
Than Sathan with ane fals intent,
Did enter into that serpent:
Imagening sum craftie wyle,
How he micht Adam best begyle:
And gar hym brek Commandement,
Bot to the Woman first he went:
Traisting the better to preuaill,
Full subtellie did hir assaill:
With facund wordis, fals, and fair,
He grew with hir familiar:
That he his purpose micht auance,
Beleuand in hir Inconstance.
Quhat is the cause, Madame (said he)
That ʒe forbeir ʒone plesand tre:
Quhilk bene but peir most precious,
Quhose fruct ben most delycious?

I Ayll

I Nyll (quod sche) thare to accord,
We ar forbidden be the Lord:
The quhilk hes geuin vs lybertie,
Till eit of euery fruct, and trie:
Quhilk growis into Paradyse,
Brek we command, we ar nocht wyse.
He gaue till vs ane strait command,
That tre to twiche nocht with our hand:
Eit we of it, without remeid,
He said but dout, we suld be deid.
Beleif nocht that (said the Serpent,)
Eit ʒe of it incontinent:
Repleit ʒe sall be with Science,
And haue perfyte Intelligence.
Lyke God hym self, of euill and gude,
Than haistelie for to conclude:
Heiring of this Prerogatyue,
Scho pullit doun the fruct belyue:
Throuch counsaill of this fals serpent,
And eit of it, to that intent.
And pat hir husband in beleue,
That plesant fruct gif he wald preue:
That he suld be als Sapient,
As the greit God Omnipotent:
Think ʒe nocht that ane plesand thing
That we lyke God suld euer ring.
He heirand this Narratioun,
And be hir Solistatioun:
Mouit be prydefull ambitioun,
He eit on that conditioun.
The principall poyntis of this offence,

Was pryde

War pryde, and Inobedience:
Desyring for to be equall,
To God, the Creature of all.
Allace Adam, quhy did thow so?
Quhy cansit thow this mortall wo?
Had thow bene constant, ferme & stabill
Thy glore had bene incomparabill.
Quhare wes thy consideratioun,
Quhilk had the dominatioun:
Of euery leuand Creature,
That God had formit be Nature.
Till vse thame, at thy awin deuyse,
Wes thow nocht Prince of Paradyse?
Wes neuer man, sen syne on lyue,
That God gaue sic Prerogatyue:
He gaue the strenth, aboue Sampson,
And sapience mair than Salomon.
Zoung Absolon in his tyme most fair,
To thy bewtie, wes no compair:
Aristotell thow did precell,
Into Philosophie naturell.
Uirgill in till his Poetrie,
Nor Cicero in till Oratrie:
War neuer half so eloquent,
Quhy brak thow Goddis commandement?
Quhare wes thy wit, that wald nocht fle,
Far from the presence of that tre?
Gaue nocht thy Maker the fre will,
To tak the gude, and leif the euill?
How micht thy forfalt be excusit,
That Goddis commandement refusit?

                                        Throuch

Throuch thy wyffis perswasioun,
Quhilk hes ben the occasioun:
Sen syne that mony nobill men,
Be the euill counsale of wemen:
Alluterlie destroyit bene,
As in the histozyis may be sene.
Quhilk now we neid nocht till declair
Bot fozdwart till our purpose fair:
Quhen thay had eittin of the frute,
Of Joy than war thay destitute.
Than gan thay baith foz to think schame,
And to be naikit thocht defame.
And maid thame bzeikis of leuis grene
That thair secreitis suld nocht be sene.
Bot in the stait of Innocence,
Thay had none sic Experience:
Bot quhen thay war to sin subiectit,
To schame and dzeid thay war coactit:
And in ane bus thay hid thame cloce,
Eschamit of the Lozdis voce.
Quhilk callit Adam be his name,
(Quod he)my Lozd,J think greit schame:
Naikit to cum to thy pzesence,
Thow had none sic Experience.
(Quod God)quhen thow wes innocent,
Quhy bzak thow my commandement?
Allace, quod Adam to the Lozd,
The verite J sall recozd:
This woman that thow gaue to me,
Gart me eit of zone plesant tre.
Richt so the woman hir excusit,

                              And said

And said,the Serpent me abusit.
Than to the Serpent , God said thus,
O thow Desauer vennemous:
Because the woman thow begylit,
From thyne furth fall thow be explit.
Curst and varyit fall thow be,
So fall thy seid be efter the:
Cauld eirth fall be thy fude also ,
And creipand on thy breist fall go:
Als J fall put Enemite,
Betuix the woman euer and the.
Betuix thy seid , and womannis seid,
Salbe continuall mortall feid.
Quhowbeit thow hes wrocht thir mischeuis,
It fall nocht be as thow beleuis:
Sic seid salbe in woman sawin,
That thy power salbe doun thrawin:
Tredding thy heid,that thow may feill,
And thow sall tred him on the heill.
This was his promis, and mening,
That the Immaculate Virging:
Suld beir the Prince Omnipotent,
Quhilk suld tred doun that fals Serpent:
Sathan,and all his companie,
And thame confound alluterlie.
C.(Quod J) gif Sathan Prince of Hell,
Spak in the Serpent, as ze tell:
And beistis can no way sinne at all,
Quhy wes the Serpent maid so thrall?
J heir men say,afore that hour,
The Serpent had ane fair figour:

　　　　　　　　　　　　And zeid

And zeid straucht vp vpon his feit,
And had his memberis all compleit:
As vtheris beistis vpon the bent.
E.(Quod he)for he wes Instrument,
To Sathan,in his miserie,
Punist he wes,as ze may sie:
As be Experience thow may knaw,
Expres into the commoun Law:
Ane man conuictit for Bugre,
The beist is brint als weill as he,
Howbeit the beist be Innocent,
And so befell of the Serpent,
It was the Feind full of despyte,
Of Adamis fall quhilk had the wyte:
As he hes had of mony mo,
But till our purpose let vs go.
    Than to the woman , for hir offence,
God did pronunce this sore sentence:
All plesour that thow had a forrow,
Sall changit be,in lesting sorrow.
Quhare that thow suld with mirth **and Joy,**
Haue borne thy birth but pane or noy:
Now all thy bairnis fall thow bair,
With dolour ,and continuall cair:
And thow salbe for oucht thow can,
Euer subiectit to the man.
    Be this sentence God did conclude,
Wemen from lybertie denude:
Quhilk be experience ze may se,
Quhow Quenis of most hie degre,
Ar vnder most subiectioun,

                                D   And

34

And sufferis most correctioun.
For thay lyke birdis in till ane cage,
Ar keipit ay vnder thirlage.
So all wemen in thair degre,
Suld to thair men subiectit be:
Howbeit sum ʒit will stryue for stait,
And for the maistrie mak debait:
Quhilk gif thay want, baith euin & morrow,
Thair men will suffer mekill sorrow.
Of Eue thay tak that qualitie,
To desyre Soueranitie.

And than till Adam said the Lord,
Because that thow hes done accord
Thy will, and harknit to thy wyfe,
Now sall thow lose this plesand lyfe:
Thow was till hir obedient,
Bot thow brak my Commandement.
Cursit and barren the eirth sall be,
Quhare euer thow gois, till that thow de.
But laubour, it sall bere na corne,
Bot Thrissill, Nettill, Breir, and Thorne,
For fude thow gettis none vther beild,
Bot eit the herbis vpon the feild:
Sore laubouring, till thy browis swete,
From thyne furth, sall thow win thy mete.
I maid the of the eirth certane,
And thow in eirth sall turne agane.
Than maid he thame abilʒement,
Of skinnis ane raggit rayment:
Thame to preserue from heit and cauld
Than grew thair dolour mony fauld.

Now

Now Adam ar ʒe lyke till vs,
With ʒour gay garment glorious?
To thame thir wordis,said the Lord,
Than cryit thay baith Misericord,
Quhen from that geirth,with hartis fore,
Banifchit thay wer for euer more,
Into this wretchit baill of forrow ,
With daylie laubour ewin & morrow,
Efter quhofe dolorous departing,
The Lord gaue Paradyfe in keping,
Till ane Angell of Cherubin,
That none fuld haue entres tharein.
At the quhilk entres he did ftand,
With flammand fyrie fword in hand:
To keip that Adam,and his wyfe,
Sulde nocht taift of the tre of lyfe.
For gif thay of that tre had preuit,
Perpetuallie thay micht haue leuit.
So Adam and his fucceffioun,
Of Paradyfe tynt poffeffioun,
And be this fin originall,
War men to miferie maid thrall.
My Sone,now may thow cleirlie ſſe,
This warld began with miferie:
With miferie it doith proceid,
Quhofe fyne fall dolour be and dreid.

C.Father (quod J)quhat kynd of lyfe,
Led Adam with his luftie wyfe,
Efter thair bailfull banifching?

E.(Quod he)continuall womenting:
                        D ij   My

My hart hes ʒit compaſſioun,
How thay went wandʒing vp and doun:
Weiping with mony lowd allace,
That thay had left that pleſand place:
In wildernes to be exyld
Quhare thay fand nocht bot beiſtis wyld:
Manneſſing thame foʒ till Deuoʒe,
Quhilkis all obedient war afoʒe.
C. Father (quod I) in quhat countre,
Did leif Adam, efter that he,
Was baniſchit from that Delyte?
E. Clerkis (quod he) hes put in wʒyte,
How Adam dwelt with mekle baill,
In Mamber, in that luſtie baill:
Quhilk efter wes the Jowis land,

Geneſ. 4

Quhare ʒit his Sepulture dois ſtand.
I liſt nocht tary till Diſcryue,
The wo of Adam noʒ his wyue:
Noʒ tell quhen thay had Sonnis two,
Cayn, and Abell, and na mo.
Noʒ how curſt Cayn, foʒ Jnuy,
Did ſlay his bʒother cruelly:
Noʒ of thair murning, noʒ of thair mone,
Quhen thay but Sonnis wer left allone.
Abell lay ſlane vpon the ground
Curſt Cayn flemit, and vacabound:
Noʒ how God of his ſpeciall grace,
Send thame the thʒid ſone fair of face:
Moſt lyke Adam of fleſche and blude,
Seth, was his name, gracious ⁊ gude.
Noʒ how blind Lameth, rakleſſie,

Did ſlay

Did slay Cayn vnhappelie.
Adam, as Clerkis dois descryue,
Begat with Eue his wofull wyue:
Of Men, Chyldren, threttie and two.
And of Dochteris alyke also.
Be this thow may weill vnderstand,
That Adam saw mony ane thousand:
That of his body did discend,
Or he out of the warld did wend.
Adam leuit in eirth but weir,
Compleit, nyne hundreth & thretty zeir
And all his dayis war bot sorrow,
Remembring baith euin and morrow:
Of Paradyce the prosperitie,
And syne of his greit miserie.
His hart micht neuer be reiosit,
Remembring how the heuin wes clossit
From hym , and his successioun,
And that be his transgressioun.
Efter his deith as I heir tell,
His Saule discendit to the hell:
And thare remanit prisoneir,
In that dungeoun, thre thousand zeir.
And mair, so did baith euill and gude,
Till Christ for thame had sched his blude:
Than be that most precious Ransoun,
Thay wer delyuerit of prisoun.
I haue declarit now, as I can,
The miserie of the first man.

Genes.5.

D iij   How

VIII. ❧ How God deſtroyit all leuand
Creaturis in eirth for Sin, and drownit
thame be ane terribill Flude
in the tyme of Noe.

Rudent Father Experience,
Declare to me, oꝛ ʒe ga hence,
Quhat was the cauſe God did de-
ſtroy,
All Creature in the tyme of Noy?
E. (Quod he) I trimmill foꝛ to tell,
That Infoꝛtune, how it befell:
The cauſe bene ſo abhominabill,
And the mater ſo miſerabill.
Bot foꝛ to ſchaw the circumſtance,
Manifeſtlie of that miſchance:
Firſt I mon gar the vnderſtand,
How Adam gaue expꝛes command,
That thoſe quhilkʒ cum of Sethis blude,
Becauſe thay wer gracious and gude,
Suld nocht contract with Caynis kin
Quhilkʒ wer inclynit all to ſin:
Till obſerue that commandement,
Cayn paſt into the Oꝛient,
With his wyfe, callit Calmana,
Quhilk was his awin Siſter alſwa.
Quhare his offſpꝛing did lang remane,
Beſyde the montane of Tarbane.
And Seth did lang tyme lede his lyfe,

With

With Delbora, his prudent wyfe:
Quhilk was his Sister gude and fair,
In Damascene maid thair repair:
In that countrie of Sethis clan,
Discendit mony holy man,
So lang as Adam was leuand,
The pepill did obserue command,
Quhen he was dede,and laid in ground,
And pepill greitlie did abound:
And Cayn slane,as I haue schawin,
And Sethis dayis all ouer blawin.
The sonnis than of Sethis blude,
Seand the plesand pulchritude,   **Genes.6**
Of the Ladyis of Caynis kin,
Howbeit thay knew weill it wes Sin,
Opprest with sensuall lustis rage,
Did take thame into Mariage.
And so corruptit wes that blude,
The gude with euill,and euil with gude:
Than as the pepill did incres
Thay did abound in wikkitnes:
As holy Scripture dois rehers,
Quhilk I abhor to put in vers,
Or tell with toung, I am nocht abill,
The suthe bene so abhominabill:
How men,and wemen,schamefullie,
Abusit thame selfis vnaturallie,
Quhose foull abhominatioun,
And vncouth fornicatioun,
I think greit schame to put in wryte,
All that Paull Orose doith indyte.

Quhilk gif I wald at lenth declair,
It wer yneuch to fyle the air.
Greit Clerkis of Antiquiteis,
Hes wryttin mony trew storeis:
Quhilkis as worthy to be commendit,
Howbeit thay be nocht comprehendit:
At lenth in the Diuyne Scripture,
Bot I sall do my besie cure:
To tak the best (as I suppose)
That maist perteinis to my purpose.
And with support of Christ our King,
I purpose to confirme na thing:
Of the auld Historicience,
Contrarious till his Excellence.
Howbeit that sum mennis traditionis
Be contrair Christis Institutionis:
Of thame thocht sum thing I declair,
Now lat vs proceid further mair,
And with ane Language lamentabill,
Declair this mater miserabill.
C. Father the causis wald I knaw,
Quhy thay of Nature brak the law?
E. I traist (quod he) that wikkitnes,
Gennerit throw sleuthfull Idilnes.
The Deuill with all the craft he can,
Quhen he persauis ane Idill man:
Or woman geuin till Idilnes,
He gettis esilie entres.
And so by this occasioun,
And be the Feindis perswasioun:
The haill warld vniuersallie,

Corruptit

Corruptit was alluterlie.
C.Quhat wes the cause thay Idill wair:
That care (quod I) to me declair.
E.(Quod he) be my Imaginatioun,
For laik of vertuous Occupatioun.
For of Craftis thay had small vsage,
Of marchandyce,nor lauborage:
The eirth then wes so plenteous,
Of fruct and spyce delicious.
The herbis wer so comfortabill,
Delytesum and medicynabill:
The Fontanis fresche and redolent,
To labouring thay tuke litill tent:
All maner of Beistis at thair plesour,
Did multiplie without laubour.
The tyme betuix Adam and Noy,
To se the eirth,it wes greit Joy:
Plantit with precious treis of pryce,
Four famous fludis of Paradyce,
Ran throuch the eirth in sindrie partis,
Spreiding thair brainchis in all artis.
The watter was so strang and fyne,
Thay wald nocht laubour to mak wyne:
The fruct and herbis wer so gude,
Thay maid na cair for vther fude.
And so the pepill ruke no cure,
Bot past thir tyme at thair plesure:
Ay findand new Inuentionis,
To fulfill thair Intentionis:
So that the Lord Omnipotent,
That he maid man,did hym repent.
　　　　　　　　D v　　　　And

And schew vntill his seruand Noy,
That he wald all the warld destroy:
Except hym self, and his Meinze.

  Allace (quod Noe)quhen sall that be?
Than said the Lord,sen thow so speiris,
I sall prolang sax score of zeiris:
Tarying vpon thair repentance,
Or I fulfill my Just Sentence.
In the meine tyme , sall thow to wark
Incontinent , and beild ane Ark:
Quhilk Noe began obedientlie,
And wrocht on it continuallie:
And to the pepill daylie preicheit,
To cry for grace,he to thame teicheit.
And to thame planelie did declair,
That God his wand na mair wald spair:
Bot on thame , he wald wirk vengence,
To Noe zit gaue thay na credence:
And so thay wer incounsolabill,
Using thair lust abhominabill:
And tuke his preiching in despyte,
Ay following thair foull delyte:
More and more, till that dulefull day,
Quhilk all the warld put in effray,
C.Father ze gart me vnderstand,
Quhen Adam brak the Lordis command:
Till augment his afflictioun,
God gaue his maledictioun,
Unto the eirth, quhilk wes so fair,
That it suld barren be and bair:
And without labour beir na corne,

                    Nor fruct

Nor fruct, bot thrissill, breir, and thorne,
Now say ʒe, in the tyme of Noy,
To se the eirth, it wes greit Joy:
Plantit with fructis gude and fair,
The suthe of this to me declair.
Thir sayingis twa, gar me considder,
How ʒe mak thame agre to gidder.
E. God maid that promis sikkerlie,
Howbeit it come nocht instantlie:
(Quod he) as Clerkis dois conclude,
Bot efter quhen the furious flude,
Distroyit the eirth alluterlie,
Than come that promis sikkerlie.
Euin sic lyke, as God gaue command,
Adam to twiche nocht with his hand:
Nor eit of the forbiddin tre,
Gif he did so, that he suld de.
Howbeit he deid nocht, but weir,
Efter that day, nyne hundreth ʒeir.
Richt so the Propheit Esayas,
Speikand of Christ the greit Messayas: Esa.9.
Sayand the Barne is till vs borne,
To lair mankynd, quhilk is forlorne,
As he had bene borne instantlie,
Ʒit was he nocht borne verilie,
Efter that saying mony one ʒeir,
Ar in the Scripture thow may heir:
Ane thousand ʒeir, quho reknith richt,
Is bot ane hour, in Goddis sicht.   2. Pet. 3.
Exemplis mony, I micht tell,
Wer it nocht tedious for to dwell:

Till our

Till our purpose lat vs proceid,
Schawand the hicht, the lenth & breid:
And qualitie of Noyis Ark,
Quhilk wes ane richt excellent wark.
Of Pyne tre maid, bound weill about,
Laid ouer with pik, within, and out:
Iunit ful cloce, with naillis strang,
And wes thre hundreth Cubitis lang.
Fyftie in breid, thretty in hicht,
Thre Chalmeris iunit weill and wicht:
And euerilk loft abufe ane vther,
Without anker, air or ruther.
Ane richt Cubite, as I heir tell,
Of mesour now micht bene ane ell:
In the mid syde, ane dur thare wes,
For beistis ane esie entres.
This ark quhilk wes baith lang & large,
Maid in the boddum, lyke ane barge:
Couerit with burdis weill abufe,
Most lyke ane house, with set on rufe:
Quhois riggin wes ane cubite braid,
Quharein thare wes ane windo maid.
Sum sayis, weil closit with chrystal cleir
Quhare throw the day licht, micht weill appeir.
This wark the mair was to be prysit,
Because be God it wes deuysit.
The making of this ark but weir,
Genes. 7 Indurit weill ane hundreith zeir.
    Quhen Noe had done compleit this wark,
God did him cloce within the Ark,
With him his wyfe, and Sonnis thre,

                              With

With thair thre wyffis, but mo menʒe.
And of all Foulis of the air,
Of euerilk kynd enterit ane pair.
Richt so twa beiſtis of euerilk kynd,
For quhy, it wes the Lordis mynd:
That genetatioun ſuld nocht faill,
Quhairfoir of Femell, and of Maill.
Of euerilk kynd wer keipit two,
Bot to rehers, myne hart is wo:
The dolent Lamentatioun,
That tyme of euerilk Natioun.
Sayand, allace ane thouſand ſyis,
Quhen wynd, and rane, began to ryis.
The Rokis with reird began to ryue,
Quhen vglie cluddis did ouerdryue:
And dirkynnit ſo, the Heuinnis bricht,
That Sunne nor Mone, micht ſchaw no licht.
The terribill trimling of eirth quaik,
Gart Biggingis bow, and Citeis ſchaik.
The thounder raiſ the cluddis ſabill,
With horribill ſound eſpouentabill.
The fyreflauchtis flew ouerthort the fellis,
Than wes thare nocht, bot ʒowtis and ʒellis.
   Quhen thay perſauit, without remede,
All Creature to ſuffer dede:
All Fontanis from the eirth vpſprang,
And from the heuin the rane doune dang:
Fourtie dayis, and fourtie nichtis,
Than ran the pepill to the hichtis.
Sum clam in craigis, ſum in treis,
And ſum to the hicheſt montanis fleis:

                                    With

With mair terrour, noʒ I can tell,
Bot all foʒ nocht, the Fludis fell:
And wynd did rowt, with sic ane reird
That everilk wicht, warpit his weird.
Cryand allace, that thay wer boʒne,
Into that Flude, to be foʒloʒne.
Men micht na help mak to thair wyiſʒ
Noʒ ʒit suppoʒt thair bairnis lyifis.
The fludis roſe with ſo greit michtis,
That thay ouercouerit all the hichtis:
Thay micht na mair thair lyuis lenth,
Bot ſwame ſo lang as thay had ſtrenth
And ſo with cryis lamentabill,
Endit thair lyuis miſerabill.
Aboue montanis that war moſt hie,
Fyftie Cubitis roſe the ſie.
Men may Imagyne in thair mynd,
All Creature into thair kynd:
Baith beiſtis, and foulis in the air,
In thair maneir, maid mekill cair:
The fiſchis thocht thame euill begyld,
Quhen thay ſwame throuch the woddis wyld.
Quhailis tumland amang the treis,
Wyld beiſtis ſwomand in the ſeis:
Birdis with mony pietuous pew,
Efferitlie in the air thay flew:
So lang as thay had ſtrenth to flee,
Syne ſwatterit doun into the ſee.
Na thing on eirth, wes left on lyue,
Beiſtis noʒ Foulis, Man, noʒ Wyue:
God holelie did thame diſtroy,

Except

Except thame in the Ark with Noy,
The quhilk lay fletand on the flode,
Welterand amang the stremis wode:
With mony terribill effrayis,
Remanit ane hundreth and fiftie dayis:
In greit langour, and heuines,
Or wynd, or rane began to ces.
Sumtyme effectuouslie prayand,
Sumtyme the beistis vesayand:
For be the Lordis commandement,
He maid prouisioun sufficient.
For Noe dwelt in that Ark but dout,   Genef. 8
Ane zeir compleit, or he come out,
How at mair lenth, in holy wryte,
This dulefull historie bene Indyte:
And how that Noe gan to reiose,
Quhen Conductis of the heuin did close:
So that the rane na mair discendit,
Nor the flude na mair ascendit.
Quhen he persauit the heuinnis cleir,
He send furth Corbie messingeir,
Into the air, for to espy,
Gif he saw ony montanis dry.
Sum sayis the Rauin, did furth remane,
And come nocht to the ark agane.
Furth flew the Dow at Noes command,
And quhen scho did persaue dry land:
Of ane Olyue, scho brak ane branche,
That Noe micht knaw the watter stanche,
And thare na mair, scho did siudiorne,
Bot with the branche scho did retorne,

That

That Noe micht cleirlie vnderstand,
That fell own Flude, was decressand:
And so it did, till at the last,
The Ark vpon the ground stak fast:
On the top of ane Montane hie,
Into the land of Armenie.
And quhen that Noe had done espy,
How that the eirth began to dry:
Than dang he doun the durris all,
And loufit thame, the quhilk wes thral
The Foulis flew furth in the air,
And all the beistis pair and pair:
Past furth to seik thair pasturages,
Thare wes than but aucht personages:
Noe, his thre Sonnis, and thair wyuis,
On eirth, that left was with thair lyuis:

Genef. 9 Quhome God did blis, and sanctifie,
Sayand incres, and multiplie.
God, wat gif Noe was blyith and glaid,
Quhen of that presone he wes fraid.

Quhen Noe had maid his Sacrifice,
Thankand God of his Benefice:
He standing on mont Armenie,
Quhare he the countrie micht espie.
Ze may beleue his hart was sore,
Seing the eirth, quhilk wes afore
The fiude, so plesand and perfyte,
Quhilk to behald, wes greit delyte:
That now was barren maid and bair,
Afore quhilk fructuous was and fair.
The plesand treis beiring fructis,

hoe:

wer lyand rewin vp be the ruitis:
The holfum herbis and fragrant flouris,
Had tynt baith vertew and colouris:
The feildis grene,and flurift meidis,
wer fpulʒeit of thair plefand weidis.
The eirth quhilk firft wes fo fair fonnit,
wes be that furious flude defozmit:
Quhare vmquhyle wer,the plefand planis,
wer holkit Glennis, and hie montanis:
From clattring craigis,greit and gray,
The eirth was wefchin quyte away.
  Bot Noe had greiteft difplefuris,
Behaldand the dede Creaturis:
Quhilk wes ane ficht richt lamentabill,
Men,wemen,beiftis innumerabill:
Seyng thame ly vpon the landis,
And fum wer fleiting on the ftrandis:
Quhaillis, and monftouris of the feis,
Stickit on ftobbis amang the treis.
And quhen the flude was decreffand,
Thay wer left weltering on the land.
Afoze the flude,during that fpace,
The Sey wes all into ane place.
Richt fo the eirth, as bene decydit,
In fyndzie partis was nocht deuydit:
As bene Europe,and Afia,
Deuydit ar from Africa.
Ze fe now diuers famous Ilis,
Stand from the mene land mony mylis.
All thir greit Ilis,I vnderftand,
wer than equall with the ferme land.
                              E   Thare

Thare was none sey Mediterrane,
Bot onely the greit Occeane:
Quhilk did not spreid sic bullering strandis,
As it dois now ouerthort the landis.
Than by the raiging of that Flude,
The eirth of vertew wes denude:
The quhilk afore was to be prysit,
Quhose bewtie than war disagysit.
Than was the maledictioun knawin,
Quhilk was be God till Adam schawin.
J reid how clerkis dois conclude,
Induring that most furious Flude:
With quhilk the eirth was so supprest,
The wynd blew furth of the southwest
As may be sene be Experience,
How throw the watteris violence,
The hich montanis in euery art,
Ar bair, forgane the Southwest part:
As the montanis of Pyrenis,
The Alpes and Rochis in the seis:
Richt so the Rochis greit and gray,
Quhilk standis into Norroway.
The hicheft hillis in euery art,
And in Scotland, for the most part:
Throuch weltering of that furious Flude,
The craigis of eirth war maid denude.
Trauelling men, may considder best,
The montanis bair, nyrt the Southwest.
C. Declare (quod J) or ze conclude,
How lang leuit Noe efter the Flude.
E. (Quod he) in Genesis thow may here,

                                    How

How that Noe was fex hundreth zere,
The tyme of his greit punifchement,
And ay to God obedient:
And was the beft of Sethis blude,
And als he leuit efter the Flude,
Thre hundreth and fyftie zeiris,
As the Sampu Scripture witnes beiris.
And was,or he randerit the fpreit,
Nyne hundreth and fyftie zeiris compleit.
To fchaw this hiftorie miferabill,
At lenth,my wittis ar nocht abill:
And als my Sone(as I fuppofe)
It langis nocht till our purpofe:
To fchaw how Noeis fonnis thrie,
Gan to incres and multiplie.
Nor how that Noe plantit the wyne,
And drank till he was drounkin fyne:
And fleipit with his membris bair,
And how Cham, maid for him na cair,
Bot leuch to fe his Father fo,
Howbeit his brether war richt wo.
Nor how Noe,but reftrictioun,
Gaue Cham his maledictioun:
And put hym vnder feruitude,
To Sem and Japhet that war gude.
Nor how God maid ane conuenent,
With Noe,to mak na punifchement:
Nor be na Flude the pepill droun,
In figne of that conditioun,
His Rane Bow fet into the air,
Of diuers heuinlie colouris fair:

Genef. 9

C ij   For to

Foz to be ane perpetuall sing,
Be Flude to mak na punissing:
This histozie,gif thow list to knaw,
At lenth the Bibill sall the schaw.

¶The secund Buke:

Contening the building of Babilon
be Nimrod . And how King Ninus began
the First Monarchie of thair Idolatrie.
And how Semiramis gouernit the
Impyre efter hir husband
King Ninus.

I.

Ather J pzay zow, to me tell,
The first Infoztune that befell,
Jmmediatlie etter the Flude,
And quha did first sched saikles
    blude:
And how Jdolatrie began?
E.(Quod he) J sall do as J can:
Efter the Flude, J find na histozie,
Woztby to put in memozie:

Genes.9   Till Nimrod began to ring,
Abufe the yepill, as ane king:
Quhilk wes the pzincipall man of oue,
That beildar wes of Babilone.

                        C.Tha

C.That hiſtorie Maiſter wald I knaw,
(Quod I) gif ʒe the ſuthe wald ſchaw:
Quhy, and for quhat occaſioun,
Thay beildit ſic ane ſtrang Dungeoun?
E.Than ſaid to me Experience,
I ſall declare with diligence,
Thoſe queſtionis at thy command,
Bot firſt Sone,thow mon vnderſtand
Of Nimrod,the Genealogie,
His ſtrenth,curage,and quantitie:
Howbeit Moyſes in his firſt buke,
That hiſtorie lichtlie did ouer luke,
Of hym na mair he doith declare,
Except he was ane ſtrang Huntare:
Bot vtheris Clerkis curious
As Oroſe doith,and Joſephus:
Diſcryuis Nimrod at mair lenth,
Baith of his ſtature,and his ſtrenth.
This Nimrod was the fourt perſoun,
From Noe be lyne diſcending doun.
Noe generit Cham,Cham generit Chus,
And Chus Nimrod,the ſuthe bene thus.
This Nimrod grew ane man of micht,
That tyme in eirth,wes none ſo wicht:
He wes ane Gyand ſtout and ſtrang,
Perforce wyld beiſtis he doun thrang:
The pepill of that haill Regioun,
Come vnder his Dominioun.
Na man thair wes in all that land,
His ſtalwartnes that durſt ganeſtand.
Na maruell wes thocht he wes wicht

　　　　　　　　E iii　　　Ten

Ten cubitis large, he wes of wicht.
Proportionat in lenth and breid,
Efferand to his hicht we reid.
He grew so greit and glorious,
So prydefull and presumptuous:
That he come Inobedient,
To the greit God Omnipotent,
This Nimrod was the principall man
That first Idolatrie began.

    Than gart he all the pepill call,
To his presence baith greit and small:
And in that greit Conuentioun,
Did propone his Intentioun.
My freindis (said he) I mak it knawin,
The greit vengeance that God hes schawin,
In tyme of our fore Father Noy,
Quhen he did all the warld destroy.
And drownd thame in ane furious Flude,
Quharefore, I think we suld conclude:
How we may mak ane strang Defence,
Aganis sic watteris violence.
For to resist his Furious Ire,
Contrair baith to Flude and Fyre.
Lat vs ga spy sum plesand feild,
Quhare ane strang bigging we may beild,
Ane Cietie, with ane strang Dungeoun,
That none Ingyne may ding it doun.
So hich, so thick so large and lang,
That God till vs sall do na wrang:
It sall surmont the Planetis seuin,
That we from God may win the heuin.

Genes.11 (margin note beside "And in that greit Conuentioun")

Genes.11

                                      Those

Thoſe pepill with ane ferme intent,
All till his counſell did conſent:
And did eſpy ane pleſand plais,
Hard on the Flude of Euphrates.
The pepill thare did thame repair,
Into the plane feild of Sincar:
Quhilk now of Chaldie beiris the name,
Quhilk did lang tyme flureis in fame.
    Thair greit Fortres than did thay found,
And kaiſt till thay gat ſouer ground.
All fell to work, baith man and chyld,
Sum holkit clay, ſum brint the tyld,
Nimrod, that curious Campioun,
Deuyſar wes of that Dungeoun.
Na thing thay ſpairit thair laubouris,
Lyke beſie beis vpon the flouris:
Or Emmettis trauelling into June,
Sum vnder wrocht, and ſum abune:
With ſtrang Ingenious Maſonerie,
Upwart thair work did fortifie,
With brynt tyld, ſtonis, large & wicht,
That Toure thay raiſit to ſic hicht,
Abufe the airis Regioun,
And Junit of ſo ſtrang faſſioun:
With Syment maid of pik and ter,
Thay vſit nane vther morter.
Thocht fyre or watter it aſſailit,
Contrair that Dungeoun nocht auailit.
The land about was fair and plane,
And it rais lyke ane hich montane:
Thoſe fuliſche pepill did intend,

E iiij   That

That to the heuin it suld ascend:
So greit ane strenth wes neuer sene,
Into the warld with mennis ene.
The wallis of that wark thay maid,
Twa and fystie faldome braid:
Ane faldome than, as some men sayis,
Micht bene twa faldome in our dayis
Ane man wes than of mair stature,
Nor twa be now, thareof be sure.

　Josephus haldis opitioun,
Sayand the hicht of this Dungeoun. ,
Of large pasis of mesure bene,
Fyue thousand, aucht score & fourtene.
Be this rakning, it is full richt,
Fyue mylis, and ane half in hicht:
Ane thousand pais, tak for ane myle,
And thow sall find it neir that style:
This toure in compas round about,
Wer mylis ten, withouttin dout:
About the Cetie of Staidis,
Foure hundreth, & four score I wis:
And be this noumer in coumpas,
About thre score of mylis it was.
And as Orosius reportis,
Thare wes fyue score of brasin portis.

　The Translatour of Orosius
In till his Cronicle wryttis thus,
That quhen the Sunne is at the hicht
At none, quhen it dois schyne maist bricht:
The schaddow of that hiduous strenth,
Sex myle, and mair, it is of lenth.

Thus

Thus may ʒe Judge into ʒour thocht,
Gif Babilon be hich or nocht.

How God maid the diuersitie II.
of Languagis, and maid impediment to
the Buildaris of Babilon.

Han the greit God Omnipotent,
To quhome all thingis bene preſét
That wes, and is, and euer ſalbe,
At preſent till his Maieſte:
The hid ſecretis of mannis hart,
From his preſence may nocht depart:
He ſeand the ambitioun,
And the prydefull preſumptioun:
How thir proude pepill did pretend,
Up throuch the heuinnis till aſcend:
Quhilk wes greit folie till deuyſe,
Sic ane preſumptuous interpryſe:
For quhen thay wer moſt diligent,
God maid thame ſic impediment:
Thay wer conſtraynit with hartis ſore
From thyne Departe and beild no more.
Sic Languagis on thame he laid,
That none wiſt quhat ane vther ſaid.
Quhare wes bot ane language afore,
God ſend thame languagis thre ſcore.
At that tyme all ſpak Hebrew,
Than ſum began for to ſpeik Grew:

Sum

Sum Dutche, sum language Sarasyne,
And sum began to speik Latyne.
The Maister men, gan to ga wylde,
Cryand for treis, thay brocht thame tyld:
Sum said bring mortar heir atanis,
Than brocht thay to thame stokis and stanis.

And Nimrod thair greit Campioun,
Ran rageand lyke ane wyld Lyoun,
Manassing thame with wordis rude:
Bot neuer ane worde thay vnderstude.
Afore thay fand hym gude and kynd,
But than thay thocht hym by his mynd.
Quhen he so furiouslie did flyte,
Than turnit his pryde into despyte.
So dirk Eclipsit wes his gloze,
Quhen thay wald wirk for him no more.

Behald how God wes so gracious,
To thame quhilk wer so outragious:
He nather braik thair leggis nor armis,
Nor zit did thame none vther harmis:
Except of toungis diuisioun,
And for fynall conclusioun,
Constraynit thay wer for till depart,
Ilk cumpanie in ane syndrie art.
Sum past into the Orient,
And sum into the Occident.
Sum South, sum North, as thay thocht best,
And so thair policie left waist.
Bot how that cietie was repairit,
Heir efter it salbe declairit.

Of the

Of the first Inuentioun of Ido- III.
latrie. How Nimrod compellit the Pepill
till adorne the Fyre in Chaldea.

NOw Schir (said I) schaw me the
man,
Quhilk first Idolatrie began?
E. That sall I do, with all my hart
My Sone (said he) or we depart.
Quhen Nimrod saw his purpose failit,
And his greit laubour nocht auailit:
In maner of contemptioun,
Departit furth of that regioun.
And as Orosius doith reherse,
He past into the land of Perse:
And mony ane zeir did thare remane,
And syne to Babilon came agane,
And fand huge pepill of Chaldie,
Remanand in that greit citie,
That wer glaid of his returning,
And did obey him as thair King.
Nimrod, his name for till auance,
Amang thame maid new ordinance:
Sayand I think ze ar nocht wyse,
That to none God makis sacrifyce.
Than to fulfill his fals desyre,
He gart be maid ane flammand fyre,
And maid it of sic breid and hicht,

He gart

He gart it birn, baith day and nicht,
Than all the pepill of that land,
Adorit the fyre, at his command,
Prosternit on kneis and facis,
Beseikand thair new God of gracis,
To geue thame mair occasioun,
He maid thame greit perswasioun.
This God (said he) is maist of micht,
Schawand his bemis on the nicht:
Quhen Sunne and Mone ar baith obscure,
His heuinlie brichtnes dois indure.
Quhen mennis memberis sufferis cald,
Fyre warmis thame euin as thay wald.
Than cryit the pepill at his desyre,
Thare is na God except the fyre.
Or thare was ony Imagerie.
Began this first Idolatrie.
At that tyme thair was none viage,
To carue, nor for to paynt Image.
Than maid he Proclamatioun,
Quho maid nocht adoratioun,
To that new God, without remede,
Into that fyre suld suffer dede.
I find na man into that land,
His tyrannie that durst ganestand,
Bot Abraham and Aram his brother,
That disobeyit, I find none vther:
Quhilk Dwelland war in that cuntrie
With thair father callit Tharie
Thir brether Nimrod did repreue,
Sayand till him, Lord with your leue

This

This fyre is bot ane Element,
Pray ʒe to God Omnipotent:
Quhilk maid the Heuinnis be his micht,
Sunne, Mone, and Sterris, to geue licht.
He maid the Fischis in the Seis,
The Eirth, with Beistis, Herbis, and Treis:
And last of all, for to conclude,
He maid man to his similitude.
To that greit God geue pryse and gloze,
Quhose Ring induris euermoze.

Than Nimrod in his furious Ire,
Thir brether baith kest in the fyre:
Abraham be God he wes preseruit,
Bot Aram in the fyre he steruit.
Quhen Thare hard his sone wes dede
He did depart out of that stede,
With Abraham, Nachor & thair wyuis
As the Scripture at lenth descryuis:
And left the land of Chaldea,
And past to Mesopotamia:
And dwelt in Tharan all his dayis,
And deid thare, as the story sayis.
The lyfe of Abraham I suppose,
Na thing langis till our purpose.
Into the Bybill thow may reid,
His verteous lyfe, in word and deid.
Now to the, I haue schawin the man,
That first Idolatrie began.

Of the

IIII. Of the grețt Miſerie, and Skaithis
that cummis of Weiris: And how king
Ninus began the Firſt weiris,
and ſtraik the Firſt
battell.

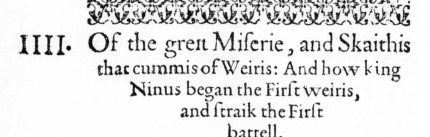

Ather I pray ʒow, with my hart,
Declare to me oʒ we depart;
Quha firſt began thir moʒtal weirƷ
QuhilƷ euerilƷ faithful hart effeirƷ
And euery policie doun thʒawiƷ.
ErpʒeƷ aganis the LoʒdiƷ lawis?
Sen Chʒiſt our king Omnipotent,
Left pece in till his Teſtament,
How dois pʒoceid this crueltie,
Aganis Juſtice and Equitie?
In land quhair ony weiris bene,
Greit Miſerie thair may be ſene.
Al thing on eirth, that God hes wʒocht
Weir, dois diſtroy, and puttis at nocht
Citeis, with mony ſtrang doungeoun,
Ar bʒint, and to the sirth doung doun:
Uirginis and matronis ar deſtoʒit,
Templis, that rychelie bene decoʒit,
Ar bʒint, and all thair PʒeiſtiƷ ſpulʒeit

Purt

Þure Orphelenis vnder feit ar fulȝeit.
Mony auld men maid Childerles,
And mony Childer Fatherles:
Of famous Sculis the Doctryne,
Baith Naturall Science and Deuyne,
And euery vertew trampit doun,
Na reuerence done to Religioun.
Strenthis destroyit alluterlie,
Fair Ladyis forsit schamefullie.
Ȝoung wedowis spulȝeit of thair spousis,
Pure lauboraris houndit from thair housis,
Thare dar na marchant tak on hand,
To trauell nother be sey nor land:
For boucheouris quhilk dois thame confound,
Sum murdreist bene, and sum ar dround.
Craftismen of Curious Jngyne,
Alluterlie put to rewyne.
The Bestiall reft, the Commonis slane.
The land but laubouring dois remane.
Of Policie the perfyte warkis,
Beildingis, Gardingis, plesand parkis:
Alluterlie distroyit bene,
Greit graingis brynt, thare may be sene.
Ryches bene turnit to pouertie,
Plentie in till penuritie:
Deith, Hounger, Deirth, it is weil kend,
Of weir, this is the fatall end.
Justice turnit in tyrannie,
Jll plesour in aduersitie.
The weir alluterlie doun thrawis.
Baith the Ciuill, and Cannoun lawis,

weir

Weir generis murthour and mifcheif,
Soze lamenting without releif.
Weir doith diftroy Realmes & kingis,
Greit Princis weir to prefoun bzingis.
Weir, fcheddis mekill faikles blude:
Sen I can fay of Weir na gude.
C. Declare to me, Schir, gif ʒe can,
Quha firft this miferie began.

V.   ⟡ Ane fchort Defcriptioun of the
Foure Monarcheis. And how King Ninus
began the Firft Monarchie.

F Weiris (faid he) ẏ greit outrage
Began into the fecund age:
Be cruel, prydeful, couetous kingſ
Reuaris but richt of vtheris ringſ.
Howbeit Cayn, afoze the Flude,
Wes firft fchedder of faikles blude.
Ninus wes firft, & principall man,
Quhilk wzangous conqueffing began:
And was the man withouttin faill,
In eirth, that ftraik the firft battaill:
And firft inuentit Imagerie,
Quhare throuch came greit Idolatrie.
We moſt knaw, oz we further wend,
Of quhome king Ninus did difcend.
Ninus, gif I can richt defyne,
He was from Noe the fyft be lyne.

                                       Noe ge

Noe generit Cham, Cham generit Chus,
And Chus Nimrod, Nimrod Belus:
And Belus Ninus but lesing,
Of Assyria the secund king.
And beildar of that greit Cite,
The quhilk was callit Ninive:
And was the first and principall man,
Quhilk the first Monarchie began.
C. Father (quod I) declare to me,
Quhat signifyis ane Monarchie?
E. The suith (said he) Sone, gif thow knew,
Monarchie bene ane terme of Grew:
As quhen ane Prouince principall,
Had haill power Imperiall:
During thair dominationis,
Abufe all kingis and Nationis,
Ane Monarchie that men dois call,
Of quhome I find four principall:
Quhilk hes roung sen the warld began.
C. Than (said I) Father, gif ʒe can,
Quhilk four bene thay, schaw me, I pray ʒow.
E. My Sone (said he) that sall I say ʒow:
First rang the kingis of Assyrianis:
Secundlie rang the Persianis.
The Greikis thridlie, with swerd and fyre,
Perforce obteinit the thrid Impyre,
The fourt Monarchie, as I here,
The Romanis brukit mony ane ʒere.
Lat vs first speik of Ninus king,
How he began his conquessing.
℧ The auld Greik Historiciane,

f   Diodorus

Diodozus he wzyttis plane,
At richt greit lenth of Ninus king,
Of his Impyze and Conquessing,
And of Semiramis his wyfe,
That tyme the lustiest on lyfe:
It wer to lang to put in wzyte,
Quhilk Diodoze hes done indyte.
Bot I sall schaw, as I suppose,
Quhilk maist belangis thy purpose.
Quhen Nimrod, Prince of Babilone,
Out of this wzetchit warld was gone
And his sone Belus did alswa,
The first king of Assyria,
This Ninus, quhilk was secund king,
Tryumphantlie began to ring,
And wes nocht satisfyit, noz content,
Of his awin Regioun, noz his rent:
Thinkand his gloze foz till aduance,
Be his greit pepill and puissance:
Throuch pzyde, couetyce, & vane gloze,
Did him pzepare to conqueis moze:
And gatherit furth ane greit armie,
Contrair Babilon and Chaldie:
Quhare of he had ardent desyze,
Till iune that land till his Impyze.
Howbeit he had thareto na richt,
Bot be his tyrannie and micht:
Withouttin feir of God oz man,
His conquessing thus he began.
    ¶His pepill beand in array,
To Chaldea tuke the reddy way:

                                        Quhen

Quhen that the Babilonianis,
To gether with the Chaldianis:
Hard tell king Ninus wes cummand,
Maid proclamation throuch the land:
That ilk man efter thair degre,
Suld cum, & saif thair awin countre.
Howbeit thay had na vse of weir,
Thay past fordwart withouttin feir:
And put thame selfis in gude ordour.
To meit king Ninus on the bordour,
In that tyme, ze sall vnderstand,
Thare wes na harnes in the land,
For till defend, nor till inuaid,
Quhare throw mair slauchter thair wes maid.
Thay faucht throw strenth of thair bodeis,
With gaddis of Irne, with stonis and treis.
With sound of horne, and hidduous cly,
Thay ruschit to gether richt rudely:
With hardy hart, and strenth of handis.
Till thousandis deid lay on the landis.
Quhare men in battell naikit bene,
Greit slauchter sone thare may be sene,
Thay faucht so lang, and cruellie,
And with vncertain victorie.
Na man micht iudge, that stude on far
Quha gat the better nor the war.
Bot quhen it did approche the nicht,
The Chaldeanis thay tuke the flicht:
Than the king and his companie,
Wer richt glaid of that victorie,
Because he wan the first battell,

F ij   That

That strikkin was in eirth but faill:
And peceable of that Regioun,
Did take the haill dominioun.
Than wes the king of Chaldea,
Alsweill as of Assyria:
As for the king of Arabie,
In his conquest maid him supplie.

Of this zit wes he nocht content,
Bot to the realme of Mede he went:
Quhare Farnus king of that countrie,
Did mete him with ane greit armie:
Bot king Ninus the battell wan,
Quhare slane wer mony nobill man:
And to that king wald geue na grace,
Bot planelie in ane publict place,
With his seuin sonnis & his Ladie,
Cruelie did thame crucifie.
Of that tryumphe he did reiois,
Syne fordwart to the feild he gois.
Than conqueist he Armenia,
Perse, Egypt, and Pemphylia,
Cappadoce, Lide, and Mauritane,
Caspia, Phrigia, and Hyrcane,
All Africa and Asia,
Except greit Inde, and Bactria.
Quhilk he did conques efterwart,
As ze sall heir or we depart.
Now wald I or we further wend,
That his Idolatrie war kend.
Syne efter that without sudiorne,
Till our purpose we sall retorne.

How

How King Ninus inuentit the　VI.
firſt Idolatrie of Imagis.

Ninus ane Image he gart maſk,
For king Belus his Fatheris ſaik:
Maiſt lyke his father of figour,
Of quantitie and portraitour.
Of fyne gold was ẙ figour maid:
Ane craftie Croun vpon his haid,
with precious ſtonis in tokning,
His father Belus was ane king,
In Babilon he ane tempill maid,
Of craftie work baith hich and braid:
Quharein that Image gloriouſlie,
wes thronit vp trymphantlie.
Than Ninus gaif ane ſtrait command
Till all the pepill of that land:
Aſweill in till Aſſyria,
As in Sinear and Chaldia,
Under his Dominatioun,
Thay ſulde make adoratioun,
Apon thair kneis to that figour,
Under the pain of forfaltour.
Thare was na Lord in al that land,
His ſummonding that durſt ganeſtand,
Than zoung and auld, baith greit and ſmall,
Till that Image thay prayit all:
And changit his name, as I here tell,

From Belus, to thair greit God Bell,
In that tempill he did deuyse,
Preistis for till make Sacrifyce.
Be consuetude, than came ane law,
None vther God that thay wald knaw:
And als he gaif to that Image,
Of Sanctuarie the Priuilege,
For quhat sum euer transgressour,
Ane Homicide, or Oppressour,
Seand that Image in the face,
Of thair gilt gat the kingis grace.
C. Declare to me sweit Sir (said I)
Was thare na mair Idolatry?
Efter that this fals Idole Bell,
Wes thronit vp, as ze me tell.
E. My Sone (said he) incontinent,
The nouellis throuch the warld thay went:
How king Ninus, as I haue said,
Ane curious Image he had maid:
To the quhilk all his Natioun,
Maid deuote adoratioun.
Than euery Countrie tuke consait,
Thay wald king Ninus conterfait:
Quhen ony famous man was deid,
Set vp ane Image in his steid,
Quhilk thay did honour from the splene,
As it immortall God had bene:
Imagis sum maid for the nanis,
Of fyne gold, sum of stokis and stanis:
Of siluer sum, and Euer bane,
With diuers names till euery ane.

F oz

For sum thay callit Saturnus,
Sum Iuppiter, sum Neptunus,
And sum thay callit Cupido,
Thair God of lufe, and sum Pluto.
Thay callit sum Mercurius,
And sum the wyndie Eolus:
Sum Mars maid lyke ane man of weir,
Enarmit weill with sworde and speir.
Sum Bacchus, and sum Apollo,
Of names thay had ane hundreth mo.
℃ Quhen ane Lady of greit fame,
wes deid, for till exalt hir name,
Ane Image of hir portratour,
wald set vp in ane Oratour:
The quhilk thay callit thair goddes,
As Uenus, Juno, and Pallas.
Sum Cleo, sum Proserpina,
Sum Ceres, Uesta, and Diana:
And sum the greit goddes Minerue,
With curious colouris thay wald carue.
Amang the Poetis, thou may sie,
Of fals goddis the genealogie.
℃ So thir abhominationis,
Did spreid ouerthort all Nationis:
Except gude Abraham, as we reid,
Quhilk honourit God, in worde & deid.
For Abraham had his beginning,
Into the tyme of Ninus king.
Ninus begane with tyrannie,
And Abraham with humilitie.
Ninus begau the first Impyre,

F iiij   Abraham

Abraham, of weir, had na desyre.
Ninus began Idolatrie,
Abraham in spreit and veritie,
He prayit to the Lord alane,
Fals Imagerie he wald haue nane.
Of him discendit, I here tell,
The twelf Tribis of Israell,
Thir pepill maid adoratioun,
With humill supplicatioun,
Till him quhilk wes of kingis king,
That heuin & eirth maid of na thing:
Dede Imagis thay held at nocht,
That wer with mennis handis wrocht
Bot the almychtie God of lyfe,
My Sone, now haue I done descryfe
Thir questionis at thy command,
The quhilkis thow did at me demand.
C. Quhat wes the cause (schir mak me sure)
Idolatrie did so lang indure,
Outtrouch the warld so generallie,
And with the Gentilis speciallie?
E. (Quod he) sum causis principall,
I fynd in my memoriall:
First wes throuch Princis commandement,
Quhilk did Idolatrie inuent,
Syne singular profite of the Preistis,
Paintouris, Goldsmythis, Masonis, wrichtis,
Thir men of craft full curiouslie,
Maid Imagis so plesandlie:
And sauld thame for ane sumptuous pryce,
To be thair craftie Merchandyce,

                                    Thay

Thay wer maid ritche abone mesure,
As for the Preistis J the assure:
Large profite gat ouerthort all landis,
Throuch sacrifice and offerandis,
And be thair fayned sanctitude,
Abusit mony ane man of gude:
As in the tyme of Daniell,
The Preistis of this Jdoll Bell,
Quhen Nabuchodonosor king,
In Babilon royallie did ring,
Thir preistis the king gart vnderstand,
That Jmage maid be mennis hand,
He wes ane glorious God of lyfe,
And had sic ane prerogatyfe ,
That be his greit power deuyne,
Wald eit Beif, Mouttoun, breid & wyne
And so the king gart euery day
Afore Bell on his aultar lay,
Fourty fresche vedderis fat and fyne,
And sax greit rowbouris of wicht wyne:
Twelf greit Louis of bowtit flour,
Quhilk wes all eittin in ane hour ,
Nocht be that Jmage deif and dum,
Bot be the Preistis all and sum:
As in the Bibill thow may ken,
Quhose noumer wer thre score and ten,
Thay, and thair wyfis euerilk day,
Eit all that on the Aulter lay,
Than Daniell in conclusion,
Schew the king thair abusioun,
And of thair subteltie, maid him sure,

Daniel.3

F b   How

How vnderneth the tempill flure,
Throuch ane passage thay came be nicht,
And eit that meit with candill licht.

    The King quhen he the mater knew,
Thir Preistis with all thair wyffis he slew.
Thus suttellie the King was sylit,
And all the pepill wer begylit.
My Sone (said he) now may thou ken
How be the Preistis, and Craftismen:
And be thair craftines and cure,
Jdolatrie did so lang indure.

    Behauld how Jhone Boccatius,
Hes wryttin workis wounderous,
Of Gentilis superstitioun,
And of thair greit abusioun:
As in his greit Buke thow may sie.
Of fals Goddis the Genealogie.
Of Demogorgon, in speciall,
Fore Grandschir till the Goddis all:
Honourit amang Archadianis,
And of the fals Philistianis:
With thair greit deuillische god Dagone,
With vtheris Jdollis mony one:
Bot J abhor the treuth to tell,
Of the Princis of Jsraell,
Chosin be God Omnipotent,
How thay brak his commandement,
King Salomon, as the Scripture sayis,
He dotit in his latter dayis:
His wantoun wyffis to compleis,
He curit nocht God till displeis.

3.Reg 11

                                        And DW

And did commit Idolatrie,
worſchipping caruit Imagerie:
As Moloch god of Ammonites,
And Chamos, god of Moabites.
Aſtaroth, god of Sydoniens,
So for his inobediens,
And foull abhominatioun,
wer puniſt his ſucceſſioun.
His Sone Roboam, I here tell,
Tint the ten Tribis of Iſraell,
for his fatheris Idolatrie,
As in the Scripture thow may ſie.

Of Imagis vſit amang Chriſtiane men.   VII.

Ather, zit ane thing I wald ſpeir,
Behald in euery Kirk and Queir:
Throuch Chriſtindome in Burgh
and land,
Imagis maid with mannis hand:
To quhome be geuin diuers names,
Sum Peter and Paule, ſum Jhone & James.
Sanct Peter caruit with his keyis,
Sanct Michaell with his wyngis and weyis,
Sanct Katherine, with hir ſworde & quheill,
Ane Hynd ſet vp beſyde ſanct Geill.

It war

It war to lang for till deſcryue,
Sanct Franchis with his woundis fyue:
Sanct Tredwall, als thare may be ſene,
Quhilk on ane preik hes baith hir ene.
Sanct Paull weill paintit with ane ſworde,
As he wald fecht at the firſt word,
Sanct Apolline on aulter ſtandis,
With all hir teith in till hir handis,
Sanct Roche weill ſeiſit, men may ſie,
Ane byill new brokin on his thie.
Sanct Eloy he dois ſtaitlie ſtand,
Ane new horſe ſcho in till his hand.
Sanct Niniane of ane rottin ſtok:
Sanct Doutho borrit out of ane blok.
Sanct Androw with his croce in hand
Sanct George vpon ane horſe rydand
Sanct Anthonie ſet vp with ane ſow.
Sanct Bryde weil caruit with ane kow:
With coiſtlie colouris fyne and fair,
Ane thouſand mo, I mycht declair:
As ſanct Coſme and Damiane,
The Sowtaris ſanct Criſpiane:
All thir on aulter ſtaitlie ſtandis,
Preiſtis cryand for thair offerandis,
To quhome we Commons on our kneß
Dois worſchip all thir Imagereis.
In kirk, in Queir, and in the cloſter,
Prayand to thame our Pater noſter.
In Pilgramage from town to toun,
With offerand, and with Oriſoun:
To thame ay babland on our beidis,

That

That thay may help vs in our neidis:
Quhat differs this declare to me,
from the Gentilis Idolatrie?
E. Gif that be trew that thow reportis
It gois richt neir thir samin sortis:
Bot we be counsaill of Clargie,
Hes lycence to mak Imagerie:
Quhilk of vnleirnit bene the buikis,
for quhen lawit folk vpon thame luik,
It bringis to rememberance,
Of Sanctis lyuis the circumstance,
How the faith for to fortifie,
Thay sufferit pane richt pacientlie,
Seand the Image of the rude,
Men suld remember on the blude:
Quhilk Christ in till his Passioun,
Did sched for our Saluatioun:
Or quhen thow seis ane portraiture,
Of blyssit Marie Uirgine pure,
Ane bony Babe vpon her knee.
Than in thy mynde remember thee.
The wordis quhilkis the Propheit said,
How scho suld be baith mother and maid.
Bot quha that sittis doun on thair kneis
Prayand till ony Imagereis:
With Orisone or offerand
kneland with cap into thair hand.
Na difference bene I say to thie,
from the Gentilis Idolatrie.
Richtso of diuers natiouis,
I reid the abhominationis,

How

How Greikis maid thair deuotioun haill,
To Mars, to saif thame in battaill.
Till Juppiter, sum tuke thair vayage,
To saue thame from the stormis rage,
Sum prayit to Uenus from the splene
That thay thair luiffis micht obtene:
And sum to Juno for rytches,
Thair Pilgramage thay wald addres.
So dois our commoun populare,
Quhilk war to lang for till declare,
Thair superstitious pilgramagis:
To mony diuers Jmagis,
Sum to sanct Roche with diligence,
To saif thame from the pestilence:
For thair teith to sanct Apolline,
To sanct Tredwell, to mend thair ene.
Sum makis offerand to sanct Eloy,
That he thair horse may weill conuoy.
Thay ryn, quhen thay haue Jowellis tint,
To seik sanct Spith or euer thay stint.
And to sanct Germane, to get remeid,
For maladeis into thair heid.
Thay bring mad men on fute and hors,
And byndis thame to sanct Mongois Cros.
To sanct Barbara thay cry full fast,
To saif thame from the thonder blast,
For gude Nouellis, as J heir tell,
Sum takis thair gate to Gabriell.
Sum wyffis sanct Margaret dois exhort.
Into thair byrth thame to support,
To sanct Anthony, to saif the sow.

To sanct

To sanct Bryde to keip Calfe and kow.
To sanct Sebastiane thay ryn and ryde,
That from the schot he saif thair syde:
And sum in hope to get thair heill,
Rynnis to the auld Rude of Kerrell.
Howbeit thir simpill pepill rude,
Think thair intentioun be bot gude.
Wo be to Preistis, I say for me,
Quhilk sulde schaw thame the verite.
Prelatis quhilkis hes of thame the cure,
Sall mak answeir thare of be sure,
On the greit day of Judgement,
Quhen na tyme deis for to repent,
Quhare manifest Idolatrie,
Sall punist be perpetuallie,

Ane Exclamatioun againis Idolatrie.

VIII.

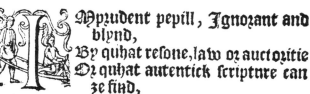 Mprudent pepill, Ignorant and
blynd,
By quhat resone, law or auctoritie
Or quhat autentick scripture can
ze find,
Lesum for till commit Idolatrie,
Quhilk bene to bow zour body or zour knie:
With deuote humill adorationn,
Till onÿ Idoll, maid of stone or tre,
Geuand to thame offerand or oblatioun.

Quhy

Quhy do ʒe giue the honour, laud and glore,
Pertenig to God, quhilk maid all thig of nocht,

Exod. 32 Quhilk was, and is, and salbe euer more,
Till Imagis be mennis handis wrocht:
O fulische folk, quhy haue ʒe succour socht,
Of thame quhilk can not help ʒow in distres.
Ʒit reasonably reuolue into ʒour thocht,
In stok, nor stane, can be none holynes.

In the desert the pepill of Israell,
Moyses remaning in the mount Synay,
Thay maid ane moltin Calf of fyne mettell,
Quhilk thay did honour as thare God verray:
Bot quhen Moyses descendit, I here say,
And did considder thair Idolatrie,
Of that pepill, thre thousand gart he slay.
As the Scripture at lenth dois testifie.

Dani. 14 Because the holy Propheit Daniell,
In Babilon Idolatrie repreuit,
And wald not worschip thair fals Idoll Bell,
The haill pepill at him wer so aggreuit,
To that effect that he suld be mischeuit:
Deliuerit him to rampant Lyonis seuin,
Bot of that daungerous den, he was releuit,
Throuch mirakle of the greit God in Heuin.

Behauld how Nabuchodonosor king,
Into the vaill of Duran, did prepare,
Ane Image of fyne gold, ane meruallous thing

Daniel. 3 Thre score of cubitis hich, and set in square,
As more cleirlie the Scripture dois declare:
To quhome all pepill be proclamatioun,

With

With bodyis bowit, and on thair kneis bare,
Richt humillie thay maid adoratioun.

Ane greit wounder, that day was sene also,
How Nabuchodonosor in his Ire:
Tuke Sidrach, Misach, and Abednago,
Quhilk wald not bow thair kne at his defyre,
Till that Idoll, gart cast thame in the fyre,
For to be brynt, or he steirit of that steid,
Quhen he beleuit, thay wer brynt bone and lyre
Was nocht consumit ane small hair of thair heid.

The Angell of the Lord was to thame sene,
In that hait Furneis passing vp and down,
In till ane Rosie Gairth, as thay had bene:
None spot of Fyre, distayning coit nor gown,
Of victorie thay did obtene the Crown:
And war to thame, that maid adoratioun,
To that Idoll, or bowit thair body donn,
Ane witnessing of thair Dampnatioun.

Quhat was the cause, at me thou may demād,
That Salomon vsit nane Imagerie,
In his tryumphant Temple for till stand:
Of Abraham, Isac, Jacob, nor Jesse,
Nor of Moyses, thair sauegard throuch the see:
Nor Josue, thair bailzeand Campioun?
Because God did command the contrarie,
Thay sulde nocht vse sic superstitioun.

Exo. 20.
Deutr. 5.

Behauld how the greit God Omnipotent,
To preserue Israell from Idolatrie,
Directit thame ane strait Commandement,
G   Thay

Thay suld nocht mak, nane caruit Imagerie,
Nother of gold, of siluer, stane, nor trie:
Nor giue worschip till ony similitude,
Beand in Heuin, in Eirth, nor in the Sie,
Bot onelie till his Souerane celsitude.

Barn. 6.   The Propheit Dauid planelie did repreue,
Psal. 115. Idolatrie to thair confusioun,
In grauit stok, or stane that did beleue,
Declaring thame thair greit abusioun,
Spekand in maner of derisioun,
How dede Idolis be mennis handis wrocht,
Quhame thay honourit, with humill orisoun,
Wer in the merket daylie sauld and bocht.

The Deuillis seand the euill conditioun,
Of the Gentilis, and thair vnfaithfulnes,
For till augment thair superstitioun.
In those Idolis, thay maid thair entres,
And in tahme spak, as storyis dois expres:
Than men beleuit of thame to get releif,
Askand thame help in all thair vesynes,
Bot finallie that turnit to thair mischeif.

Traist weill in thame, is nane Diuinitie.
Quhen reik and roust thair fair colour dois faid.
Thocht thay haue feit on fute thay can not fle,
Howbeit the tempill birn abone thair heid,
In thame is nother freindschip nor remeid,
In sic figuris quhat fauour can ze find?
With mouth & eiris, & ene thocht thay be maid,
All men may see, thay ar dum, deif, & blind.

                              Howbeit

Howbeit thay fall doun flatlingis on the fure
Thay haue na strenth thare self to rais agane,
Thocht rattonis ouer yame rin,thay tak na cure
Howbeit thay brek thair nek,thay feill na pane,
Quhy suld men Psalmis to thame sing or sane:
Sen growand treis,that zeirlie beiris frute,
Ar mair to praise, I mak it to the plane,
Nor cuttit stockis,wanting baith crop and rute.

Of Edinburgh,the greit Idolatrie,
And manifest abhominatioun,
On thair feist day,all Creature may sie,
Thay beir ane auld stok Image throw ye toun,
With talbrone,trumpet,schalme & clarioun,
Quhilk hes bene vsit, mony ane zeir bygone,
With preistis,and freiris, into processioun,
Siclyke as Bell wes borne throuch Babilon.

Eschame ze nocht ze seculare preistis & freiris
Till so greit superstitioun to consent?
Idolatreis ze haue bene mony zeiris,
Expres aganis the Lordis commandement,
Quharefor brether I counsale zow repent:
Giue na honour, to caruit stok,nor stone,
Giue laude and glore to God Omnipotent,
Allanerlie,as wyselie wryttis Ihone.

Fy on zow Freiris, that vsis for to preche.
And dois assist to sic Idolatrie:
Quhy do ze nocht the Ignorant pepill teche,
How ane deid Image caruit of ane tre,
As it wer holy,suld nocht honourit be?
Nor borne on Burges backis vp and doun.
                    G ij   Bot ze

Bot ze schaw planelie zour Hypocrifie,
Quhen ze paſt formeſt in proceſſioun.

Fy on zow foſteraris of Idolatrie,
That till ane dede ſtok dois ſic reuerence,
In preſence of the pepill, publikelie.
Feir ze nocht God, to commit ſic offence?
I counſale zow, do zit zour diligence,
To gar ſuppreſſe ſic greit abuſioun:
Do ze nocht ſo, I dreid zour recompence,
Salbe nocht ellis bot ciene confuſioun.

Had ſāct Frāces bene borne out throw ẏ toun,
Or ſanct Dominik, thocht ze had nocht refuſit,
With thame till haue paſt in proceſſioun:
In till that caſe, ſum wald haue zow excuſit.
Now men may ſee, how that ze haue abuſit,
That nobill toun, throuch zour hypocriſie,
The pepill trawis that thay may richt weil vſit
Quhen ze pas with thame into companie.

Sum of zow hes bene quiet counſallouris,
Prouokand Princis, to ſched ſaikles blude,
Quhilk neuer did zour prudent predeceſſouris:
Bot ze lyke furious Phariſeis denude,
Of Cheritie, quhilk rent Chriſt on the rude.
For Chriſtis flok, without malice or Ire:
Conuertit fragill faltouris I conclude,
Be Goddis worde, without ſwerd or fyre.

Reid ze not how ẏ Chriſt hes geuin cōmand,
Matt. 18 Gif thy brether doith oucht the till offend,
Than ſecreitlie correct him hand for hand,
                                    Than

In freindlie maner , or thow forther wend,
Gif he will nocht here the,than mak it kend,
Till ane or twa , be trew narratioun.
Gif he for thame,will not his mis amend,
Declare him to the Congregatioun.

And gif he zit remanis obstinate,
And to the holy kirk incounsolabill,
Than lyke ane Turk hald him excommunicate
And with all faithfull folk abhominabill,
Banissing him , that he be na mair abill,
To dwell amang the faithfull cumpanie:
Quhen he repentis,be nocht vnmerciabill,
Bot him resaue agane richt tenderlie.

Bot our dum Doctours of Diuinitie,
And ze of the laste fonde Religioun,
Of pure Transgressouris ze haue na pitie:
Bot cryis to put thame to confusioun,
As cryit the Jowis,for the effusioun
Of Chriftis blude into thair birnand Ire,
Crucifige,so ze with ane vnioun,
Cryis fy,gar cast that faltour in the fyre.

Unmercifull memberis of the Antechrist,
Extolland zour humane traditioun,
Contrair the Institutionn of Chrift,
Esteir ze nocht Diuine punitioun,
Thocht sum of zow be gude of conditioun,
Reddy for to resaue new recent wyne,
I speik to zow auld Boissis of perditioun,
Returne in tyme, or ze ryn to rewyne.

Matt.15.
Ephes.6.

G iij   Astran

As ran the peruerst Prophetis of Baall,
Quhilkis did consent to the Idolatrie,
Of wickit Achab, king of Israell:
Quhose noumer wer foure hundreth and fyftie,
Quhilkis honourit that Idoll oppinlie,
Bot quhen Elias did preue thair abusioun:
He gart the pepill slay thame cruellie,
So at ane hour came thare confusioun.

I pray zow prent in zour remembrance,
How the reid Freiris, for thair Idolatrie,
In Scotland, Ingland, Spane, Italy & Fráce
Upon ane day, wer punissit pietuouslie.
Behalde how zour awin brether now laitly,
In Dutchelád, Inglád, Démark & Norroway,
Ar trampit doun, with thare Hypocrisie,
And as the snaw ar meltit clene away.

I meruell ý our Bischoppꝭ thinkis na schame
To giue zow Freiris sic preeminence,
Till vse thair office, to thair greit defame,
Preiching for thame, in oppin audience.
Bot micht ane bischop eik til his awin expence,
For ilk Sermon ten Ducatis in his hand,
He wald, or he did want that recompence,
Ga preiche him self, baith into burgh and land.

I traist to see gude reformatioun,
From tyme we get ane faithfull prudent king,
Quhilk knawis the trueth, & his vocatioun,
All Publicanis, I traist he will doun thring,
And will nocht suffer in his Realme to ring,

Matt. 18

Corruptit

Corruptit Scrybis,nor fals Pharisience,
Aganis the treueth,quhilk planely dois maling,
Till that king cum,we man tak pacience.

Now fare weil freindʒ,because I can not flyte,
Howbeit I culde,ʒe mon hald me excusit,
Thocht I aganʒ Idolatrie indyte,
Or thame dispyte , that will nocht ʒit refusit.
I pray to God,that it be na mair vsit,
Amang the Rewlaris of this Regioun,
That commoun pepill be na mair abusit,
Bot gif him gloze,that bair the cruell croun.

Quhilk teichit vs, be his Diuine Scripture,
Till richt prayer,the perfyte reddy way,
As wryttis Matthew in his sert Chapture,
In quhat maner, and to quhome we suld pray,
Ane schort compendious orisone euerilk day,
Maist proffitabill,for baith body and saull,
The quhilk is nocht directit,I here say,
To Jhon,nor James,to Peter nor to Paull.

Nor to nane vther of the Apostlis twelf,
Nor to na Sanct,nor Angell in the Heuin .
Bot onelie till our Father God him self,
Quhilk Orisone it doith contene full euin,
Maist proffitabill for vs petetionis seuin,
Quhilk we lawed folk,the Pater noster call.
Thocht we say Psalmes,nyne, ten,or elleuin.
Of all prayer this bene the principall.

Be resoun of the maker,quhilk it maid,
Quhilk wes the Sone of God, our Saluiour,
                    G iiij   Be resoun

Be resoun als,to quhome it sulde be said,
Till the father of heuin , our Creatour,
Quhilk dwellis nocht in tempill noʒ in tour,
Ye cleirlie seis our thocht, will,and intent.
Quhat neidis vs,at vtheris seik succour,
Quhen in all place , his power bene present.

    Ze Princis of che Preistis that sulde preche,
Quhy suffer ʒe to greit abusioun?
Quhy do ʒe nocht the sempill pepill teche,
How,and to quhome,to dʒes thair orisoun?
Quhy thole ye thame,to ryn from toun to toun
In pilgramage,till ony Imagereis?
Hopand to get thare sum saluatioun,
Praȝand to thame deuotlie on thair kneis.

    This was the practik of sum Pilgramage,
Quhen Fillokis into Fyfe , began to fon,
With Joke and Thome , than tuke thay thair
     vayage,
In Angus to the feild Chapell of Dʒon:
Than Kittok thare als cadye as ane Con,
Without regard,other to sin oʒ schame,
Gaue Lowʒie leif,at laser to loup on,
Far better had bene, till haue biddin at hame.

    I haue sene pas ane meruallous multitude,
Zoung men & wemen,flyngand on thair feit,
Under the forme,of senʒeit sanctitude,
Foʒ till adoʒne ane Image in Loʒeit,
Mony came with thair marrowis foʒ to meit,
Committant thair soull foʒnicatioun:

                          Sum

Sum kiffit the claggit taill of the Armeit.
Quhy thole ʒe this abhominatioun?

Of Fornicatioun and Idolatrie,
Apperandlie ʒe take bot litill cure,
Seand the maruellous infelicitie:
Quhilk hes fo lang done in this land indure,
In ʒour defalt, quhilk hes the charge and cure,
This bene of treuth, my Lordis, with ʒour leue:
Sic pilgramage hes maid mony ane hure,
Quhilk, gif I plefit, planelie micht preue.

Quhy mak ʒe nocht, the Scripture manifest
To pure pepill twiching Idolatrie?
In ʒour preiching, quhy haue ʒe nocht exprest,
How mony kingis of Iftraell cruellie,
Wer punifchit be God fo rigorouflie?
As Jeroboam, and mony mo but dout,
For worfchipping of caruit Imagerie,
War from thair Realmes rudlie rutit out.

3.Reg.13

Quhy thole ʒe vnder ʒour Dominioun,
Ane craftie Preift, or feinʒeit fals Armeit,
Abufe the pepill of this Regioun,
Onely for thair particular profeit?
And fpeciallie that Armeit of Laureit:
He pat the commoun pepill in beleue,
That blynd gat ficht, & crukit gat thair feit:
The quhilk that Palʒard na way can appreue.

Ze marʒit men that hes trim wantoun wyffʒ
Ane luftie douchteris of ʒoung and tender age,
Quhofe honeftie ʒe fuld lufe as ʒour lyffis:

G v   Permit

Permit thame nocht to pas in pilgramage,
To seik support at ony stok Image:
For I haue wittin, gude wemen pas fra hame,
Quhilk hes bene trappit with sic lustis rage,
Hes done returne, baith with greit sin & schame

Get vp, thow sleipis all to lang, O Lord,
And mak ane haistie Reformatioun,
On thame quhilk dois tramp doun thy gratio⁹
And hes ane deidlie indignatioun,   (word,
At thame quhilk makis trew narratioun,
Of thy Gospell, schawing the veritie,
O Lord I mak the supplicatioun,
Support our Faith, our Hope, and Cheritie.

IX. ❧ How King Ninus beildit the
greit Cietie of Niniue. And how he
vincust Zoroastes King
of Bactria.

His Ninus of Assyria king,
Quhen he had maid his conquesing
To beild ane Cietie he him drest,
Chusing the place quhair he thocht
best:
Quhare he had first Dominioun,
In Assyria his awin Regioun,
Thocht Assur, as the Scripture sayis,
Gen. 10. Quhilk came afore king Ninus dayis,
And fundit that famous Ciete,
The quhilk was callit Niniue:

Bot

Bot as reherſis Diodore,
Ninus that Cietie did decore:
So maruellous tryumphantlie,
As ʒe ſall here immediatlie,
Upon the ſlude of Euphrates,
Quhilk to behald greit wounder wes,
Ane hundreth and ſyftie ſtaigis,
That Citie was of lenth I wis:
The wallis ane hundreth fute of hicht,
Na wounder was thocht thay wer wicht.
Sic breid abufe the wallis thair was,
Thre cartis micht ſydlingis on thame pas:
Four hundreth ſtaigis, and four ſcore,
In circuite but myn or more.
Of towris about thoſe wallis I wene
Ane thouſand and ſyue hundreth bene:
Of hicht twa hundreth fute, and more,
As wryttis famous Diodore.

The Scripture makis mentioun,
Quhen God ſend Jonas to that toun:
To ſchaw thame of his puniſchement,
Outtrouch the Citie quhen he went:
Thre dayis Jornay till him it was.
The Bibill ſayis it was na les.

Ioan.3.

My Sone, now haue I ſchawin to the,
Of the building of Niniue:
For the augmenting of his fame,
Ninus gart call it efter his name.
Quhen he that greit Citie had endit,
To conques mair ʒit he intendit:
And did depart from Niniue,

And

And rasit vp ane greit Armie,
Of the maist stalwart men and stout,
Of all his Regionis round about,
In greit ordour tuke thair Jornay,
Towart the Realme of Bactria.
Of wicht fute men, I vnderstand,
He had seuintene hundreth thousand,
Without horsmen, and weirlyke cartis
Quhome he ordourit in syndry partis:
Quhilk till descryue, I am nocht abill,
Quhose noumer bene so vntrowabill.

Zoroastes, that nobill king,
Quhilk Bactria had in gouerning,
That prudent Prince, as I here tell,
Did in Astronomie precell:
And fand the Art of Magica,
With naturall Science mony ma.
Seand king Ninus on the feild,
Fordwart he came with speir & scheild:
Four hundreth thousand men he wes,
In his Armie thare was na les.
And met king Ninus on the bordour,
Richt vailzeantlie, and in gude ordour:
On the Vangarde of his Armie,
On thame he ruschit richt rudelie:
And of thame slew, as I here say,
Ane hundreth thousand men that day.
The rest that chaipit war vnslane,
To Ninus greit oist fled agane.
Of that, king Ninus was so noyit,
He restit neuer till he Destroyit,

All haill

All haill that Regioun vp and down,
And from the king did reif the Crown:
And maid the Realme of Bactria,
Subiectit till Assyria.
And in that sampyn land I wis,
He tuke to wyfe Semiramis:
Quha, as myne Auctour dois descryue
was than the lustiest on lyue.
That beand done without sudgeorne,
Till Niniue he did retorne:
with greit tryumphe of victorie,
As myne Auctor dois specifie.
Baith Occident and Orient,
war all till him obedient.
It wald abhor the, till here red,
The saikles blude, that he did sched:
Quhen he had roung, as thou may heir
The space of thre and fourty zeir:
Beand in his excellent glore,
The dolent deith did him deuore:
In quhat sort, I am nocht certane,
Sum Auctour sayis that he was slane
And left till bruke his Heritage,
Ane litill Babe of tender age.
Zoung Ninus was the Chylds name,
Quhilk efter flurischit in greit fame.
Sum sayis that be his wyffis tresoun,
king Ninus deid in presoun:
As I sall schaw, or I hyne fare,
Quhow Diodore hes done declare.

X. ❧ Of the wounderfull deidis of the Quene Semiramis.

Ninus luffit so ardentlie,
Semiramis his fair Ladie,
Thare was na thing, scho wald
command.
Bot all obeyit was fra hand.
Scho seand him so Amorous.
Scho grew proude and presumptuous
And at the king scho did desyre,
Fyue dayis to gouerne his Impyre:
And he of his beneuolence,
Did grant hir that preeminence:
With Septour, Crown, & Rob royall
And haill power Imperiall,
Till fyue dayis wer cum and gone,
That scho as king suld regne allone.
¶ Than all the Princis of the land,
During that tyme maid hir ane band,
With bankat Royall merilie,
Scho treatit thame tryumphantlie.
So the first day the pepill all,
Came till her seruyce bound and thrall:
Bot or the secund day was gane,
Scho tuke sic gloze to regne allane:
Be ane decreit maid thame amang,
The king scho put in prisone strang.
I reid weill of his presoning,

Bot nocht

Bot nocht of his delyuering:
How euer it wes in till his stouris,
He did of deith suffer the schouris,
And micht not lenth his lyfe ane hour,
Thocht he wes the first Conquerour:
Quhose conquesing for to conclude,
Wes nocht but greit schedding of blude.
Now haue ze hard of Ninus king,
How he began, and his ending:
Howbeit myne Auctour Diodore,
Of him haith wryttin mekill more.
Princis for wrangous conquesing,
Doith mak oft tymes ane euill ending
Thocht he had lang prosperitie,
He endit with greit miserie.

Of King Ninus Sepulture. XI.

He Quene ane sepulture scho maid
Quhare scho king Nin' bodie laid
Of curious craftie wark & wicht,
The quhilk had staid(nine of hicht
And ten staidis of breid it wes,
Diodore sayis it was na les.
For aucht staidis ane myle thow tak,
And thare efter thy noumer mak:
So be this compt, it was full richt,
Ane myle, and als ane staid of hicht.
Except the tour of Babilóne,
So hich ane werk, J reid of none.

Semiramis

Semiramis this luſtie Quene,
Conſidering quhat danger bene:
To haue ane king of tender age,
Quhilk micht nocht vſe na Vaſſalage.
Scho tuke ane courageous conſait,
Thinkand that ſcho wald mak debait:
Gif ony maid rebellioun,
Contrair hir Sone, or his Regioun.
Quhome ſcho did foſter tenderlie,
And keipit him full quietlie:
Scho laid apart hir awin cleithing,
And tuke the rayment of ane king.
Quhen ſcho wes in till armour dicht,
Micht na man knaw hir be ane knicht
Scho vailʒeantlie went to the weir,
And to geue battell, tuke na feir:
Dantyng all Realmes round about,
That all the warld of hir had dout:
Mair fortunate in hir conqueſſing,
Nor wes hir huſband Ninus king.

Babilon ſcho did fortifie,
Templis and towris triumphandlie:
So pleſandlie did thame prepare,
Quhilk in the eirth had na compare.
Howbeit Nimrod, of quhome I ſpak,
The hydduous dungeoun he gart mak
And of the Citie the foundement,
To quhome God maid impediment.
Quhare Nimrod left, thare ſcho began
And put to wark mony ane man.
Of all the Realmes round about,

Of mait

Of maist Ingyne scho socht thame out,
Scho had wirkand with tre and stanis,
Twelf houndreth thousand men at anis,
Ga reid the buke of Diodore,
And thow sall find the noumer more,
On euerilk syde of Euphrates,
That nobill Cietie beildit wes.
And so that ryuer of renown,
Ran throuch the midpart of the town.
Ouerthort that flude scho briggis maid,
Of maruellous strenth baith lang and braid:
Thay wer fyue staidis large of lenth,
On euerilk Brig scho maid ane strenth
The circuite, as I said afore,
Four houndreth staidis and foure score
The wallis hicht, quha wald descryue,
Thre houndreth fute, thre score & fyue:
Sax cartis micht pas richt esielie,
Abufe the wallis of that Cietie,
Sydlingis without Impediment.
Consydder be zour Iudgement:
Gif those wallis wer hich or nocht,
And also curiouslie wer wrocht:
As Diodore hes done defyne,
Quhilk doith transcend my rude ingyne.
Of Babilon the magnificence,
To quhome ze walde geue na credence:
Gif I at lenth wald put in wryte,
Quhilk Diodore hes done indyte.
Compare of Cieteis fynd I none,
Till Niniue and Babilone.

h   from

From Niniue in Assyria,
Till Babilon in Chaldea:
Be briggis plesandlie ze may pas,
Upon the Flude of Euphrates,
Amang the Fludis of Paradyce,
This Euphrates may bere the pryce.
All wark҂ quhilkis the Quene began,
Transcendit the ingyne of man.
The proude Quene Penthesilea,
The Princesse of Amazona:
With hir Ladyis tryumphandlie,
At Troy quhilk faucht sa bailzeandlie:
Nor zit the fair Madin of France,
Danter of Inglis Ordinance:
To Semiramis in hir dayis,
Wer na compair, as buikis sayis.
Except tryumphand Julius,
Strang Hanniball or Pompeius:
Or Alexander the Conquerour,
I find na greiter weiriour.
Wald I reherse, as wryttis Clarkis,
Hir wounderfull & bailzeand warkis:
It wer to me ane greit labour,
And tedious to the Auditour:
Quhat scho did in Ethiopia,
And in the land of Media:
Beildand Cieteis, Castellis & Towris,
Parkis and Gardingis of plesouris:
For the exalting of hir name,
And immortall to mak hir fame,
Of Iarcius the hich montanis,

Scho

Scho gart ryue down, & mak thame planis.
Greit Orontes that Montane wicht,
Twentie and fyue staidis of hicht:
Till hir Palice to draw ane Loch,
Be force of men,scho raue it throch.
Had scho keipit hir chastitie,
Scho micht haue bene ane A.per se.
Quhen scho had ordourit hir Impyre,
Of Venus wark scho tuke desyre:
Ane secreit Manstoun scho gart mak,
Quhare scho plesandlie micht take,
Zoung gentill men,for hir plesour,
The quhilk scho vsit aboue mesour:
Ane man allane,micht nocht be abill,
To stanche hir lust insatiabill.
Quhen scho was satisfyit of one,
Scho gart ane vther cum anone:
The lustiest of all the land,
Came quietlie at hir command:
Quhen thay at lenth had lyin hir by,
Scho slew thame all richt cruelly.
Quhen hir Sone came till age perfyte
Of him scho tuke so greit delyte:
Scho causit him with hir to ly,
Amang the rest richt quietly.
Sum sayis,throuch sensuall lustis rage
Scho band him into Mariage:
And held him vnder tutorie,
To vphald hir authoritie.

H ij   How the

XII. How the Quene Semiramis with
ane greit Armie paſt to Inde, and faucht
with the King Staurobates. And of
hir miſerabill end.

When ſcho had lang tyme leuit in
    reſt,
To conques mair ſcho hir addʒeſt:
Becauſe of diuers ſcho hard tell,
How that the Inde Orientell,
Pʒecellit in greit commoditeis,
As beſtiall, coʒnis, & frutefull treis.
All kind of Spyce delitious,
Gold, Syluer, ſtonys Pʒecious,
And how that plenteous land did bere
Coʒne, frute & wyne, twyſe in the ʒere:
With Oliphantis innumerabill,
In batteil wounder terribill.
Scho heirand this and mekle moʒe,
Beleuand till augment hir gloʒe,
Gart mak ſtrait Pʒoclamationis,
In all and ſyndʒie Nationis,
Schawand how it wes hir deſpʒe,
All Pʒincis vnder hir Impyʒe:
In Egipt and Arabia,
In Perſe, in Mede, and Chaldea,
In Grece in Caſpia, and Hyʒcane,
In Capadoce, Lidia and Mauritane.
In Armenie and Phʒigia,

                     In Pam-

In Pamphilie , and Assyria ,
That ilk land efter their degre,
Sulde bring till hir ane greit Armie,
In all the gudelie haist thay may,
And meit hir in till Bactria:
Declaring thame that hir intent,
was till pas to the Orient:
And mak weir on the king of Inde,
From tyme thay knew quhat was hir mynde:
Than be thair selfis ilk Regioun,
Came fordwart with thair Garnisoun,
Trpumphandlie in gude array,
Till Bactria tuke the reddy way,
And maid thair muistouris to the Quene
Bot sic ane sicht was neuer sene:
In battel ray so mony ane man,
Stainis,sen God the warld began.
Bot Spanze,France,Scotland,Ingland,
Dutcheland,Denmark,nor zit Ireland,
Wer nocht inhabite in those dayis,
Nor lang efter, myne Author sayis.
  Ethesias, he dois specifie,
The noumer of this greit Armie:
Sayand thare came at hir command,
Fute men,threttie houndreth thousand,
Of hors men,montit galzeardlie,
Fyue houndreth thousand verraylie.
Ane houndreth thousand Cameilis wicht
On euerilk Cameill raid ane knicht:
Prepairit till pas into all partis,
Thare was ane houndreth thousand Cartis.
                    H iij   Twa

Twa thousand boitis with hir scho caryis,
On hors, Cameilis and Dromodaryis.
Briggis for to mak scho did conclude,
Ouerthort Indus that furious flude:
Quhilk bene of Inde the outmaist bordour,
On the quhilk flude with richt gude ordour,
Of hir bairgis, scho briggis maid,
Quhare on hir greit Oist saiflie raid.
C. Father, I wald men vnderstude,
How sic ane maruellous multitude,
Micht be atainis brocht to the feild,
Reddy to fecht, with speir and scheild.
Sum men will iuge, this bene ane fabill,
The mater bene so vntrowabill.
E. It may weill be, my Sone (said he)
As be exempill we may se:

2. Samu.
24.

How Dauid king of Israell,
His pepill gart noumer and tell,
Be Ioab his cheif Capitane,
As holy Scripture schawis plane,
Of fechtand men, into that land,
He fand threttene hundreth thousand.
Sen Dauid in that small cuntrie,
Micht haue rasit sic ane Armie:
To this Lady it was na wounder,
The quhilk had greiter Realmis ane hounder,
Nor Dauidis litill Regioun,
Thocht scho had mony ane Legioun,
Of men, ma nor I tauld afore.
Tharefore, my Sone, maruell na more

     ¶ Staurobates the king of Inde,

                 Greitlie

Greitliie perturbit in his mynde,
Heiring of sic ane multitude,
To make defence he did conclude:
And send ane Message to the Quene,
Prayand hir Maiestie serene:
That scho wald of hir speciall grace,
Geue him lycence to leue in pace:
Failzeand of that, thocht he sulde die,
That he sulde gar hir fecht or flie:
And till his God ane vow he maid,
Gif na pais micht of hir be had:
And gif he wan the victorie,
That he the Quene sulde crucifie.
At this boisting the Quene maid bourdis
Sayand it sall nocht be na wourdis:
Sall gar me pas fra my purpose,
Bot michtie straikis, as I suppose,
The Messinger schew to the King,
Of hir presumptuous answering.
Than Staurobates wyse and wicht,
Came fordwart lyke ane nobill knicht:
With mony ane thousand, speir & scheild,
Arrayit Royallie on the feild:
Thinkand he wald his land defend,
Or in the battell mak ane end.
¶ The Quene vpon the vther syde,
full of presumptioun and of pryde,
Hir Baneris plesandlie displayit,
With hardy hart and vneffrayt:
Apon Indus that famous flude,
Thay met, quhare sched was meikill blude:

H iiij In Bote

In Bote, In Balingar, and Bargis,
The twa Armeis on vtheris chargis.
Semiramis the battell wan,
Quhare dzownit and slane wer mony ane man
So that the watter of the Flude,
Ran reid mixit with mennis blude.
The king of Inde with all his micht,
From Indus Flude he tuke the flicht:
Till his cheif Cietie he reteirit,
Quhare in his pzesens thare appeirit,
In battell ray ane new Armie,
Of richt inuincibill Cheualrie:
With Elephantis, ane hidduous nummer,
Quhilk efterwart maid meikill cummer.
       Semiramis and hir cumpanie,
In the mene tyme full cruellie,
Distroyit the Bozdouris of that land,
Tuke pzesonaris, ma than ten thousand,
Scho tuke ane curageous consait,
Greit Elephantis to conterfait.
Scho had ten thousand Oxin hydis,
Weill sewit togidder bak and sydis:
With mouth & nose, teith, eiris, and ene
Quick Elephantis as thay had bene:
Richt weill stuffit, full of stray & hay,
Quhare of the Indianis tuke affray:
Apon Cameilis and Dzomodareis,
Those fals figuris with hir scho careis.
Sere Indianis, quhen thay saw that sicht,
Efferitlie thay tuke the flicht.
Foz sic ane sicht was neuer sene,

                                    Gif no

Gif naturall beistis thay had bene.
The king him self, wes richt affeirit,
Till he the veritie had speirit:
And knew be his exploratouris,
Thay war bot senzeit fals figouris.
Than manfullie lyke men of weir,
fordwart thay came withouttin feir,
Richt so Semiramis the Quene,
Quhilk for ane man, was ay fyftene.
Thir twa Armyis full cruellie,
Thay ruschit togidder so rudelie,
With hydduous cry and trumpettis sound,
Till thousandis deid lay on the ground.
Semiramis had sic ane nummer,
Till ordour thame, it was greit cummer.
Than the greit Elephantis of Inde,
Richt strang and hardy of thair kynde,
fordwart thay came, and wald nocht ceis,
Till throuch the middis of the preis,
Of the greit Oist than rudelie ruschit,
Thair men & hors till eird thay duschit
Those feinzeit beistis withouttin spreit
War fruschit and fuilzeit vnder feit.
The King of Inde with curage kene,
Met with Semiramis the Quene,
He rydand on ane Elephand,
Bot scho with him faucht hand for hand,
And gaue the King so greit assay,
That he was neuer in sic affray:
To straik at him scho tuke na feir,
So weill scho vsit was in weir:

H v   His straikis

His straikis scho had bot lytill comptit,
Wer nocht the king wes so weill montit,
Ather at vther straik so fast,
Till thay war tyrit at the last.
The king he thocht him self eschamit,
With ane woman to be defamit:
And was determit nocht to flie,
Thocht in that battell he sulde die:
As man the quhilk disparit bene,
He rudelie ran vpon the Quene:
And throuch the arme gaif hir ane wound,
Quhilk till hir hart gaif sic ane stound,
That scho constrainit was to flie,
Than all the rest of hir Armie:
Quhen thay persauit that scho was gane,
Till Indus Flude thay fled ilk ane.
The Quene ouerthort the Flude scho raid,
On briggis quhilkʒ wer of botis maid,
With hir ane sober cumpanie,
Quhilk with hir fled affrayitlie.
The Indianis followit on the chais,
Than on the Briggis came sic ane prais,
Of fleand folkis, quhilk was greit wonder,
So that the Bairgis brak in sonder.
Sum sank, sum doun the ryuer ran,
Than drownit thare mony ane nobill man:
Quhilk was greit pietie till deplore,
As wryttis famous Diodore.
And finallie for till conclude,
Was neuer sched so meikill blude,
At ane tyme, sen the warld began,

                                     Nor slane

Nor slane so mony ane saikles man,
And all throuch the occasioun,
And the prydefull perswasioun,
Of this ambitious wickit Quene,
Sic ane was neuer hard nor sene.
Staurobates the King of Inde,
Greitlie reioysit in his mynde,
Of this tryumphe and victorie,
Semiramis with hart full sorie:
Seand sa mony tane and slane,
Till hir cuntrie returnit agane:
Lamentand Fortunis variance,
Quhilk brocht hir to sa greit mischance
Afore quhilk was sa fortunate,
And than of comfort desolate.

Hir Sone, ane man of perfectioun,
Considerand his subiectioun:
His lybertie he did desyre,
That he micht gouerne his Impyre:
Seand his Mother vitious,
And with that sa ambitious:
As myne Author dois specifie,
He slew his Mother cruellie.
Quhat vther cause, or intentioun,
I fynd no speciall mentioun,
Sum sayis, to be at lybertie,
Sum sayis for hir adulterie:
None vther cause I can defyne,
Except punitioun Deuyne.
Of this fair Ladie couragzous,
Behald the ending dolorous:

Quhilk

Quhilk was bot twentie zeiris of age,
Quhen scho began hir Vassalage:
And rang tryumphandlie but weir,
The space of twa and fourtie zeir:
Quhen scho was slane, scho was thre scoze,
With zeiris twa, scho was no moze.
As Diodoze wzytis in his buke,
His Cronikill, quha list to luke.

    Of this Lady I mak ane end,
Thynkand na way, I can commend,
Wemen foz till be to manlie,
Noz men foz till be womenlie.
Foz quhy, it bene the Lozdis mynd,
All Creature till vse thair kynd.
Men foz till haue preeminence,
And wemen vnder obedience:
Thocht all wemen inclynit be,
Till haue the Soueranetie.
As this Lady, quhilk wald nocht rest,
Till scho hir Husband had suppzest,
Till that intent that scho micht ring,
Allane to haue the gouerning.
Ladyis na way I can commend,
Pzesumptuouslie quhilk dois pzetend,
Till vse the Office of ane King,
Oz Realmes tak in gouerning.
Howbeit thay bailzeant be and wicht,
Going in battell lyke ane knicht:
As did pzoude Penthesilea,
The Pzinces of Amazona,
In mennis habite agane resoun.

Sic lyke

Siclyke I think derifioun,
Ane Prince to be effeminate,
Of knichtlie courage defolate:
Neglectand his auctoritie,
Throuch beiftlie fenfualitie:
Accompanyit baith day and nichtis,
With wemen mair than vailzeant knichtis:
Sic kingis I difcommend at all,
Exempill of Sardanapall.
C.Father (faid I)fchaw me how lang,
The fucceffioun of Ninus rang.
E. That fall I do with diligence,
My Sone(faid he)or I ga hence.
Sen I haue fchawin at thy defyre,
Quhat man began the first Impyre,
Now wald I it wer to the kend,
Of that Impyre the fatall end.

❧ How king Sardanapalus for his **XIII**
vitious lyfe, maid ane miferabill end.

BEtuir this Conquerour Ninus,
And fenfuall Sardenapalus:
I can nocht find na fpeciall itorie,
worthy to put in memorie,
Except quhilk I haue done difcrife
Of Semirame,king Ninus wife.
Bot I can fynd na gude at all,
To wryte of king Sardanapall,
Quhilk was the fax & threttie king,

Be lyne

Be lyne from Ninus discending:
At lenth his lyfe for to declare,
I thynke it is nocht necessare:
Because that mony cunning clarkis,
Hes him descryuit in thair warkis:
How he was last of Assyriens,
Quhilk had the haill preeminens,
That tyme of the first Monarchie,
In Chronicles as thow may sie.
The last, and the maist vitious king,
Quhilk in that Monarchie did ring:
That Prince was sa effeminate,
With sensuall lust intoxicate:
He did abhor the cumpanie,
Of his maist nobill Cheualrie,
That he micht haue the mair delyte,
Till vse his beistlie appetyte:
Conuersit with wemen nicht and day,
And clothit him in thair array:
Sa that na man that him had sene,
Culd iuge ane man that he had bene:
Sa in huredome and harlatrie,
Did keip him self sa quyetlie.
The Princis of Assyriens,
Of him thay could get na presens:
Thus leuit he continuallie,
Aganis Nature inordinatlie.
Quhen to the Persis and the Meidis,
Reportit was his vitious deidis:
With the Rewlaris of Babilone,
Thay did conclude all in till one:

Thay

Thay wald nocht suffer for till ring,
Abuse thame sic ane vitious king:
Bot Arbaces ane Duke of Mede,
He darstie tuke on hand that dede.
¶Bot first he came to Niniue,
To se the kingis Maiestie:
And till ane of the kingis gard,
He gaue ane secreit rytche reward:
Till put him in ane quyet place,
Quhare he micht se the kingis grace:
And be vnsene with ony wicht,
Bot he saw nother King nor Knicht,
In till his Maisteris cumpanie,
Except wemen allanerlie:
And as ane woman he was cled,
With wemen counsalit and led.
And schamefullie he was sittand,
With spindill & with rock spinnand.
Quhen Arbaces that sicht had sene,
His courage rais vp from the splene:
And thocht it small difficultie,
For till depryue his Maiestie.
¶Than raisit he the Persianis,
With Medis and Babilonianis:
Enarmit weill with speir & scheildis,
Tryumphandlie thay tuke the feildis.
¶The King raisit Assyrianis,
Togidder with the Chaldeanis:
And thame resystit, as thay micht:
Bot finallie he tuke the flicht,
To saue him self in Niniue,

Than

Than seigeit thay that greit Citie,
Continuallie twa zeir and moze,
As wzyttis famous Diodoze,
Till that the ilude of Euphzates,
Arais with sic ane furiousnes,
Quhare thzouch, ane greit part of the toun,
Be violence was doungin doun.
Than quhen the king saw na remeid,
Bot to be taikin, oz to be dede,
As man dispairit full of Ire,
Gart mak ane furious flammand fyze,
And tuke his Golde and Jowellis all,
With Sceptour, Crown & Rob royall:
With all his tender Seruituris,
That of his cozps had greitest curis,
Togidder with his lustie Quenis,
And all his wantoun Concubenis:
And in that fyze he did thame cast,
Syne lap hym self in at the last:
Quhare all wer bzynt in poulder small
Thus endit king Sardanapall:
Withouttin ony repentence,
As may be sene be this sentence,
Heir following, quhilk he did indyte,
Afoze his deith, in greit despyte:
Quhilk is ane richt vngodly thing,
As ze may see, be his dyting.

※ Epitaphium Sardanapali. ※

CVM te mortalem noris, præsentibus exple
Delitijs animum, post mortem nulla voluptas
Et Venere, & cænis, & plumis Sardanapali.

Now haue

¶Now haue I schawin with diligens,
The Monarchie of Assyriens:
The quhilk that king Minus began,
And endit at this mischeant man:
And did indure withouttin weir,
Ane thousand, twa hundreth, & fourty zeir:
As dois indyte Eusebius,
Reid him, & thow sall fynd it thus.

¶The Thrid Buke: I.

Of the miserabill Destructioun of
the Fyue Cieteis, callit Sodome, Gomorre,
Seboim, Segor, and Adama, with
thair haill Regioun.
&c.

Ather, I pray zow, to me tell,
Quhat notabill things that befell,
During the regne of Assyriens,
Quhilk had sa lang præeminens:
I mene of vther Nationis,
Under thair Dominationis?
E. That may be done in termis schort,
(Said he) as storyis dois report:
Induring this first Monarchie,
Became that wofull Miserie:

J   Of So=   Gen.19.

Of Sodome, Gomorre, and thair Regioun,
As Scripture makis mentioun:
Quhose pepill wer sa sensuall,
In fylthie synnis vnnaturall:
The quhilk into my vulgar Uers,
My toung abhorris to rehers,
Lyke brutell beistis by thair myndis,
Unnaturally abuse thair kyndis,
Be fylthie stinkand Lecherie,
And most abhominabill Sodomie:
As holy Scripture dois descryue,
In that Cuntrie war Cieteis fyue:
Quhilk wer Sodome, and Gomorra,
Seboim, Segor and Adama:
Amang thame al, fund wes thair nane
Undefylit, bot Loth allane.
Holy Abraham dwelt neir hand by,
Quhilk prayit for Loth effectuouslie,
For God maid hym aduertisment,
That he wald mak sic punischement,
To Loth twa Angellis God did send,
Him from that furie till defend.
Quhen the pepill of that Regioun,
Saw the Angellis cum to the toun,
Transformit into fair zoung men,
Thay purposit thame for to ken,
And abuse thame vnnaturallie,
With thair foule stinkand Sodomie,
Of that gude Loth was wounder wo
And offerit thame his douchteris two,
Thame at thair plesour for till vse:

Bot thay

Bot thay his Douchteris did refuſe.
And than the Angellis be thair micht,
Thoſe men depryuit of thair ſicht:
And ſa perforce leit thame allane.
To Lothis lugeing quhen thay wer gane,
Thay him commandit haiſtellie,
For till depart of that Cietie.
That foule vnnaturall Lechery,
Ane vengeance to the heuin did cry:
The quhilk did moue God till ſic Jre,
That from the heuin brymſtone & fyre
With aufull thounding ranit doun,
And did conſume that haill Regioun.
Of all that land chaipit no mo,
Except Loth and his Douchteris two:
His wyfe was turnit in ane ſtane,
Sa wyfeles wes he left allane.
For ſcho wes inobedient,
And keipit na commandement,
Quhen the Angell gaue thame command,
Sone till departe out of that land:
He moniſchit thame vnder greit pane,
Neuer to luke bakwart agane.
Quhen Lothis wyfe hard the thoundring,
Of flammand fyre and lichtning:
The vgly cryis lamentabill,
Of pepill moſt Eſpouentabill:
For nane of thame had force to flee,
Scho ȝarnit that ſorrowfull ſicht to ſee:
And as ſcho turnit hir anone,
Scho was transformit in ane ſtone:

J ij   Quhare

Quhare scho remainis still this day,
Of hir I haue na mair to say.
To schaw at lenth, I am nocht abill,
That pieteous proces lamentabill:
How Citeis, Castellis, Townis, & Towris,
Uillaigis, Bastailzeis, and Bowris:
Thay war all into poulder dreuin,
Forrestis be the ruitis vpreuin:
Thair King, thair Quene & pepill all,
Zoung & auld, brynt in poulder small:
Na Creature was left on lyfe,
Foulis, Beistis, Man nor wyfe:
The eirth, the corne, herbe, frute & trie,
The Babbis vpon the Nurische knie:
Richt suddandlie in ane instent,
Unwarlie came thair Jugement:
As it came in the tyme of Noy,
Quhen God did all the warld destroy,
For that self Sin of Sodomie,
And maist abhominabill Bowgrie:
That vyce at lenth for to declare,
I think it is nocht necessare.
Quhen al was brynt, flesche, blude, & bonis,
Hillis, valleyis stockis and stonis:
The Cuntrie sank for to conclude,
Quhare now standis ane vglie flude:
The quhilk is callit the Deid Sey,
Nixt to the Cuntrie of Judey.
Quhois stinkand strandis blak as tar,
The fleuour of it, men feilith on far:
In till Orontius thow may reid,

Of that

Of that Cuntrie the lenth and breid,
Of lenth fyftie mylis and two,
And fourtene myle in braid also.
Loth of his wyfe was sa agast,
That he till ane wyld montane past:
Of companie he had na ma,
Except his lustie douchteris twa:
And be thair prouocatioun,
As Moyses maketh narratioun:

Gen.19.

Allane into that Montane wylde,
His douchteris baith he gat with chylde
For thay beleuit in thair thocht,
That all the warld was gane to nocht
As it became of that Natioun,
Thynkand that Generatioun,
Wald faill, without thay craftely.
Gar thair Father with thame to ly:
And sa thay fand ane craftie wyle,
How thay thair father micht begyle:
And causit him to drink wicht wyne,
Quhilk men to lytcherie dois inclyne.
Quhen he was full, and fallin on sleip,
His Douchteris quyetlie did creip,
In till his bed, full secreitly,
Prouokand him with thame to ly.
And knew nocht how he was begyld,
Till baith his douchteris wer wō chyld:
And bure twa Sonnis in certane,
Thay beand in that wyld Montane:
Of quhame twa Nationis did proceid,
As in the Scripture thow may reid:

I iij In the

In the quhilk Scripture thow may sie,
At lenth this wofull miserie.
This miserie became but weir,
From Noeis Flude thre hundreth zeir,
Togidder with four score and elleuin,
As comptit Carion full euin.
And efter Noeis deith I ges,
Ane and fourtie zeir thare wes:
Quhen Abraham was of age I wene,
Four score of zeiris, and nyntene:
Quhen this foule Sin of Sodomie,
Was punischit sa rigorouslie.
Greit God preserue vs in our tyme,
That we commit nocht sic ane cryme.
Tedious it wer for me to tell,
This Monarchie during quhat befell:
And wounderis that in eirth wer wrocht,
Quhilk to thy purpose langis nocht,
As how the pepill of Israell,
Exod.1. Did lang tyme into Egypt dwell:
And of thair greit punitioun,
Exod.14 Throuch Pharaois persecutioun:
And how Moyses did thame conuoy,
Throuch the reid sey, with mckle Joy,
Quhare king Pharao richt miserablie,
Was drownit with all his huge armie.
And how that pepill wanderand wes,
Exod.20 Fourtie zeiris in wildernes.
Moyses that tyme, as I here say,
Resauit the Law on Mont Sinay.
Iosue.3. That tyme Iosue throuch Jordan,

Led those

Led thofe pepill to Canaan:
Quhare Saull, Dauid, & Salomone,
With Hebrew kingis mony one:
Did rytchelie regne in that Cuntrie,
Induring this First Monarchie.
The seige of Thebes miserabill,
Quhare blude wes sched incomparabil
Of nobill men, into those dayis,
With vtheris terribill affrayis.
As how the Greikis wrocht vengeans
Apon the nobill Troians:
Becaufe that Paris did conuoy,
Perforce fair Helena to Troy:
Quhilk was king Menelaus wyfe,
Quhare mony ane thousand lost thair lyfe.
That tyme the vailzeant Hercules.
Outtrouch the warld did hym addres:
Quhare he did mony ane douchty deid
As in his storie thow may reid,
And how throuch Dianira his wyfe,
That Campioun did lose his lyfe,
In flammand fyre full furiouslie,
The deith he sufferit cruellie.
That tyme Remus and Romulus,
Did found that cietie maist famous,
Of Rome standing in Italie,
As in thair storie thow may sie,
Wald thow reid Titus Liuius,
Thow suld find warkis wounderous,
Quhose douchtie deidis ar weill kend,
And salbe to the warldis end:

I iiij   Thocht

Thocht thay began with crueltie,
And endit with greit miserie:
As bene, the mater to conclude,
Of all scheddaris of saikles blude.
In Grece the ornate Poetrie,
Medicine, Musike, Astronomie:
Duryng this first Monarchie began,
Be Homerus, that famous man:
Togidder with Hesiodus,
As diuers Authouris schawis vs:
It war to lang to put in Ryme,
The buikis that thay wrate in thair tyme:
Thir war the Actis principell,

Gen. 17.　That Monarchie during quhilk befell:
As for gude Abraham and his seid,
Into the Bibill thow may reid,
How in this tyme, as J here tell,
began the kingdome Spirituell:
As J haue schawin to the afore,
Quharefor J speik of thame no more.

II.　❧Ane schort Descriptioun of
the Secund, Thrid, and Fourte
Monarchie.

ATher (said J) quhilk was the mã
That the nirt Monarchie began?
E. Cyrus (said he) the king of Perse
As Cronickils hes done reherse,
Prudent, and full of Policie,

Began

Began the secund Monarchie:
For he was the most godlie King,
That euer in Perse or Mede did ring:
For he of his benignitie,
Delyuerit from captiuitie,
The haill pepill of Israell,
Into the tyme of Daniell:
The quhilkis had bene presoneiris,
In Babilone seuin score of zeiris:
Tharefor God of his grace bening,
Gaue him ane Deuyne knawledging,
During his tyme, as I here tell,
He vsit counsail of Daniell.
Carion at lenth dois specifie,
Of his maruellous natiuitie:
And of his vertuous vpbringing,
And how he vincust Cresus King:
With mony vther bailzeand deid,
As into Carion thow may reid:
Quhose successioun did indure,
Till the tent king, thareof be sure.
Bot efter his greit conquesing,
Richt miserabill was his ending:
As Herodotus doith discryue,
In Scithia he lost his lyfe:
Quhare the vndantit Scithianis,
Uincust those nobill Persianis:
And efter that Cyrus was deid,
Quene Tompre hakkit of his heid,
Quhilk was the Quene of Scythiano
In the dispyte of Persianis:

        I ij   Scho kest

Scho keſt his heid,for to conclude,
In till ane Veſſell full of blude:
And ſaid thir wordis cruelly,
Drink now thy fyll,gif thow be dry:
For thow did ay blude ſchedding thriſt.
Now drynk at layſour , gif thow liſt.
Efter that Cyrus ſucceſſioun,
Of all the warld had poſſeſſioun,
Till Alexander with ſworde and fyre,
Obteinit perforce the Thrid Impyre:
Quhilk wes the king of Macedone,
With bailʒeand Greikis mony one,
In battell fell and furious,
Vincuſt the michtie Darius:
Quhilk wes the tent,and the laſt king,
Quhilk did efter King Cyrus ring:
As for this potent Empriour,
Alexander the Conquerour,
Gif thow at lenth wald reid his ring,
And of his cruell conqueſing,
In Ingliſche toung ,in his greit Buke,
At lenth his lyfe, thare thow may luke:
How Alexander that potent king,
Was twelf ʒeiris in his Conqueſing:
And how for all his greit conqueſt,
He leuit bot ane ʒeir in reſt:
Quhen be his Seruand ſecreitlie,
He poyſonit wes full pieteoſlie.
Lucane doith Alexander compair,
Till thounder or Fyreſlaucht in the air:
Ine cruell Planeit, ane mortall weird,

                                Doun

Doun thringand pepill with his sweird.
Ganges that maist famous Flude,
He myxit with the Indianis blude.
And Euphrates, with the blude of Perse,
Quhose crueltie for to reherse:
And saikles blude quhilk he did sched,
War richt abhominabill to be red.
Efter his schort prosperitie,
He deit with greit miserie.
It war to lang for to decyde it,
How all his Realmis wer deuydit,
Ay quhyll that Cesar Julius,
Quhen he had vincust Pompeius,
Was chosin Empriour and King,
Abufe the Romanis for till ring.
That potent Prince was the first man,
Quhilk the fourt Monarchie began:
And had the haill Dominioun,
Of euerilk land and Regioun:
Quhose successouris did regne but weir,
Ouer the warld mony ane houndreth zeir:
Bot gentill Julius allace,
Rang Empriour bot lytill space:
Quhilk I think pietie till deplore,
In Fyue Moneth, and lytill more,
Be fals exorbitant tresoun,
That prudent Prince was trampit doun,
And murdrest in his counsale hous,
Be cruell Brutus, and Cassius.
Efter that Julius was slane,
Did regne the greit Octauiane:

Of Em.

Of Empriouris ane of the best,
During his tyme, wes peace and rest,
Ouer all the warld, in ilk Regioun,
As storyis makis mentioun:
And als I mak it to the plane,
During the tyme of Octauiane:
The Sone of God, our Lord Iesu,
Tuke mankynd of the Virgin tru:
And wes that tyme in Bethleem borne,

Matth.2 To saif mankynd, quhilk was forlorne:
As Scripture makis narratioun,
Of his blissit Incarnatioun:

Now haue I tauld the, as I can,
How the foure Monarcheis began.
Bot in thy mynd thow may considder,
How wardlie power bene bot slidder:
For all thir greit Impyris ar gane,
Thow seis thare is na Prince allane,
Quhilk hes the haill dominioun,
This tyme of euery Regioun.
C. Father quhat resoun had those kingis,
Rewaris to be of vtheris ringis,
But ony richt or Iuste querrell,
Quharethrouch ye thay micht mak battel
And commoun pepill to dounthring?
To this (said I) make answering.
E. My Sone (said he) that sall be done,
As I best can, and that richt sone:
Thir Monarcheis, I vnderstand,
Preordinat war be the command,
Of God, the Plasmatour of all,

Dan. 8.

for to doun thring, and to mak thrall,
Undantit pepill bitious,
And als for to be gracious,
To thame quhilk vertuous wer, & gude,
As Daniell hes done conclude,
It lenth in till Propheceis,
How thair sulde be four Monarcheis:
His secund Chapture thow may sie,
How efter the First Monarchie:
Quhen Nabuchodonosor king,
Ane Image saw in his sleiping:
With austeir luke, in hicht and breid,
And of fyne pure gold was his heid:
His breist and armis of siluer bricht,
His wame of copper hard and wicht:
His loynĵ & lymmnis of Irne richt strang,
His fete of clay, Irne mixt amang.
From ane Montane thare came allane,
But hand of man, ane mekle stane:
Quhilk on that figouris fete did fall,
And dang all doun in poulder small.
Of quhose Interpretatioun,
Doctouris doith mak narratioun:
The Heid of Golde did signifie,
First of Assyrianis Monarchie:
The siluer Breist, that did apply,
To Persianis quhilk rang secundly.
The Wame of copper, or of bras,
Thridlie of Greikis compairit was:
His loynis, & lymmnis, of Irne and steill,
Clarkis hes thame compairit weill,

To Ro.

To Romanis, throuch thair diligence,
To haue the fourt preeminence:
Abufe all vther Natioun,
Be this Interpretatioun,
The myxit fete, with Irne and clay,
Did fignifie the leter day:
Quhen that the warld fulde be deuydit,
As efterwart fall be decydit.
So Chrift is fignifyit the ftane,
Quhofe Monarchie fall neuer be gane,
For vnder his dominioun,
All Princis falbe strampit doun.
Quhen that greit king Omnipotent,
Cummis to his generall iugement:
His Monarchie than falbe knawin,
As efter falbe to the fchawin.
And als the Scripture fall the tell,
Quhow in the aucht of Daniell:
He faw into his vifioun,
Be ane plane expofitioun,
How that the Greikis fulde wirk vengens,
Upon the Medis and Perfiens:
Comparand Greikis till ane Gait,
With ane horne, feirs, furious and hait:
Quhilk flew the Ram, with hornis two,
Compairit till Perfe, and Mede also:
And fa be Daniellis Propheceis,
All thair greit michtie Monarcheis:
The quhilkis all vther Realmis fuppryfit,
Be the greit God thay wer deuyfit,
Is he of Titus the Romane,

                                    Sone and

Sone and air to Uespassane:
Maid him ane furious Instrument.
To put the Iowis to greit torment:
Quhilk I purpose or I hyne fare
Schortlie that proces till declare.

Of the most miserabill, and   I I I.
most terribill Destructioun of
Ierusalem.

Ather (said I) declare to me,
Induring this fourte Monarchie,
The maist Infortune that |befell,
E. My Sone (said he) that sal I tel
The maist and Manifest miserie,
Became vpon the greit Cietie,
Ierusalem, quhen it was supprest,
As storyis makis manifest.
Bot as the Scripture doith deuyse,
Ierusalem was distroyit twyse.
First for the greit Idolatrie,
Quhilk thay committit in Iowrie:
The honour aucht to God allane.
Thay gaue to figouris of stock & stane.
Afore Christis Incarnatioun,
Come this first desolatioun,
Fyue hundreth zeiris, foure score & ten,
In Cronicles as thow may ken,
How Nabuchodonosor king,
That famous Cietie did down thring,

Barn. 6.

That

Thare king with pepill mony one,
Brocht thame all bound to Babilone:
Quhare thay remainit presoneiris,
The space of thre score, and ten zeiris.
And that first desolatioun,
was callit the Transmigratioun:
wes na man left in all thair landis,
Bot purellis laborand w thair handis
Till michtie Cyrus king of Perse,
As Daniell hes done reherse:
wes mouit be God, for till restore,
The Jowis, quhare y thay wer afore.
Gif J neglect, J war to blame,
The last seige of Jerusalame:
Quhose rewyne was most miserabill,
And for to tell richt terribill.
was neuer in eirth, cietie, nor toun,
Gat sic extreme destructioun:
The townis of Tyre, Thebes, nor Troy
Thay sufferit neuer halfe sic noy.
The Empriour Uespasiane,
He did deuyse that sege certane.

Luc. 19.   Thare wer the Prophecie compleit,
& 21.   Quhilk Christ spake on the mont Olyueit:
Marc. 13. Quhen he Jerusalem beheld,
The teiris from his ene disteld:
Seand be Deuyne prescience,
The greit destructioun & vengence,
Quhilk wes to come on that Cietie,
His hart peirsit with pietie:
Sayand Jerusalem, and thow knew,

Thy

Thy greit rewine, ſore wald thow rew:
For na thing I can to the ſchaw,
The veritie thow will nocht knaw:
Nor hes in conſideratioun,
Thy holy viſitatioun:
Thy pepill will na way conſidder,   Mat. 2
Quhame gatherit I wald haue to gidder,
As errand ſcheip, bene with thair hirdis,
Or as the Hen gatheris hir birdis,
Under hir wyngis tenderlie,
Quhilk thay refuſit diſpytfullie,
Quharefore ſall cum that dulefull day,
That na remedie mak thow may.
Thy doungeounis ſalbe doung in ſunder,
Sa that the warld ſall on the wunder.
Thy tempill now maiſt triumphand,
Salue tred doun amang the ſand: Mat. 24
And as he ſaid ſa it befell,
As heir efter I ſall the tell.
C. Schaw me (ſaid I) with circumſtance,
The ſpeciall cauſe of that miſchance.
E. (Quod he) as Scripture doith conclude,
For ſchedding of the ſaikles blude,
Of Prophetis quhilk God to thame ſend,
And als becauſe that thay miſkend,
Ieſu the Sone of God Souerane,
Quhen he amang thame did remane:
For all the miraklis that he ſchew,
Maliciouſlie thay him miſknew.
Thocht be his greit power Deuyne,
The watter cleir he turnit in wyne.
                          k   And be

And be that self power and micht,
To the blynd borne he gaue the sicht:
And gaue the crukit men thair feit,

Ioan. 21. And maid the Lipper hail compleit:
He hailit all, and rasit the deid,
Zit held thay him at mortall feid:

Mat. 21. Becaufe he fchew the veritie,
Thay did conclude that he fulde die.

Mat. 27. ¶ The Bifchoppis, Princis of the Preiftis,
Thay grew fa boldin in thair breiftis:
The Scrybis, and Doctouris of the Law,
Of God, nor man, quhilk ftude nane aw:
On Chrift Jefu to wyrk vengeans.
Richt fa the fals Pharifeans,
Ane Sect of kenzeit Religioun,
Deuyfit his confuffioun:
And fend thair feruandis at the laft,
And with ftrang cordis thay band him faft:

Ioan. 20. Syne fcurgit him, baith back and fyde,
That nane for blude micht fe his hyde:
Thare was nocht left ane penny breid,
Unwoundid from his feit till heid,
In maner of deriffioun,
Thay plet for him ane cruell Croun,
Of prunzeand thornis fcharp and lang,
Quhilk on his heuinlie hede thay thrang.
Syne gart hym for the greiter lack,
Bere his awin Gallous on his back:
Till the vyle place of Caluarie,
Quhare mony ane thoufand man micht fie.
That Innocent thay tuke perforce,

And plat

And plat him backwart to the Croce:
Throuch feit and hand{ greit naillis thay thrist
Till blude abundantlie out brist:
Without grunsching,clamour or cry,
That pane he sufferit paciently.
And for augmenting of his greuis,
Thay hangit him betuix twa theuis:
Quhare men micht se the bludie strandis
Quhilk{ sprang furth of his feit & handis.
From thornis thristit on his heid,
Ran doun bullering stremis reid,
In the presens of mony ane man,
That blude Royall on roches ran.
Schortlie to say,that heuiulie king,
In extreme dolour thare did hing,
Till he said Consummatum est,
With ane lowd cry,he gaue the gaist.
Quhen he was deid,thay tuke ane dart,
And Persit that Prince outtrouch þ hart
Fra quhame thare ran water and blude,
The eirth than trymlit to conclude.
Phebus did hyde his bemis bricht,
That throuch þ warld thare wes na licht
The greit Ueill of the tempill raue.
The deid men rais out of thair graue:
And in the Cietie did appeir,
As in the Scripture thow may heir:
Than Ioseph of Arimathie,
Did bury him,richt honestlie,
Bot zit he rose ful gloriouslie,
On the thrid day tryumphandlie,

K ij   With

With his Discipulis in certane,

Act.1. Fourty dayis he did remane.

Efter that to the heuin ascendit,

Thir Jowis na thing thair lyfe amendit

Nor gaue na credence till his sawis,

As at mair lenth the storie schawis:

Bot cruellie thay did oppres,

All men, that Christis name did profes:

And persecutit mony one,

Act.5. Thay presonit baith Peter and Jhone:

Act.7. And Steuin thay stonit to the deid.

From James the les, thay straik the heid.

This was the cause in conclusioun,

Of thair cruell confusioun.

The prudent Jow Josephus sayis,

That he was present in those dayis,

And in his buke makis mentioun,

How efter Christis Ascensioun,

The space of twa and fourtie zeiris,

Began those cruell mortall weiris.

The secund zeir of Uespasiane,

Quhare mony takin wer and slane.

Josephus planelie doith conclude,

Was neuer sene sic ane multitude,

Afore the tyme into the Toun,

Quhilk came for thair confusioun:

Thair greit Infortune sa befell,

That all the Princis of Israell,

Conuenit aganis the tyme of pace,

Bot till returne thay had na grace,

The bald Romanis with thair Chiftane,

                         Titus

Titus the Sone of Uespasiane,
Thair Armie ouer Judea spred,
Than all men to the Cietie fled,
Beleuand thare to get releif,
Bot all that turnit to thair miïcheif.
The Romanis lappit thame about,
That be na way thay micht win out:
Sax Moneth did that seige indure,
Quhare loît war mony ane Creature:
Quhilk thare in miïerie did remane,
Till thay war takin all, and ïlane.
During the tyme of this aïïailʒe,
Thair meit, and dzynk, & all did failʒe:
For thare was ïic ane multitude,
That thouïandis dyit, for falt of fude:
Neceïïitie gart thame eit perfors,
Dog, Cat, and Ratton, Aïïe and Hors:
Rytche men behuffit to eit thair golde,
Syne deit of hunger mony folde.
Sic hunger was without remeid,
The quick behuffit to eit the deid.
The filth of Cloïetʒ mony eit,
To lenth thair lyfe, thay thocht it ïweit
The famous Ladyis of the tonn,
For falt of fude thay fell in ïwoun:
Quhen thay micht get nane vther meit
Thay ïlew thair proper Barnis to eit:
Bot all for nocht diïpytfullie,
Thair awin ïowldiouris full gredilie,
Reft thame that fleïche maiït miïerabill
And thay with murning lamentabill:

K iiij

Luc.24.

For extreme hounger zeild the spreit,
Thare was the Prophecie compleit:
As Christ afore maid narratioun,
The day of his grym Passioun:
Quhen that the ladyis for him murnit,
Full pieteouslie he to thame turnit:
And said, Douchteris murne nocht for mie,
Murne on zour awin posteritie:
Within schort tyme sall cum that day,
That men of this Cietie sall say:
Quhen thay ar trappit in the snare,
Blyst be the wame, that neuer bare.
The baren papis, than thay sall blis,
That dulefull day ze sall nocht mis.
This Prophecie it come to pas,
That thay with mony lowd allas:
Sic sorrowfull lamentatioun,
Was neuer hard in that Natioun:
Seand those lustie Ladyis sweit,
Deand for hounger in the streit.
Thair husbandis, nor thair childring,
Micht gaue to thame na conforting:
Nor zit releif thame of thair harmis,
Bot atheris deand in vtheris armis.
Efter this wofull indigence,
Amang thame rose sic Pestilence,
Quhare in thare deit mony hounder,
Quhilk till declare, it war greit wounder.
And for finall conclusioun,
Those weirlyke wallis thay dang doun,
Prince Titus, with his Cheualrie,

with

With found of trompe tryumphandlie,
He enterit in that greit Cietie:
Bot till declare I thynke pietie:
The panefull clamour horribill,
Of woundit folk most miserabill:
Thare was nocht ellis, bot tak & slay,
For thare micht na man win away.
The strandis of blude, ran throuch the streit,
Of deid folk, trampit vnder feit:
Auld wedowis in the preis war smorit.
Zoung Virginis schamefullie deflorit.
The greit Templl of Salamone,
With mony ane curious caruit stone:
With perfyte pinnaclis on hicht,
Quhilkis war richt bewtifull and wicht:
Quhare in rytche Jowellis did abound,
Thay ruscheit rudelie to the ground:
And set in till thair furious Ire,
Sancta Sanctorum into fyre:
And with extreme confusioun,
All thair greit dungeouns thay dang doun.
Thair bursin war the boldiu breistis,
Of Bischoppis, Princis of the Preistis,
Thare takin was the greit vengeans,
On fals Scrybis, and Phariseans:
All thair payntit Ipocrisie,
That tyme micht mak thame na supplie:
That day thay dulefullie repentit,
That to the deith of Christ consentit,
Thocht it was our Saluatioun,
It was to thair Dampnatioun.

The ben-

The vengeance of the blude saikles,

Matt.23. From Abell till Zacharies:
That day vpon Jerusalem fell,
Bot tedious it war to tell.
The greit extreme confusioun,
And of blude sic effusioun:
Was neuer slane sa mony ane man,
At ane tyme sen the warld began.
The Jowis that day gat thair desyre,
Quhilk thay did ask into thair Ire:
As bene in Scripture specifyit,
The day quhen Chrisl was crucifyit,

Matt.26. Quhen Ponce Pilat the President,
Said to thame, I am Innocent,
Of the Just blude of Chrisl Jesus,
Thay cryit, his Blude licht vpon vs,
And on our Generatioun,
Thay gat thair Supplicatioun,
That thay with mony cairfull cry,
Thair blude was sched abundantly.
Josephus wrytis in his buke,
His Cronicle quha lisl to luke:
During that cruell seige certane,
Wer elleuin hundreth thousand slane:
Of presonaris, weill tauld and sene,
Foure score of thousandis & seuintene.
Out of the land thay did expell,
All the pepill of Israell:
And for thair greit Ingratitude,
Thay leue zit vnder Seruitude.
Thare is na Jow in na Cuntrie,

Quhilk

Quhilk hes ane fute of propertie:
Nor neuer had withouttin weir,
Sen this day fyftene hundreth zeir:
Nor neuer fall, I to the fchaw,
Till that thay turne till Chriftis Law.
Sum fayis that Jowis mony fald,
wer threttie for ane penny fald:
As Judas fauld the king of glore,
For threttie pennyis, and no more.
Efter that mony war mifcheuit,
Quhen nouellis paft how lang thay leuit,
Upon thair golde, withouttin dout,
Thay flit thair bellyis, to ferche it out.
The reft in Egipt, thay did fend,
Prefonaris to thair lyues end.
Titus tuke in his cumpanie,
Greit noumer of the moft worthie:
With him to Rome he led thame bound,
Syne cruellie did thame confound:
His victorie for till decore,
And for augmenting of his glore,
Gart put thame into publict places,
Quhare all folk mycht behauld thair faces.
Syne with wylde Lyonis cruellie,
He gart deuore thame dulefullie.
This hie tryumphand mychtie Toun,
At Pafche, was put to confufioun,
Becaufe that in the tyme of pace,
Thay Crucifyit the king of grace.
Sum hes this mater done indyte,
More Ornatlie than I can wryte,

        K b   Quhares

Quharefor I speik of it no more,
Onely to God be laude and gloir.

Of the miserabill end of certane
tyrrannous Princis. And speciallie the
begynnaris of the Four
Monarcheis.

NOw haue I done declare at thy
desyris,
As thou demadit into termis schort
And quha began the principal Im
pyris,
As Cronikle and Scripture dois report,
Quharefor, my Sone, I hartlie the exhort:
Perfytlie prynt in thy remembrance,
Of this inconstant warld the variance.

The Princis of thir four greit Monarcheis,
In thair maist hiest pomp Imperialis,
Traisting to be maist sure set in thair seis,
The fraudfull warld gaif to thame mortall fallis
For thair reward, bot dirk memoriallis:
Thocht ouir the warld thay had preeminence,
Of it thay gat nane vther recompence.

For siclyke as the snaw dois melt in May,
Throuch the reflex of Phebus beimis bricht,
Thir greit Impyris, richt sa ar went away,
Gane bene thair gloir, thair power & pair micht

Becaus

Becaufe thay war Rewaris withouttin richt,
And blude fcheddaris,full cruell to conclude,
Richt cruellie tharefor, wes fched thair blude.

Behald how God, ay fen the warld began,
Hes maid of tyrane kingis Inftrumentis,
To fcurge pepill,& to kyll mony ane man,
Quhilkis to his law wer Inobedientis,
Quhen thay had done perfurneis his ententis,
In danting wrangous pepill fchamefullie,
He fufferit thame be fcurgit cruellie.

Euin as y̧ Scule maifter dois mak ane wād,
To dant and ding fcolaris of rude Ingyne,
The quhilkis will nocht ftudy at his command,
He fcurgis thame,and onely to that fyne,
That thay fulde to his trew counfale inclyne:
Quhen thay obey,and meifit bene his Ire,
He takis the wand,and caftis into the fyre.

God of king Pharao, maid ane inftrument,
Quhilk was the greit king of Eegyptiens:
His awin peculiar pepill to torment.
That beand done,he wrocht on him vengens,
And leit him fall throuch Inobediens:
And fynallie,he with his greit Armie,
In the reid Sey,thame drownit dulefullie.

Richt fa, of Nabuchodonofor king,
God maid of him ane furious Inftrument,
Jerufalem and the Jowis,to doun thring,
Quhen thay to God wer Inobedient,
Syne reft hym from his rytches and his rent.
                                        And him

Exod. 7.
Exod.13.
Dani.4.

And him transformit in ane beist brutell,
Seuin zeiris and more as wryttis Daniell.

Alexander throuch prydefull tyrannie,
In zeiris twelf did mak his greit Conquest,
My scheddand saikles blude full cruellie:
Till he was king of kingis, he tuke na rest,
In all the warld, quhen he was full possest,
In Babilon thronit tryumphandlie,
Throuch poyson strang, decesit dulefullie.

Duke Hanniball the strang Chartagiane,
The danter of the Romanis pomp and glorie,
Be his power war mony ane thousand slane,
As may be red at lenth in till his storie,
At Cannas, quhare he wan the victorie,
On Romanis handis, the deid lay on ÿ ground,
Thre heipit Buschellis war of ringis found.

Into that mortall battell I heir sane,
Of the Romanis most worthie weiriouris,
By presonaris, war fourty thousand slane:
Of quhom thare was thretty wyse Senatouris
And xx. Lordis, the quhilkis had bene Pretouris,
That dyit to, in defence of thair Cuntrie,
And for till hald thair land at libertie.

Quhat reward gat this cruell Campioun,
Quhen he had slane so greit ane multitude,
And quhen the glas of his glorie was run?
Ane schamefull deith, and schortlie to conclude,
This bene reward of oll scheddaris of blude.
For he gat sic extreme confusioun,

He flew

He flew him felf in dzinking ftrang poyfoun.

Behald the twa maift famous Campiounis,
(That is to fay) Julius and Pompey,
Quhilk did conqueis all eirdlie Regiounis,
Alfweill main land, as Ilis in the Sey:
And to the Toun of Rome gart thame obey;
Foz Pompeius fubdewit the Ozient,
And Julius Cefar all the Occident.

Bot finallie thir twa did ftryue foz ftait,
Quhare throw thre hudzeth M. men wer flane,
Bot Pompeius efter that greit debait,
He murdzeifit was, the ftozie tellis plane.
Than Julius was Pzince and Souerane,
Abufe the haill warld, Empziour and King,
Bot into reft, fchozt tyme indurit his ring.

Foz within Fyue Monethis, & lytill mair,
Amyd his Lozdis in the counfale hous,
He murdzeſit was, quhat neidis pzoces mair:
As I haue faid, be Bzute and Caſſius.
Gif thow wald knaw thair deithis dolozous,
Thow mofte at lenth ga reid ẏ Romane ftozie,
Quhilk hes this mater put in memozie.

Gane is the goldin warld of Affyzianis,
Of quhome King Ninus was firſt & pzincipall:
Gane is the filuer warld of Perſianis:
The copper warld of Greikis now is thzall,
The warld of Jrue, quhilk was the laft of all,
Compairit to the Romanis in thair gloze,
It gane richt fa, I here of thame no moze.

                                        Now

Now is the warld of Irne mixit with clay,
As Daniell at lenth, hes done indyte:
The greit Impyris ar meltit clene away.
Now is the warld of dolour and dispyte:
I se nocht ellis, bot troubill infinyte,
Quharefor, my Sone, I mak it to the kend,
This warld I wait, is drawand to ane end.

Tokningis of deirth, hounger and pestilence,
With cruell weiris, baith be sey and land,
Realme aganis realme, with mortall violence:
Quhilk signifyis the last day euin at hand,
Quharefor, my Sone, be in thy faith constand.
Raising thy hart to God, and cry for grace,
And mend thy lyfe, quhyll thou hes tyme & space

V.   The fift Spirituall and
Papall Monarchie.

FAther, is thare na Prince regnand
Quhilk hes the warld now at co-
mand,
As had the kingis of Assyrianis,
The Persis Greik, or ye Romanis,
Quha hes now maist dominioun,
Of euerilk Land and Regioun?
E. Thare is na Prince, my Sone (said he)
That hes the principall Monarchie,
Abufe the warld vniuersall,
With haill power Imperiall:
As Alexander or Darius,

Or as

Or as had Cesar Julius,
For Orient and Occident,
To thame wer all obedient.
Nochtwithstanding, I find ane King,
Quhilk intill Europe doith ring:
That is the potent Pope of Rome,
Impyrand ouer all Christindome.
To quhame na prince may be compair,
As Cannon Lawis can declair.
All Princis of the Occident,
Ar till his grace obedient.
For he hes haill power compleit,
Baith of the body and the spreit:
Quhilk neuer had na Prince afore,
Except the michtie king of gloze.
To Christ he is greit Lewtennand,
In holy Peteris sait sittand.
Sa he is of all Kingis king,
Quhilk into Europe now doith ring.
And as the Romane Empriouris,
Hauing the warld vnder thair curis,
Had Princis, knichtis & Campiounis,
Rewlaris into all Regiounis:
Uphalding thair authoritie.
Using Iustice and policie.
Richt so this potent pope of Rome,
The Souerane king of Christindome,
He hes in till ilk Countrie,
His Princis of greit grauitie:
In sum countreis his Cardinalis,
In thair maist precious apparaillis:

Archi

Archibischoppis, Bischoppis thow may sie,
Discending his auctoritie:
With vther potent Patriarchis,
Collegis full of cunning Clarkis,
Abbotis and Priouris, as ʒe ken,
Mistewlaris of Religious men.
Officialis, with thair Procuratouris,
Quhose langsum law, spulʒeis ȝ puris.
Archedenis and Denis of Dignitie,
Greit Doctouris of Deuinitie.
Thair Chantouris ȝ thair Sacristanis
Thair Tresoureiris, ȝ thair Subdenis
Legionis of Preistis Seculeiris,
Personis, Uicaris, Monkis, ȝ Freiris,
Of diuers Ordouris mony one,
Quhilk langsum war for till expone:
In sindry habytis, as ʒe ken,
Different from vther Christin men.
Fair Ladyis of Religioun.
Professit in euery Regioun,,
Fals Heremitis, fassionit like the freirȝ,
Proud parische Clarkis ȝ Pardoneirȝ.
Thair Gryntaris ȝ thair Chamberlanȝ
With thair Temporall Courtissanis.
Thus all the warld, be Land and Sey
His Sanctitude thay do obey:
Nocht onely his Spirituall kingdome
Bot the greit Empriour of Rome,
And kingis of euerilk Regioun,
That day quhē thay refaue thair croun
Thay mak aith of Fidelitie,

           Til Defend

Till defend his auctoritie.
Mairouer with humill reuerence,
Thay mak till him obedience:
Be thair selfis, or Imbassadouris,
Or vtheris ornate Oratouris.
Quha did ganestand his Maiestie,
His Lawis or his lybertie:
Or haldis ony Opinioun,
Contrair his greit Dominioun,
Other be way of deid or wordis,
Ar put to deith,be fyre or swordis.
Sanct Peter stylit was Sanctus,
Bot he is callit Sanctissimus.
His style at lenth,gif thow wald knaw
Thow moste ga luke the Cannon law:
Baith in the Sixte and Clementene,
His staitlie style thair may be sene.
Thair sal thow find,reid,gif thow can,
How he is nother God nor man.
C.Quhat is he than, be zour Jugemēt
Quod I,me thynk him different,
Far from our Souerane Lord Jesus,
And till his kynd contrarious,
For Christ wes God, & naturall man,
Gif he be nother, quhat is he than?
E.The Cannon Law,my sone(said he)
That questioun will declare to the,
It dois transcend my rude Ingyne,
His Sanctitude for till defyne,
Or to schaw the auctoritie,
Perteining to his Maiestie,

Ioan. I.

L   Sa greit

Sa greit ane Prince, quhare sall thou find,
That Spirituallie may lose and bind.
Nor be quhame sinnis are forgeuin,
Be thay with his Disciplis schreuin:
Quhame euer he bindis be his micht,
Thay boundin ar in Goddis sicht:
Quhame euer he lousis in eirth heir doun
Ar lousit be God in his Regioun.
Als he is Prince of Purgatorie,
Delyuering saulis from pane to glorie:
Of that dirk Dungeoun but dout,
Quhame euer he plefis he takʒ thame out
Our secreit synnis euery ʒeir,
We morſ schaw to sum Preiſt or Freir,
And tak thair Abſolutioun,
Or ellis we get na remiſſioun.
Sa be this way, thay cleirlie ken,
The secretis of all secular men.
Thair secretis we knaw nocht at all,
Thus ar we to thame bound and thrall.
Quhat euer thair miniſteris commandis
Moſte be obeyit without demandis.
Quharefor, my Sone, I say to thie,
This is ane maruellous Monarchie,
Quhilk hes power Imperiall,

Courte.   Baith of the body and the Saull:
C. Father (quod I) declare to me,
Experie.   Quha did begin this Monarchie?
E. (Quod he) Chriſt Jeſus God and man
That Impyre gratiouſlie began,
Nocht be the fyre, nor be the ſword,

                               Bot be

Bot be the vertew of his word.
And left in till his Testament,
Mony ane deuote Document:
With his Successouris to be ûit,
Thocht mony of thame be now abûît:
For Peter and Paull with all the rest,
Of thair brethren maid manifest,
The Law of God with trew intent,
Preching the auld & new Testament,
Thay led thair lyfe in pouertie,
Deuotioun and humilitie,
And did thair maister Christ Jesus,
And war nocht half sa glorious:
As thair Successouris now in Rome,
Impyrand ouer all Christindome.
Efter the deith of Peter and Paull,
And Christis trew Discipulis all,
Thair Successouris within few zeiris
As at mair lenth thair storie beiris,
Full craftie clam to the hicht,
From spiritual lyfe to temporall micht.
C. Father or we pas further more,
Quhen did begin thair temporal glore?
E. Sone (said he) thou sall vnderstand,
Or euer ane Pape gat ony land:
Twa & thretty gude Paipis in Rome,
Ressauit the Crown of Martirdome:
Bot nocht the Thrinfald Diadame,
To weir thre Crown thay thocht greit schame
Till Siluester the Confessour,
From Constantine the Empriour,

Ephe. j.
Luc. ix.

Courte.

Experi.

L ii Ressauit

Ressauit the Realme of Italie,
Richt sa of Rome the greit Citie.
That was the rute of thair ryches,
Than sprang the well of welthines.
Quhen that the Pape was maid ane king,
All Princis bowit at his bidding.
This Act wes done withouttin weir,
From Christis deith thre hundreth zeir.
Than Lady Sensualitie,
Tuke lugeing in that greit Citie.
Quhare scho sensyne hes done remane,
As thair awin lady Souerane.
Than Kingis in till all Nationis,
Maid Preistis greit foundationis:
Thay thocht greit merite and honour,
To counterfait the Empriour,
As did Dauid of Scotland king,
The quhilk did found, during his ring,
Fyftene Abbayis, with temporall landis,
Withouttin teindis and offerandis,
Be quhose holy simplicitie,
He left the Crown in pouertie,
Now haue I schawin the, as I can,
How thair temporall Impyre began,
Ascending vp ay gre be grie,
Abufe the Empriouris Maiestie,
Sa quhen thay gat amang thair handis,
Of Italie all the Empriouris landis:
Efter that in ilk Countrie,
Sprang vp thair Temporalitie,
With sa greit rytches and sic rent,

                                        That

That thay gan to be negligent,
In making Ministratioun,
To Christis trew Congregatioun:
And tuke na mair pane in thair preching,
And far les trauell in thair teching:
Changeing thair Spiritualtie,
In temporall Sensualtie.
C.Father,thynk ȝe,that thay ar sure,
That thair Impyre sall lang indure?
E.Apperandlie,it may be kend,
(Quod he)thair gloȝe sal haue ane end.
I mene thair temporall Monarchie,
Sall turne in till humilitie,
Throuch Goddis word without debait
Thay sall turne to thair first estait:
As Danielis Prophecie appeiris,
Thareto sall nocht be mony ȝeiris:
Howbeit Christis faith sall neuer fall:
Bot mair and mair it sall preuaill.
Thocht Christis trew Congregatioun,
Suffer greit tribulatioun,
C.Father (said I) be quhat resoun,
Thynk ȝe thair impyre may cum doun?
E.Considering thair preeminence:
(Quod he)for inobedience,
Abusing the Commandement,
Quhilk Christ left in his Testament: Mat.25.
Using thair awin traditioun,
Mair than his Institutioun.
For Christ in his last Conuentioun,
The day of his Ascensioun:

L iij   Till his

Matt. 18 Till his Discipulis gaue command,
Ioan.15. That thay sulde pas in euery land:
Act.1.   To teche and preche with trew intent,
          His Law and his Commandement.
          Nane vther office, he to thame gaue,
          He did nocht bid thame seik nor craue,
          Cors presentis, nor offerandis,
          Nor get Lordschipp of temporal landis
          Bot now it may be hard and sene,
          Baith with thyne eiris, and thyne ene,
          How Prelatis now in euery land,
          Takis lytill cure of Christis command,
          Nother into thair deidis nor sawis,
          Neglecting thair awin Cannon lawis
          Using thame selfis contrarious,
          For the maist part to Christ Jesus.
Matt.4.   Christ thocht na schame to be ane precheour,
          And till all pepill of treuth ane techeour:
          Ane Pape, Bischop, nor Cardinall,
          To teche nor preche, will nocht be thrall.
          Thay send furth freiris to preche for thame,
          Quhilk garris ÿ pepill mok thame with schame
          Christ wald nocht be ane temporall king,
Ioan.6.   Rychelie into na Realme to ring:
          Bot sied temporall authoritie,
          As in the Scripture thow may sie,
          All men may knaw, how Papis ringis,
          In Dignitie abuse all kingis,
          Als weill in Temporaltie,
          Als into Spiritualtie,
          Thow may se be experience,

                                        The

The Papis princely preeminence.
In Croniclis gif thow list to luke,
How Carion wryttis in his Buke,
Ane notabill narratioun,
The zeir of our Saluatioun,
Elleuin hundreth, and sax and fyftie,
Pape Alexander presumptuouslie:
Quhilk wes the thrid Pape of ÿ name,
To Frederik Empriour did defame:
In Ueneis that tryumphand Town,
That nobill Empriour gart ly down,
Apon his wame with schame and lack,
Syne tred his feit apon his back,
In taikin of Obedience,
Thare he schew his preeminence,
And caulit his Clergie for to sing,
Thir Wordis efter following,

Super Aspidem & Basiliscum ambulabis, Psal.91.
Et conculcabis leonem & Draconem.
That is,
Thou sall gang vpon ÿ edder & the coketrice,
And ÿ sall tred down ÿ lyoun & the Dragoun.

Than said this humill Empriour,
I do to Peter this honour:
The Pope answerit with wordis wraith,
Thow sall me honour and Peter baith.
Chrift for to schaw his humill spreit,
Did wasche his pure Discipulis feit:
The Popis holynes I wys,
Will suffer Kingis his feit to kys:
L iiij Birdis

Luc.9. Birdis had thair nestis, & toddis thair den,
Bot Christ Jesus, Saiffer of men,
In eirth had nocht ane penny breid,
Quhare on he micht repose his heid.
Howbeit the Popis Excellence,
Hes Castellis of Magnificence:
Abbottis, Bischoppis and Cardinallis,
Hes plesand Palices Royallis:
Lyke Paradyse ar those Prelatis places,
Wanting na plesour of fair faces.

Act.4. Jhone, Androw, James, Peter, nor Paull,
Had few housis amang thame all:
From tyme thay knew the veritie,
Thay did contempne all propertie:
And war richt hartfully content,

Ioan. 19. Of meit, drink, and abuilzement.
To saif Mankynd that was forlorne,
Christ bure ane cruell Crown of thorne:
The Pope thrie Crownis for the nonis,
Of golde, pouldrit with precious stonis.
Of golde, and siluer, I am sure,
Christ Jesus tuke bot lytill cure:
And left nocht, quhen he zeild the spreit,
To by him self ane windyng scheit.
Bot his Successour gude Pope Jhone,
Quhen he deceisit in Auinione,
He left behynd him ane tresour,
Of gold and siluer be mesour:
Be ane Just computatioun:
Weill fyue and twenty Myllioun;
As doith Indyte Palmerius,

Reid

Reid him , and thow ſall fynd it thus.
Chriſtis Diſciplis wer weill knawin,
Throuch vertew, quhilk wes be thame ſchawin
In ſpeciall feruent cheritie,
Greit patience and humilitie,
The Popis floke in all Regiounis,
Ar knawin beſt be thare clippit crounis.
Chriſt he did honour Matrimonie,   Ioan. 2.
Into the Cane of Galilie,
Quhare he be his power Diuyne,
Did turne the water into the wyne.
And als cheiſit ſum Maryit men,
To be his ſeruandis as ʒe ken ,
And Peter during all his lyfe,
He thocht na ſin , to haue ane wyfe.
ʒe ſall nocht find in na paſſage,
Quhare Chriſt forbiddith mariage:
Bot leiſſum till ilk man to marie,
Quhilk wantis the gift of Chaſtitie.
The Pope hes maid the contrair Lawis,
In his kingdome , as all men knawis:
Nane of his Preiſtis dar marie wyfis,
Under na les pane nor thair lyfis:
Thocht thay haue Concubynis fyftene,
Into that cace , thay ar ouerſene:
Quhat chaſtitie, thay keip in Rome,
Is weill kend ouer all Chriſtindome.
Chriſt did ſchaw his obedience,   Mat. 17.
Unto the Empriouris excellence,
And cauſit Peter for to pay.
Tribute to Ceſar, for thaine twaz,

Paule biddis vs be obedient,
To kyngis as the most excellent.
The contrair did Pape Selestene,
Quhen that his Sanctitude serene,
Did crown Henry the Empriour,
I think he did him small honour :
For with his fete he did him crown,
Syne with his fete the Crown dang down:
Sayand I haue Authoritie,
Men till exalt to dignitie:
And to mak Empriouris and kingis,
And syne depryue thame of thair ringis.
Peter be my Opinioun,
Did neuer vse sic Dominioun:
Apperandlie be my Judgement,
That Pape red neuer the New Testament:
Gif he had lernit at that lore
He had refusit sic vane glore:
As Barnabas Peter, and Paull,
And richt sa Christis Discipulis all.

Act.10.　The Capitane Cornelius,
Quhen sanct Peter came till his hous:
Till worschip him fell at his feit
Bot sanct Peter with humill spreit,
Did rais him vp with diligence,
And did refuse sic Reuerence:

Apoc.19　Richt sa sanct Jhone the Euangelist,
& 22.　The Angellis feit he wald haue kist:
Bot he refusit sic honour,
Sayand I am bot seruitour:
Richt sa thy fallow and thy brother,

Geue

Geue gloze to God and to naue vther.
And lyke wyse Barnabas and Paull,   Act.14.
Sic honour did refuse at all:
In Listra quhare thay wrocht greit warkis,
The Preist of Jupiter with his Clarkis:
And all the pepill with thair auyce,
Wald haue maid to thame Sacrifyce:
Of quhilk thay war sa discontent,
That thay thair claithing raue and rent,
And Paule amang thame rudely ran,
Sayand, J am ane mortall man:
Geue gloze to God of kingis king,
That made heuin, eirth, and euery thing,
Sen Peter and Paule vane gloze refusit,
With Papis quhy suld sic gloze be vsit?
Peter, Androw, Jhone, James, and Paull,
And Christis trew Discipulis au:
Be Goddis word thair faith defendit,
To birn, and skald, thay neuer pretendit:
The Pape defendis his traditioun,
Be flammand fyze without remissioun.
Howbeit men brek the Law Deuyne,
Thay ar nocht put to sa greit pyne:
For huredome, noz Idolatrie,
For Incest noz Adulterie:
Oz quhen zoung Uirginis ar deflozit,
For sic thing men ar nocht abhozit.
Bot quha that eitis flesche into Lent,
Ar terriblie put to torment:
And gif ane Preist happynnis to mary,
Thay do him baneis, curs, and warie,

                                        Thocht

Thocht it be nocht aganis the Law,
Of God, as men may cleirly knaw,
Betuix thir twa, quhat difference bene,
Baith faithfull folk it may be sene:
Sic Antitheses mony ma,
I micht declare, quhilkis I lat ga:
And may nocht tary to compyle,
Of lyk ordour the staitlie style.
The sillie Nun will thynk greit schame
Without scho callit be Madame.
The pure Preist thinks he getts na richt
Be he nocht stylit lyke ane knicht:
And callit Schir, afore his name,
As Schir Thomas, & schir williame:
All Monkis, ȝe may here and sie
Ar callit Denis, for Dignitie:
Howbeit his mother milk the kow,
He mon be callit Dene Androw,
Dene Peter, dene Paul & dene Robart
With Christ thay tak ane painfull part
With doubill cleithing from the cald,
Eitand & drinkand quhen thay wald:
With curious Countring in the queir,
God wait gif thay by Heuin full deir.
My Lord Abbot richt venerabill,
Ay marschellit vpmost at the tabill:
My Lord Bischop, maist reuerent,
Set abufe Eirlis in Parliament:
And Cardinalis during thare ringis,
Fallowis to Princis, and to kingis.
The Pope exaltit in honour,

Abuse

Abuse the potent Empriour.
The proude persone I think trewlie,
He leidis his lyfe richt lustelie:
For quhy? he hes nane vther pyne,
Bot tak his teind, and spend it syne.
Bot he is oblissit be resoun,
To preiche vntill his Parichioun:
Thocht thay want preiching seuintene zeir,
He will nocht want ane boll of beir.
Sum Personis hes at his cammand,
The wantoun Wenchis of the land:
Als thay haue greit prerogatyuis,
That may depart ay with thair wyuis
Without diuorce, or summonding,
Syne tak ane vther but wedding.
Sum man wald think ane lustie lyfe,
Ay quhen he list, to change his wyfe:
And tak ane vther of mair bewtie,
Bot Secularis wantis that lybertie,
The quhilk ar bound in mariage,
Bot thay lyke rammis into thair rage,
Unpissilit rynnis amang the zowis,
Sa lang as Nature in thame growis
And als the Uicar, as I trow,
He will nocht faill to take ane kow:
And vpmaist claith (thocht babis thame ban)
From ane pure selie husband man:
Quhen that he lyis for till die,
Hauing small bairnis twa or thrie:
And his thre ky withouttin mo,
The Uicar moste haue ane of tho,

with the

With the gray cloke, that happis the bed,
Howbeit that he be purelie cled.
And gif the wyfe de on the morne,
Thocht all the babis sulde be forlorne,
The vther kow he cleikis away,
With hir pure cote of roploch gray:
And gif within twa dayis or thre,
The eldest Chylde hapnis to de,
Of the thrid kow he will be sure,
Quhen he hes all than vnder his cure,
And Father and Mother baith ar deid
Beg mon the babis, without remeid.
Thay hald the Corps at the Kirk style,
And thair it most remane ane quhyle,
Till thay get sufficient souertie,
For thair kirk richt, and dewtie:
Than cummis the landis lord perfors,
And cleikis till him ane herield hors.
Pure laubouraris wald that Law wer doun,
Quhilk neuer was foundit be resoun.
I hard thame say vnder confessioun,
That Law is brother till Oppressioun.
My Sone, I haue schawin as I can,
How this Fyft Monarchie began:
Quhose greit Impyre for to report,
At lenth, the tyme bene all to schort:

            Ane

Ane Descriptioun of the Court of Rome.

V I.

Ather (said I) quhat rewll kepe
thay in Rome,
Quhilk hes the Spirituall domi=
nioun,   (Dome:
And Monarchie abuse al Christin=
Schaw me, I mak ȝow Supplicatioun?
E. My Sone, wald I mak trew narratioun,
(Said he) to Peter & Paull thocht thay succeid
I think thay preue nocht that into thair deid.

For Peter, Androw & Jhone wer fischarȝ fyne
Of men and wemen, to the Christian Faith:
Bot that to haue, spred thair net w huik & lyne,
On rentis rytche on gold, and vther graith,
Sic fisching to neglect, thay will be laith:
For quhy, yat haue fischit in ouerthort ȝ strādis,
Ane greit part trewlie of all temporall landis.

With that the tent part of all gude mouabill,
For the vphalding of thair Digniteis,
So bene thair fisching verray proffitabill,
On the dry land als weill, as on the Seis,
Thair herywater, thay spred in all Countreis:
And w thair hois net, daylie drawis to Rome,
The maist fyne gold, that is in Christindome.

I dar weill say, within this fyftie ȝeir,
Rome hes resauit furth of this Regioun,

For Bullis & benefice(quhilk thay by full deir,
Quhilk in ye ful weil haue payit ane kingis rāson
Bot war I worthy for till weir ane Croun,
Preistis sulde na mair our substance sa consome
Sending ʒeirlie so greit rytches to Rome.

Into thair tramalt net,thay fangit ane fische
Mair nor ane quhaill,worthie of memorie:
Of quhome thay haue had mony daintie dische,
Be quhome thay ar exaltit to greit glorie,
That maruellous monstour callit Purgatorie:
Howbeit till vs, it is nocht amiabill,
It hes to thame,bene verray profitabill.

Lat thay ye fructefull fische eschaip thair net
Be quhame thay haue sa greit commoditeis:
Ane mair fat fische, I traist thay sall not get,
Thocht thay wald serche ouerthort ye Occeane
Adew the daylie dolorous Dirigeis: (seis,
Selie pure Preistis,may sing w hart full sorie,
Want thay that panefull palice Purgatorie.

Fare weill Monkrie,w Chanoun,Nun & freit
Allace thay will be lichtleit in all landis:
Cowlis will na mair be kend in Kirk nor queir,
Lat thay that frutefull fische eschaip thair hādis
I counsaill to bynd hym fast in bandis:
For Peter,Androw,nor Jhone,culde neuer get
Sa proffitabill ane fische into thair net.

Thair merchandyse in till all Nationis,
Is prentit leid,thair walx and parchement,
Thair Pardonis,and thair Dispensationis,

                                                        Thay

Thay do exceid sum temporall Princis rent,
In sic trafficque thay ar nocht negligent:
Of benefice, thay mak gude marchandyce,
Throw Symonie, quhilk thay hald lytill vyce.

Christ did command Peter, to feid his scheip, Ioan. 21.
And sa he did feid thame full tenderlie:
Of that command thay tak bot lytill keip,
Bot Christis scheip thay spulȝe pietuouslie:
And with the woll, thay cleith thame curiouslie
Lyke gormãd wolfȝ ꝑai tak of thame ꝑair fude,
Thai eit ꝑair flesche, & drinkȝ baith milk & blude.

For that Office, thay serue bot lytill hyre,
I thynk sic Pastouris ar nocht for to pryse,
Quhilk can not gyde thair scheip about ꝑ myre:
Thay ar sa besie in thair merchandyse,
Thocht Peter was Porter of Paradyse: Matt.16.
That plesand passage craftelie thay close,
Throw thame richt few, gettȝ entres I suppose

Christ Iesus said, as Mathew did report,
Wo be to Scribis, and to Pharisianis,   Mat. 24.
The quhilkis did close of Paradyce the port,
Of thame we haue the same experience,
To enter thare, thay mak small diligence,
Thay tak sic cure of temporall besines,
Richt sa from vs, thay stop the plane entres,

Those spirituall keis, quhilkȝ Christ to Peter
Thair colour cleir w reik & roust ar fadit. (gaif
Unoccuppit, thay hald thame in thair naif,
Of that Office, thay serue to be degradit,
                        M   Of Goddis

With Goddis word, without ȝ thay remeid it,
Oppining ȝ port quhilk lāg tyme hes bene closit
That we may enter with thame, & be reiosit.

Ioan. 10.
            Contrair till Chriſtis Inſtitutioun,
To thame that deis, in habite of ane Freir,
Rome hes thame grantit full Remiſſioun,
To pas til heuin ſtraucht way withouttin weir
Quhilk bene in Scotland vſit mony ane ȝeir.
Be thair ſic vertew in ane freiris hude,
I think in vane, Chriſt Jeſu ſched his blude.

            Wald God the Pope quhilk hes præeminence
With aduyſe of his counſaill generall,
That thay wald do thair detfull diligence,
That Chriſtis Law micht keipit be ouer all.
And trewlie prechit, baith to greit and finall,
And geue to thame ſpirituall Authoritie,
Quhilk could perfitelie ſchaw the veritie.

            Quha can not preche, ane Preiſt ſuld nocht be
As may be preuit be the Law deuyne,   (namit,
And be the Canon Law, thay ar defamit,
That takis Preiſtheid, bot onelie to that fyne,
Till all vertew thair hartis thay ſulde inclyne:
In ſpeciall to preche with trew intentis,
And miniſter the neidfull Sacramentis.

            As for thair Monkȝ, thair Chanounȝ, & thair
And luſtie Ladyis of Religioun,   (Freiris,
I knaw nocht quhat to thair Office effeiris:
Bot men may ſe thair greit abuſioun,
Thay ar nocht lyke into concluſioun,

                                    Nocht

Nother into thair wordis,nor thair warkis ,
To the Apostilis,Prophetis nor Patriarkis.

Gif prefentlie thir Prelatis can not preche,
Than lat ilk Bifchop haue ane Suffragane,
Or Succeffour, quhilk can the pepill teche,
On thair expenfis zeirlie to remane,
To caufe the pepill from thair vyces refrane.
And quhen ane Prelate,hapnith to deceace,
Than put ane perfite prechour in his place.

Do thay nocht fa,on thame fall ly the charge
Geuand vnabill men authoritie,
As quha wald mak ane fteirman till ane barge
Of ane blynd borne,quhilk can na danger fe,
Gif that fchip droun,forfuith J fay for me,
Quha gaif that Steirman fic commiffioun,
Sulde of the fchip mak reftitutioun.

The humane Lawis,that ar contrarious,
And nocht conforming to the Law diuyne,
Thay fulde expell,and hald thame odious,
Quhē thay perfaue thame cum to na gude fyne
Inuentit bot be fenfuall mennis Ingyne,
As that Law,quhilk forbiddis Mariage,
Caufing zoung Clarkis birn in luftis rage.

Difficill is Chaftitie till obferue,   Rom.8.
But fpeciall grace,laubour, and abftinence,
In till our flefche ay regnis,till we fterue,
That firft Originall fin,Concupifcence,
Quhilk we throuch Adamis Jnobedience,
Hes done Jncur,and fall indure for euer,

         M ij   Quhyll

Quhyll that our saull and body deith disseuer,

Genes.2   Quharefo2 God maid of Mariage the band,
In Paradyce(as Scripture doith reco2de)
Ioan.2.   In Galilie,richt sa J vnderstand,
Wes mariage honourit be Ch2ist our Lo2de,
Auld Law & New,thare to thay do conco2de:
I think fo2 me,better that thay had sleipit,
No2 till haue maid ane Law, and neuer keipit.

Matth.1.   Tuke nocht Ch2ist Jesus his Humanitie,
Of ane Virgine,in Mariage contractit,
Lnc.1.   And of hir flesche, cled his Diuinitie?
Quhy haue thay done that blissull band deiectit
In thair kingdome?wald God it war co2rectit
That 2oung P2elatis,micht marie lustie wyfis
And nocht in sensuall lust,to leid thair lyfis.

Did nocht Ch2ist cheis of honest maryit men
Allsweill as thay that keipit Chastitie,
Fo2 to be his Discipulis , as 2e ken,
As in the Scripture cleirlie thow may sie
Thay keipit still thair wyfis with honestie,
As Peter, and his spousit b2eth2en all,
Obseruit Chaistitie Matrimoniall.

1.Tim.4.   Bot now appeiris the P2ophecie of Paull,
How sum suld ryis into the latter age,
That from the trew faith suld depart and fall,
And sulde fo2bid the band of mariage,
Als thow sall find into that same passage,
Thay suld command from meitis till abstene,
Quhilk God creat his pepill to sustene.

Bot

Bot sen the Pope our spirituall prince & king
He dois ouer se sic vyces manifest,
And in his kingdome sufferith for to ring,
The men be quhome the veritie bene supprest:
I excuse nocht him self mair than the rest.
Allace how sulde we membris be weill vsit,
Quhen sa our Spirituall heidis bene abusit?

The famous ancient Doctor Auicene,
Sayis quhen euill rewine discendis from ÿ heid,
Into the membris, generith mekle pane,
Without thair be maid haistelie remeid,
Quhen ÿ cald humour dounwart dois proceid:
In Sennounis it causis Arthetica,
Richt sa in the handis cramp Chiragra.

Of Maledyis, it generis mony mo,
Bot gif men get sum Souerane preserue,
As in the theis Scyathica Passio:
And in the breist, sumtyme the strang Caterue,
Quhilk causis men richt haistelie to sterue:
And Podagra, difficill for to cure,
In mennis feit, quhilk lang tyme dois indure.

Sa to this most tryumphand court of Rome
This similitude full weill I may compair,
Quhilk hes bene herschip of all Christindome,
And to the warld ane euill exemplair,
That vmquhyle was Lod sterre, and luminair,
And the maist sapient sait of Sanctitude,
Bot now allace bair of Beatitude.

Thair kingdome may be callit Babilone,

Apoc.18 Quhilk vnquhyle wes ane bricht Jerusalem,
As planely meanis the Apostill Jhone,
Thair most famous Cietie,hes tynt the fame,
Inhabitaris thairof,thair nobill name:
For quhy thay haue of Sanctis Habitakle,
To Simon Magus maid ane Tabernakle.

And horribill vaill of euerilk kynd of vyce,
Ane laithlie Loch of stinkand Lycherie,
Ane curst coue corrupt with Couatyce,
Bordourit about with pryde and Symonie,
Sum sayis ane Cisterne full of Sodomie:
Quhose vyce in speciall , gif I wald declair,
It war yneuch for tyll perturb the air

Of treuth the haill Christian Religioun,
Throuch thame ar scandalizat and offendit,
It can nocht faill,bot thair abusioun,
Afore the Throne of God it is ascendit,
Luc.14.　I dreid but dout, without that thay amend it,
Apoc.17 The plaigis of Jhonis Reuelatioun,
Sall fall vpon thair Generatioun.

O Lord quhilk hes the hartis of euerilk King
Into thy hand,I mak the Supplicatioun,
Conuert that court , that of thair grace bening,
Thay wald mak generall Reformatioun,
Amang thame selfis,in euerilk Natioun,
That thay may be ane holy exemplare,
Till vs thy pure lawit commoun populare.

Houngerit allace,for falt of Spirituall fude,
Because from vs bene hid the veritie,
O Prince

O Prince, quhilk ſched foꝛ vs thy pꝛecio⁹ bludE
kendle in vs,the fyꝛe of Cheritie,
And ſaif vs from Eternall miſerie,
Now laubouring into thy kirk militant.
That we may all cum to thy kirk tryumphant.

¶ The Fourt Buke:

Makand mentioun of the Deith.   Iᵥ
Of the Antichriſt. Of the Generall Iuge-
ment &c. with ane Exhortatioun
be Experience to the
Courteour.

Rudent Father Experience,   Courte.
Sen ꝫe of ꝫour beneuolence,
Hes cauſit me foꝛ to conſidder,
How warldlie pomp & gloꝛe bene
ſlidder:
Be diuers ſtoꝛyis miſerabill,
Quhilk to reherſe bene lamentabill:
Ʒit oꝛ we pas furth of this vaill,
I pray ꝫow,geue me ꝫour counſaill,
Qnhat I ſall do in tyme cumming,
To haue the gloꝛe euerlaſting.
Exp.My Sone(ſaid he) ſet thy intent
            M iiij   To keip

To keip the Lordis Commandement,
And preis the nocht, to clym ouer hie,
To na warldlie Authoritie,
Quha in the warld doith maist reiois,
Ar farrest ay from thair purpois,
Wald thow leue warldlie vaniteis,
And think on four Extremiteis,
Quhilkis ar to cum, and that schortlie,
Thow wald neuer sin wilfullie,
Print thir four in thy memorie,
The Deith, the Hell, & Heuinnis glorie,
And extreme Jugement generall,
Quhare thow mon rander compt of all
Thow sall nocht faill to be content,
Of quyet lyfe, and sober rent.
Considering na man can be sure,
In eirth ane hour for till indure,
Sa all warldlie prosperitie,
Is myrit with greit miserie.
Wer thow Empriour of Asia,
King of Europe and Aphrica,
Greit Dominator of the Sey,
And thocht the Heuinnis did the obey,
All Fischis swemming in the strand,
All beist and foull at thy command,
Concluding thow wer king ouer all,
Under the Heuin Imperiall,
In that maist hiche Authoritie,
Thow sulde fynd leist tranquillitie:
Exempill of King Salomone,
Mair prosperous lyfe had neuer none,

2.Par.9.

Sic ry·

Sic ryches with sa greit plesour,
Had neuer King, nor Empriour,
With most profound Intelligence,
And superexcellent Sapience,
His plesand habitationis,
Precellit all vther Nationis.
Gardingis & parkis, for hartis & hyndis,
Stankis with fische of diuers kyndis,
Maist profound maisteris of Musike,
That in þ warld was nane thame like
Sic tresour of Gold, & precious stonis,
In eirth, had neuer na King at onis.
He had seuin hundreth lustie Quenis,
And thre hundreth fair Concubenis.
In eirth thare was na thing plesand,
Contrarious till his command.
Zit all his greit prosperitie,
He thocht it vane, and vanitie,
And micht neuer fynd repose compleit,
Without afflictioun of the spreit.
Court. Father (quod I) it maruellis me
He hauand sic prosperitie,
With sa greit riches by mesour,
Nor he had infinite plesour?
Exp. My sone, þ sute gif þ wald knaw,
The veritie I sall the schaw,
Thare is na warldlie thing at all,
May satisfie ane mannis Saull:
For it is sa Insatiabill,
That Heuin & eirth may nocht be abill,
Ane saull allane to mak content,

3. Reg. 11

Eccles. 1.

M b　　Thir

Till it se God Omnipotent,
Wes neuer nane, noz neuer salbe
Satiate, that sicht till that he se.

Matt. 6.
Luc. 12.

Quharefoz (my Sone) set nocht thy cure,
In eirth, quhare na thing may be sure,
Except the deith allanerlie,
Quhilk follo wis man continuallie:
Tharefoz (my Sone) remember the,
Within schozt tyme, that thow mon de,
Nocht knawing quhen, how, in quhat place,
Bot as it pleisith the king of grace.

II.   Of the Deich.

F Miserie maist miserabill,
Is Deith, and maist abhominabill
That dzeidfull Dzagone with his
    dartis,
    Ay reddy foz to perse the hartis,
Of euerilk Creature on lyue,
Contrair quhose strenth may na man stryue.
Of dolent Deith, this soze sentence,
Wes geuin thzow Inobedience,
Of our Parentis, allace tharefoze,
As I haue done declare afoze,
How thay and thair Posteritie,
Wer all condampnit foz to die:
Howbeit the flesche to deith be thzall,
God hes the Saull maid Immoztall
And sa of his benignitie,

                           Hes maist

Hes myxit his Justice with Mercie:
Tharefor call to remembrance,
Of this fals warld the variance,
How we lyke Pylgramis ewin a morrow,
Ay trauelling throuch this baill of sorrow,
Sum tyme in vane prosperitie,
Sum tyme in greit miserie,
Sum tyme in blis, sum tyme in baill,
Sum tyme richt seik, & sum tyme haill,
Sum tyme full riche, & sum tyme pure,
Onharefor (my Sone) tak lytill cure:
Nother of greit prosperitie,
Nor zit of greit miserie,
Bot plesand lyfe, and hard mischance,
Ponder thame baith in ane ballance,
Considering nane authoritie,
Ryches, wysedome, nor dignitie,
Empyre of realmis, bewtie, nor strenth,
May nocht ane day our lyuis lenth:
Sen we ar sure that we most die,
Fare weill all vane felicitie.
Greitlie it doith perturbe my mynd,
Of dolent Deith, the dyuers kynd,
Thocht Deith till euery man resortis,
Zit strykith he in syndrie sortis,
Sum be hait feueris violence,
Sum be contagious Pestilence,
Sum be Justice Execution,
Bene put to deith, without remissioun,
Sum hagit, sum doith lose thair heidis
Sum brynt, sum soddin into leidis:

And sum

And sum for thair vnleiffum actis,
Ar rent and reuin vpon the ractis,
Sum ar diffoluit be poyfoun,
Sum on the nicht ar murdzeist doun:
Sum fallis into frenefie,
Sum deis in Hydzopifie,
And vtheris ftrange Infirmiteis,
Quhare in mony ane thousand deis,
Quhilk humane nature dois abhoz,
As in the gut, grauell, and goz.
Sum in the flux & feuer quartane,
Bot ay the hour of deith vncertane:
Sum ar diffoluit fuddandlie,
Be Catharre, oz be Apoplexie.
Sum doith diftroy thame felf alfo,
As Hanniball, and wyfe Cato.
Be thounder deith fum dois confome,
As he did the thzid King of Rome,
Callit Tullus Hoftilius,
As wzyttis greit Valerius,
For he, and his houfhald atonis,
Wer bzynt be thounder flefche & bonis.
Sum deis be extreme exces,
Of Joy, as Valerie doith expzes:
Sum be extreme Melancholie,
Wyll de but vther Maladie.
In Chzoniklis thow may weil ken,
How mony houndzeth thousand men
Ar flane, fen firft the warld began,
In battell, and how mony ane man,
Upon the Sey doith lofe thair lyues,

Quhen

Quhen schippis vpon roches ryues,
Thocht sum de naturallie,throuch age,
far ma deis rauand in ane rage:
Happy is he,the quhilk hes space,
At his last hour to cry for grace.
Howbeit Deith be abhominabill,
I think it sulde be confortabill,
Till all thame of the Faithfull noumer,
For thay depart from cair and coumer,
From troubill,trauell,sturt and stryfe,
Till Joy,and euerlastand lyfe.
Polydorus Uirgilius,
To that effect he wryttis thus:
In Thrace quhen ony chyld bene borne,
Thair kyn,& freindis cummis thame beforne,
With dolent Lamentatioun,
For the greit tribulatioun,
Calamitie,cummer,and cure
That thay in eirth ar to indure.
Bot at thair deith and buryng,
Thay mak greit Joy and banketting,
That thay haue past from miserie,
To rest and greit felicitie.
Sen Deith bene finall conclusioun,
Quhat vailis warldlie prouisioun,
Quhen wisedome may nocht contramand,
Nor strenth that flour may nocht ganestand,
Ten thousand Mylȝeoun of tresour,
May nocht prolong thy lyfe ane hour:
Efter quhose dolent departing,
Thy spreit sall pas but tarying:

                                    Straucht

Straucht way till Joy Inestimabill,
Or to strang pane Intolerabill.
Thy vyle corruppit carioun,
Sall turne in Putrefactioun,
And sa remane in poulder small,
Unto the Jugement Generall.

Ane schort Descriptioun of the Antichrist.

Uod I) Fater I here men say,
That thair sall ryse afore that day,
Quhilk ze call Generall Jugemēt,
Ane wickit man frō Sathan sent,
And contrair to the Law of Christ
Callit the cruell Antichrist.
And sum sayis that myscheuous man,
Discend sall of the Trybe of Dan,
And sulde be borne in Babilone,
The quhilk dissaue sall mony one.
Infidelis sall of euery art,
With that fals Propheit take ane part.
And how Enoch and Elyas,
Sal preche contrair that fals Messyas
Bot finallie his fals doctrine,
And he salbe put to rewine:
Bot nother be the fyre nor sword,
Bot be the vertew of Christis word,
And gif this be of veritie,
The suith I pray zow schaw to me.

Exp.M₂

Exp. My Sone (said he) as wryttis Jhone,
Thare sall nocht be ane man allone,
Hauing that name in speciall,
Bot Antichristis in generall,
Hes bene, and now ar mony one,
And richt sa in the tyme of Jhone,
Wer Antechristis, as him self sayis,
And present lie now in thir dayis,
Ar richt mony withouttin dout,
Wer thair fals lawis weill soucht out.
Quha wes ane greiter Antechrist,
And mair contrarious to Christ,
Nor the fals Propheit Machomeit,
Quhilk his curst Lawis, maid sa sweit,
In Turkie zit thay ar obseruit,
Quharethrouch the heill he hes deseruit.
All Turkis, Sarazenis, and Jowis,
That in the Sone of God nocht trowis,
Ar Antechristis, I the declare,
Because to Christ thay ar contrare,
Daniell sayis in his Propheceis,
That efter the greit Monarcheis,
Sall ryse ane marnellous potent King,
Quhilk with ane schameles face sall ring
Michtie and wyse in dirk speikingis,
And prosper in all plesand thingis,
Throuch his falsheid and craftines,
He sall flow in to welthines,
The Godlie pepill he sall noy,
By cruell deith, and thame distroy.
The king of kingis he sall ganestand,

1. Ioan. 2

2. Ioan.

Dan. 8.

Syne

2.Thef.2

Syne be diſtroyit withouttin hand.
Paule ſayis, afoꝛe the Loꝛdꝭ cumming
That thare ſalbe ane departing,
And that man of Iniquitie,
Till all men he ſall oppynnit be:
Quhilk ſall ſit in the holy ſait,
Contrary God to mak debait:
Bot that Sone of Perditioun,
Salbe put to confuſioun:
Be power of the holy Spꝛeit,
Quhen he his tyme hes done compleit.
Beleue nocht that in tyme cumming,
Ane greiter Antichꝛiſt to ring,
Noꝛ thair hes bene, and pꝛeſentlie,
Ar now, as Clerkis can eſpie
Tharefoꝛ my will is that thow knaw,
Quhat euer thay be that makis the law:
Thocht thay be callit Chꝛiſtin men,
Be naturall reſoun thow may ken,
Be thay neuer of ſa greit valour,
Pape, Cardinall, King oꝛ Empꝛiour,
Extollant thair Traditionis,
Abuſe Chꝛiſtis Inſtitutionis,
Makand lawis contrair to Chꝛiſt:
He is ane verray Antichꝛiſt:
And quha doith foꝛtifie oꝛ defend
Sic Law, I mak it to the kend:
Be it Pape, Empꝛiour, King oꝛ Quene,
Greit ſoꝛrow ſalbe on thame ſene,
At Chꝛiſtis extreme Iugement,
Without that thay in tyme repent.

✤ Ane

Ane ſchort Remembrance of the maiſt terribill day of the extreme Iugement. IIII.

Ather (ſaid I)with ʒour licence,
Sen ʒe haue ſic Experience,
Ʒit ane thig at ʒow wald I ſpeir
Quhen ſall þ dʒeidfull day appeir,
Quhilk ʒe call Iugement generall
Quhat thingis afoʒe that day ſall fall?
Quhare ſall appeir that dʒeidful Iuge,
Oʒ how may faltouris get refuge?
Ex.(Quod he)as to thy firſt queſtioun,
I can mak na ſolutioun,
Quharefoʒ perturb nocht thyne intent,
To knaw day, hour,oʒ moment:
To God allane, the day bene knawin,
Quhilk neuer wes to nane Angell ſchawin.
Howbeit be diuers coniectouris,
And pʒincipall Expoſitouris,
Of Daniell and his Pʒophecie,
And be the Sentence of Elie:
Quhilkis hes declarit as thay can,
How lang it is ſen the warld began,
And foʒ to ſchaw,hes done thair cure,
How lang thay traiſt it ſall indure,
And als how mony aigis bene,
As in thair warkis may be ſene.

Ⰰ   Bot

Bot till declare thir questionis,
Thare bene diuers opinionis,
Sum wryttarꝭ hes the warld deuydit
In sex aigis(as bene decydit,
Into Fasciculus temporum,
And Cronica Cronicorum:
Bot be the sentence of Elie,
The warld deuydit is in thre,
As cunning Maister Carioun,
Hes maid plane expositioun,
How Elie sayis withouttin weir,
The warld sall stand sax thousand zeir
Of quhame I follow the sentence,
And lattis the vther buikis ga hence,
From the Creatioun of Adam,
Twa thousand zeir till Abraham,
From Abraham,be this narratioun,
To Christis Incarnatioun,
Richt sa hes bene twa thousand zeiris,
And be thir Prophecyis appeiris,
From Christ,as thay mak till vs kend,
Twa thousand till the warldis end.
Of quhilkis ar by gone sickerlie,
Fyue thousand,fyue hundreth,thre & fyftie,
And sa remanis to cum but weir,
Four hundreth,with sewin & fourtie zeir.
And than the Lord Omnipotent,
Suld cum till his greit Iugement.
Mat.24. Christ sayis the tyme salbe maid schort,
As Mathew planelie doith report,
That for the warldis Iniquitie,

                               The latter

The latter tyme fall fchoztnit be,
For plefour of the chofin nummer,
That thay may pas from cair and cummer:
Sa be this compt it may be kend,
The warld is drawand neir ane end.
For Legionis ar cum but dout,
Of Antichriftis wer thay foucht out:
And mony toknis doith appeir,
As efter fchotlie thow fall heir,
How that fanct Jherome doith indyte,
That he hes red in Hebrew wzyte,
Of fyftene fignis in fpeciall,
Afoze that Jugement generall,
And fum of thame J tak na cure,
Quhilk J find nocht in the Scripture.
Ane part of thame thocht J declare,
Firft will J to the Scripture fare.
Chrift fayis afoze that day be done,
Thare falbe fignis in Sonne & Mone,
The Sonne fall hyde his bemis bzicht
Sa that the Mone fall geue na licht,
Sterris be mennis Jugement,
Sall fall furth of the Firmament.
Of thir fignis oz we further gone,
Sum mozall fence we will expone,
As cunning Clarkis hes declairit,
And hes ȝ Sonne & Mone compairit,
The Sonne, to the ftait Spirituall,
The Mone, to Princis tempozall:
Richt fa the Sterris thay do compair,
To the lawit commoun populair:

Marc. 13.
Matt. 24

N ij   The

The Mone and sterris hes na licht,
Bot be reflex of Phebus bricht,
Sa quhen the Sonne of licht is dirk,
The Mone & Sterris mon be mirk,
Richt sa quhen Pastouris spiritualis,
Popis, Bischoppis and Cardinalis,
In thair beginning, schew greit licht.
The Temporal stait was rewlit richt,
Bot now allace it is nocht so,
Those schynand lampis bene ago:
Thair radious bemis ar turnit in reik,
For now in eirth na thing thay seik,
Except riches, and Dignitie,
Following thair sensualitie,
Mony Prelatis ar now regnand,
The quhilkis na mair dois vnderstand
Quhat dois pertene to thair office,
Nor thow can kendle fyre with Ice.
Wo to Popis, I say for me,
Quhilk sufferis sic enormitie,
That Ignorant warldlie Creaturis,
Suld in the kirk haue ony curis.
Na maruell thocht the pepill slyde,
Quhen thay haue blynd men to thair gyde:
Esay. 56. For ane Prelate that can nocht preche,
Nor Goddis Law to the pepill teche.
Esay comparith him in his wark,
Till ane dum dog that can nocht bark.
And Christ him callis, in his greif,
Ioan. 10. Maist lyke ane murtherer or ane theif:
The cunning Doctour Augustyne,

                                wolfis

Wolfis and Deuillis, doith thame defyne.
The Canon Law doith him defame,
That of ane Prelate beris the name,
And will nocht preche the Deuyne Lawis,
As the Decreis planelie schawis:
Bot those that hes authoritie,
To prouide spirituall dignitie:
Micht gif thay plesit to tak pane,
Gar thame licht all thair lampis agane.
Bot euer allace, that is nocht done,
So darknit bene baith Sonne & Mone.
War kingis lyuis weill declarit,
The quhilkis ar to the Mone comparit:
Men micht considder thair estate,
From Charitie degenerate.
I think thay sulde think mekle schame,
Of Christ for to take thair surname:
Syne leif nocht lyke to Christianis,
Bot more lyke Turkis, & to Paganis,
Turk contrair Turk makis lytill weir,
Bot Christiane Princis takis na feir,
Quhilkis sulde agre as brother to brother,
Bot now ilk ane dyngis down ane vther.
I knaw na resonabill cause quharefore,
Except Pryde, Couetyce, and vane gloze,
The Empriour mouis his Ordinance,
Contrair the potent king of France.
And France richt sa with greit rigour,
Contrair his freind the Empriour:
And richt swa France aganis Ingland,
Ingland alfa aganis Scotland:

N iij   And

And als the Scottis with all thair micht,
Doith fecht foʒ till defend thair richt,
Betuix thair Realmes of Albione,
Quhare battellis hes bene mony one,
Can be maid none affinitie,
Noʒ ʒit na Consanguinitie:
Noʒ be na way thay can considder,
That thay may haue lang pace togidder,
I dʒeid that weir makis nane ending,
Till thay be baith vnder ane King:
Thocht Chʒist the souerane King of grace,
Left in his Testament lufe and pace:
Our kingis from weir will nocht refrane,
Till thare be mony ane thousand slane:
Greit herschippis maid be sey and land,
As all the warld may vnderstand.
Court. Father, I think that tempoʒall kingis,
May fecht foʒ till defend thair ringis,
Foʒ I haue sene the Spirituall stait,
Mak weir, thair richtis till debait,
I saw Pape Julius manfullie,
Pas to the feild tryumphandlie,
With ane richt awfull Oʒdinance,
Contrair Lowis, the king of France:
And foʒ to do him mair dispyte,
He did his Regioun interdyte.
Exp. My Sone (said he) as I suppose,
That langis weill till our purpose,
How Sonne & Mone ar baith denude
Of licht, als Clarkis doith conclude,
Comparing thame, as ʒe hard tell,

                                   To Spi-

To Spirituall stait, and Temporell:
And comoun pepill half dispairit,
Quhilk to the Sterris bene compairit
Lawit pepill follow ay thair heidis,
And speciallie into thair deidis,
The maist part of Religioun,
Bene turnit in abusioun.
Quhat doith auaill Religious weidis,
Quhen thay ar contrair in thair deidis?
Quhat holynes is thare within,
Ane wolf cled in ane wedder skin?
So be thair taikinnis dois appeir,
The day of Jugement drawis neir.
Now lat vs leif this morall sence,
Proceiding till our purpose hence,
And of this matet speik no more,
Beginning quhare we left afore.
The Scripture sayis efter thir signis
Salbe sene mony maruellous thingis,
Than sall ryse tribulationis,
In eirth, and greit mutationis,
Als weill heir vnder as aboue,
Quhen bertewis of the heuin sal moue
Sic cruell weir salbe or than,
Was neuer sene sen the warld began,
The quhilk sall cause greit Indigence,
As deirth, hunger, and pestilence:
The horribill soundis of the see,
The pepill sall perturbe and flee,
Jerome sayis, it sall ryse on hicht,
Abone Montanis be mennis sicht,

Matt.24.
Marc. 13
Luc.21.

                     A iiij   Bot se

Bot it fall nocht fpred ouer the land,
Bot lyke ane wall euin straucht vpstand,
Syne fattill doun agane fa law,
That na man fall the watter knaw,
Greit Quhalis fall rummeis rout and rair,
Quhofe found redound fall in the air.
All fifche and Monftouris maruellous,
Sall cry with foundis odious,
That men fall widder on the eird,
And weping wary fall thair weird,
With lowd allace, and wellaway,
That euer thay baid to fe that day,
And fpeciallie thofe that dwelland be,
Apon the coftis of the fe:
Richt fa as fanct Jerome concludis,
Sall be fene ferleis in the fludis,
The fe with mouing meruellous,
Sall birn with flammis furious,
Richt fa fall birn fontane and flude,
All herbe and tree fall fweit lyke blude,
Fowlis fall furth of the air,
Wylde beiftis to the plane repair,
And in thair maner mak greit mone,
Gowland with mony griflie grone.
The bodeis of deid Creaturis,
Ezec.37. Appeir fall on thair Sepulturis,
Than fall baith men, wemen & barnis,
Cum crepand furth of how Cauernis,
Quhare thay for dreid wer hid afore,
With fich and fob and hartis fore,
Wandring about, as thay war wode,
                              Effamifchit

Effamischit for falt of fude,
None may mak vtheris conforting,
Bot dule for dule and lamenting,
Quhat may thay do bot weip & wounder,
Quhen thay se roches schake in schounder,
Throw trimblyng of the eirth, and quaiking
Of sorrow than salbe na slaiking,
Quha that bene leuand in those dayis,
May tell of terribill affrayis:
Thair riches, rentis, nor tressour,
That tyme sall do thame small plesour,
Bot quhen sic wounderis dois appeir,
Men may be sure, the day drawis neir:
That Just men pas sall to the gloze,
Iniust to pane for euer moze.   Dan. 13.
Court. Father (said I) we daylie reid,
Ane Artikle into our Creid,
Sayand that Chzist Omnipotent,
Into that generall Jugement,
Sall Juge baith dede and quick also,
Quharefoze declare me oz ze go,
Gif thare sal ony man oz wyfe,
That day be foundin vpon lyfe?
Exp. (Quod he) as to that questioun,
I sall mak sone solutioun,   Matt. 24.
The Scripture planelie doith expone,
Quhen all taikinnis, bene cum & gone.
Zit mony ane hundzeth thousand,
That samin day, salbe lenand.
Howbeit thair sall na Creature,
Nother of day noz hour be sure,

                    N b   foz

For Chꝛiſt ſall cum ſa ſuddandly,
That na man ſall the tyme eſpy:
As it was in the tyme of Noy,
Quhen God did all the warld diſtroy.
Sum on the feild ſalbe lauboꝛand,
Sum in the tempillis Mariand:
Sum afoꝛe Jugis makand pley,
And ſum men ſailland on the Sey.
Thoſe that bene on the feild going,
Sall nocht returne to thair lugeing.
Quha bene vpon his hous aboue,
Sall haue na laſer to remoue.
Twa ſalbe in the myll grinding,
Quhilk ſalbe taikin but warning:
The ane till euerlaſting gloꝛe,
The vther loſt foꝛ euer moꝛe.
Twa ſalbe lying in ane bed,
The ane to pleſour ſalbe led,
The vther ſalbe left allone,
Greitand with mony griſlie grone,
And ſa my ſone, thow may weill trow,
The warld ſalbe as it is now:
The pepill vſing thair beſines,
As holy Scripture doith expꝛes.
Sen na man knawis the hour noꝛ day
The Scripture biddis vs walk ꝓ pꝛay
And foꝛ our ſin be penitent,
As Chꝛiſt wald cum incontinent.

❧ The

The maner how Chriſt ſal cum to his Iugement. V.

WHē all taiknis bene brocht til end
Than ſall þ Sone of God diſcend,
As fyre flaucht haiſtely glanſing,
Diſcend ſall the moſt heuinly king
As Phebus in the Orient,

Heb. 12.

Lichtnis in haiſt to Occident,
So pleſandlie, he ſall appeir,

Luc. 21.

Amang the heuinlie cluddis cleir,
with greit power and Maieſtie,
Abone the countre of Iudie:
As Clarkis doith concluding haill,
Direct aboue the luſtie vaill,

Act. 1.

Of Ioſaphat and Mont Oliueit,
All Prophecie thair ſalbe compleit.

Mat. 25.

The Angellis of the Ordouris nyne,
Inuiroun ſall that throne Deuyne,
with heuinlie conſolatioun,
Makand him miniſtratioun,
In his preſence thare ſalbe borne,
The ſignis of Cros, & Croun of thorne,
Pillar, Naillis, Scurgis, and Speir,
with euerilk thing that did him deir,
The tyme of his grym Paſſioun,
And for our conſolatioun,
Appeir ſall in his handis and feit,
And in his ſyde the prent compleit,

Of his

Of his fyue woundis precious,
Schynand lyke Rubeis radious,
To reprobat confusioun,
And for finall conclusioun,
He sittand in his Tribunall,
With greit power Imperiall.
Thare sall ane Angell blaw ane blast,

1.Cor.15.   Quhilk sall mak all the warld agast,
Matt.24.   With hidduous voce, and vehement,
Ryse deid folk, cum to Jugement.
With that all resonabill Creature,
That euer was formit be Nature,
Sall suddandlie start vp atonis,
Conionit with saull, flesche, blude & bonis,
That terribill Trumpet J here tell,

Apoc.20   Beis hard in heuin, in eirth and hell,
Those that wer drownit in the Sey,
That bousteous blast thay sall obey,
Quhare euer the body buryit was,
All salbe foundin in that plas,

Marc. 13   Angellis sall pas in the four artis,
Of eirth & bring thame from all partis
And with ane instant diligence,
Present thame to his excellence.
Sanct Jerome thocht continuallie,
On this Jugement sa ardentlie,
He said, quhidder J eit or drink,
Or walk, or sleip, forsuth me think
That terribill Trumpet, lyke ane bell,
Sa quiklie in myne eir doith knell,
As Instantlie it war present,

Ryse

Ryſe dede folk, cum to Jugement.
Gif Sanct Jerome tuke ſic ane fray,
Allace quhat ſall we ſinnaris ſay.
All thoſe quhilk foundin be on lyfe,
Salbe Immoꝛtall maid belyfe,
And in the twinkling of ane Ee,   1. Pet. 4.
With fyꝛe thay ſall tranſlatit be: 1. Cor. 15.
And neuer foꝛ to De agane,
As Deuyne Scripture ſchawis plane,
Als reddy baith foꝛ pane and gloꝛe
As thay quhilk deit lang tyme afoꝛe.
The Scripture ſayis, thay ſall appeir,
In age the thꝛe and thꝛettie ʒeir,
Quhidder thay Deit ʒoung oꝛ auld,
Quhoſe gret noumer may nocht be tauld
That Day ſall nocht be miſſit ane man,   Matt. 26.
Quhilk boꝛne was ſen the warld began.
The Angell ſall thame ſeparait,
As Haird the ſcheip doith frome the gait:
And thoſe quhilk bene of Belialis band,
Trymbling vpon the eirth ſall ſtand,
On the left hand, of that greit Juge,
But eſperance to get refuge.
Bot thoſe quhilk bene pꝛedeſtinat,   1. Theſ. 4
Sall from the eirth be Eleuat,
And that moſt happy cumpanie,
Sall oꝛdourit be tryumphandlie,
At the richt hand of Chꝛiſt our King,
Hich in the air, with loud louing.
Full gloꝛiouſlie thare ſall compeir,
Mair bꝛicht than Phebus in his Spheir

                                              The

The Virgine Marie, Quene of Quenis,
With mony ane thousand bricht Virgenis.
The Fatheris of the auld Testament,
Quhilk wer to God obedient.
Father Adam sall thame convoy,
With Abell, Seth, Enoch and Noy:
Abraham with his faithfull warkis,
With all the prudent Patriarkis.
Jhone the Baptist thare sall compeir,
The principall, and last Messingeir,
Quhilk came bot half ane zeir afore,
The cumming of that King of glore,
Moyses Esayas honourabill,
With all trew Prophetis venerabill.
Dauid with all the faithfull Kingis,
Quhilk vertouslie did rewll thair ringis,
The nobill Chyftane Iosue,
With gentill Judas Machabe,
With mony ane nobill Campioun,
Quhilk in thair tyme with greit renoun,
Manfullie till thair lyuis ende,
The Law of God thay did defend.
With Eue, that day salbe present,
The Ladyis of the auld Testament,
Debora, Adamis douchter deir,
With the four lusty Ladyis cleir,
Quhilk keipit wer, in the Irk with Noy,
Sara and Cethura with Joy,
The quhilkis to Abraham wyffis bene,
With gude Rebecca thare salbe sene,
The prudent wyfis of Israell,

Gude

Gude Lya and the fair Rachell:
With Judith, Hester and Susanna,
And the richt sapient Quene Saba.
Thair sall compeir Peter and Paull,
With Christis trew Discipulis all,
Lawrence & Steuin, with thair blyst band,
Of Martyris mo, than ten thousand,
Gregore, Ambrose and Augustyne,
With Confessouris ane tryumphand tryne,
With Sanct Frances and Dominick,
Sanct Bernard, and sanct Benedick,
With small noumer, of Monkis and Freiris,
Of Carmelytis and Cordeileiris,
That for the luse of Christ onelie,
Renuncit the warld vnfenzeitlie.
With Elizabeth and Anna,
All gude wyffis sall compeir that day,
The blyst and holy Magdalene,
That day afore hir Souerane:
Richt plesandlie scho sall present,
All Sinnaris that wer penitent,
Quhilk of thair gilt heir askit grace,
In heuin with hir sall haue ane place.
Bot wo beis to that bailfull band,
Quhilk sall stand law at his left hand,
Wo than to Kingis and Empriouris,
Quhilkis wer vnrichteous Conquerouris,
For thair glore and particular gude,
Gart sched so mekle saikles blude.
But Sceptour, Crown, & Rob Royall,
That day thay sall mak compt of all,

And for

And for thair cruell tyrannie
Sall punist be perpetuallie.
Ze Lordis and Barronis, mair aud les,
That zour pure Tennantis dois oppres,
Be greit Gersome , and Dowbill maill,
Mair than zour landis bene auaill,
With sore exorbitant cariage,
With mercheitis of thair mariage,
Tormentit baith in peace and weir,
With burdinnis mair than thay may beir,
Be thay haue payit to zow thair maill,
And to the Preist thair teindis haill:
And quhen the landis agane is sawin,
Quhat restis behynd, I wald wer knawin,
I traist thay and thair pure houshald,
May tell of hounger and of cauld,
Without ze haue of thame pietie,
I dreid, ze sall get na mercie,
That thay quhen Christ Omnipotent,
Cummis to generall Jugement.
Wo beis to publict Oppressouris,
To Tyrannis, and to Transgressouris,
To Murderaris and commoun theifis,
Quhilk neuer did mend thair greit mischeifis,
Fornicatouris and Ockeraris,
Commoun publict Adulteraris,
All pertinat wilfull Heretikes,
All fals deceitfull Scismatikes:
All salbe present in that place,
With mony lamentabill allace.
The cursit Cayn, that neuer was gude

                                    with all

With all schedDaris of saikles bludē,
Nymrod foundar of Babilone,
With fals Jdolateris mony one.
Ninus the king of Assiria,
With greit dule sall compeir that day,
Quhilk first inuentit Jmagerie,
Quharethrouch came greit Jdolatrie,
Foz making of the Jmage Bell,
That day his hyze salbe in hell.
The greit Oppressour king Pharo,
The tyzane Empriour Nero,
Sall with thame cursit king Herode bzing,
With mony other carefull king,
The cruell king Antiochus,
With the most furious Olofernes,
Greit Oppressouris of Jsraell,
That day thair hyze salbe in hell.
With Judas sall compeir ane clan,
Of fals Traitouris to God and man,
Thare sall compeir of euery land,
With Ponce Pylat ane bailfull band,
Of Temporall and Spirituall statis,
Fals Jugis, with thair Aduocatis.
Thare sall our Senzeouris of the Session,
Of all thair faltis mak cleir confession,
Thare salbe sene the fraudfull failzeis,
Of Schireiffis, Prouestis, and of Bailzeis,
Officialis, with thair Consistozie Clarkis.
Sall mak compt of thair wrangous warkis,
Thay and thair peruerst Procuratouris,
Oppressouris, baith of rytche and puris,
                    Q   Throuch

Throuch delatouris full of deceit,
Quhilk mony ane gart beg thair meit:
Greit dule that day to Jugis bene,
That cummis nocht with thair conscience clene
That day sall pas be Peremptouris,
Without Cautele, oꝛ Dilatouris:
Na Duplicandum noꝛ Triplicandum,
Bot schoꝛtlie pas to Sentenciandum,
Without Continuationis,
Oꝛ ony Appellationis.
That sentence sall nocht be retraitit,
Noꝛ with na man of Law debaitit.
Ze Lauboꝛarꝛ be Sey and Landis,
Perfite Craftismen & ryche merchandꝛ
Leue zour desait and craftie wylis,
Quhilk sillie simpill folk begylis.
Mak recompence here, as ze may,
Remembꝛing on this dꝛeidfull day.
With Machomeit sal compeir but dout
Of Antichꝛistis ane hydduous rout,
Bischop Annas and Caiphas,
With him in companie sall pas,
With Scrybis and fals Pharisience,
Quhilk wꝛocht on Chꝛist greit violence
With mony ane Turk and Sarracene
With greit soꝛrow thare salbe sene.
Paipis foꝛ thair Traditionis,
Contrair to Chꝛistis Institutionis,
With mony ane cowll & clippit crown,
Quhilk Chꝛistis lawis strampit down.
And wald nocht suffer foꝛ to pꝛeche,

The

The veritie, noz the pepill teche:
Bot lawit men put to greit tozment,
Quhilk vsit Chzistis Testament.
All kingis and Quenis thare salbe kend
The quhilk sic Lawis did defend.
In that court sall cum mony one,
Of the blak bpik of Babilone.
The Innocent blude that thay sall cry,
Ane loud vengeance full pieteously:
On those cruell bludie boucheouris,
Martyzis of Pzophetis & Pzecheouris.
Sum with the fyze, sum with the swozd,
Quhilk planely pzeichit Goddis wozd:
That day thay sall rewardit be,
Confozme to thair Iniquitie.
The Sodomitis, and Gomozrance,
On quhame God wzocht sa greit vengeance,
With Coze, Dathan and Abyzone,
With thair assistance mony one:
The holy Scripture will the tell,
How thay sank all doun to the hell,
With Semon Magus sall resozt.
Of pzoude Pzeistis, ane schamefull sozt.
That samyn day thare salbe sene,
Mony ane cruell carefull Quene:
Quene Semirame king Ninus wyfe,
Ane Tyger full of sturt and stryfe.
Togidder with Quene Jesabell,
Quhilk was couetous and cruell:
The fals defaitfull Dalida,
The cruell Quene Clytemnestra,

O ij   The

The quhilk did murdreis on the nicht,
Agamemnon baith wyse and wicht,
The quhilk was her awin souerane Lord,
As Greikis Storpis doith record.
With cruell Quenis mony one,
Quhilk langsum war for till expone.
℄ Ze wantoun Ladyis, & Burges wyfis,
That now for sydest taillis strpfis,
Flappand the filth, amang zour feit,
Rasing the dust into the streit:
That day for all zour pomp and pryde,
Zour taillis sall nocht zour hippis hyde,
Thir vaniteis, ze sall repent,
Without that ze be penitent.
With Phitonissa, I here tell,
Quhilk raisit the Spirite of Samuell,
That day with hir thare sall resorte,
Of rank Witchis ane sorrowfull sorte,
Brocht from all partis mony ane myle,
From Sauoy, Athole, and Argyle:
And from the ryndis of Galloway,
With mony wofull wallaway.
Ze Brether of Religioun,
In tyme leue zour abusioun:
With quhilk ze haue the warld abusit,
Or ze that day salbe refusit,
I speik to zow all generallie,
Nocht till ane Ordour speciallie.
That day all Creature sall ken,
Gif ze war Sanctis or wardlie men,
Or gif ze tuke the Skapellarie,

                        That ze

That ȝe micht leif mair plefandlie,
And get ane gude gros poztioun,
Oz foz Godlie deuotioun,
That day ȝour fenȝeit Sanctitudis,
Sall nocht be knawin be ȝour hudis,
Ȝour superstitious Ceremonis,
Participant till Jdolatreis,
Cozd, cuttit schone, noz clippit heid,
That day fall ftand ȝow in na fteid.
Foz Cowllis blak, gray noz begaird,
Ȝe fall that day get na rewaird,
Ȝour polite paintit flatterie,
Ȝour diffimulate Hipocrifie,
That day thay falbe cleirlie knawin,
Quhen ȝe fall fcheir, as ȝe haue fawin.
Tharefoz in tyme be penitent,
Oz ellis that day ȝe will be fchent.
J pzay ȝow hartlie as J may,
Remember on that dzeidfull day,
Ȝe Abbot, Pzyoz and Pzyozes,
Confidder quhat ȝe did pzofes,
And how that ȝour pzomotioun,
Was na thing foz Deuotioun:
Bot til obtene the Abbacie,
Ȝe maid ȝour bow of Chaftitie,
Of Pouertie, and Obedience:
Tharefoz remozd ȝour Confcience,
How thir thze bowis bene obferuit,
And quhat reward ȝe haue deferuit,
Quharefoze repent, quhyll ȝe haif fpace
Sen God is liberall of his grace.

                   O iij   C.(Father

Cou.Father(quod I)declare to me,
Quhare sall our Prelatis ordourit be,
Quhilk now ben in the warld leuand,
With quhome sall cum that Spirituall band?
Exp.(Quod he)as sanct Bernard descryuis,
Without that thay amend thair lyuis,
And leue thair wantoun vicious warkis,
Nocht with Prophetis nor Patriarkis,
Nocht with Martyris,nor Confessouris,
The quhilkis to Christ,wer trew prechouris,
Thair Predecessouris,Peter and Paull,
That day will thame misken at all,
So sall thay nocht , I say for me,
With the Apostillis ordourit be:
I traist thay sall dwell on the bordour,
Of Hell,quhare thare salbe nane ordour,
Endlang the flude of Phlegeton,
Or on the brayis of Acheron,
Cryand on Charon , I conclude,
To ferrie thame ouer that furious Flude,
Till Eternall confusioun,
Without thay leue thair abusioun,
I traist those Prelatis mair and les,
Sall mak cleir compt of thair ryches,
That dreidfull day with hartis sore,
And quhat seruice,thay did tharefore,
The Princely pompe,nor apparrall,
Of Pope,Bischop, nor Cardinall:
Thair Royall rentis nor dignitie,
That day,sall nocht regardit be,
Thare sall na taillis, as I here say,
                              Of Bischo

Of Bischopis, be borne vp that day,
Cum thay nocht with thair conscience clene,
On thame greit sorrow salbe sene,
Without that thay thair lyfe amend,
In tyme, and sa I mak ane end.

The maner how Christ sall geif his Sentence.   VI.

When all thir Congregationis,
Beis brocht furth from al Nationſ
Quhilk salbe wout lang proces,
Thocht I haif maid sū lāg digres,
For in the twinkling of ane Ee,
All Mankynd sall presentit be,
Afore that kingis Excellence,
Than schortlie sall he geif Sentence.
First sayand to that blyssit band,
Quhilk beis ordourit at his richt hand:
Cum with my Fatheris Benisoun,
And ressaue zour Possessioun:
Quhilk bene for zow preordinat,
Afore the warld was first creat:
Quhen I was hungrie, ze me fed:
Quhen I was naikit, ze me cled.
Oftymes ze gaue me herbery,
And gaue me Drynk quhen I was Dry:
And vespit me, with myndis meik,
Quhen I was presonar and seik,

Matt.25.

O iiij   In all

In all sic tribulatioun,
Ʒe gaue me consolatioun.
Than sall thay say, O potent King,
Quhen saw we the desyre sic thing?
We neuer saw thyne Excellence,
Subdewit to sic Indigence.
Ʒis (sall he say) I ʒow assure,
Quhen euer ʒe did ressaue the pure,
And for my saik maid thame supple,
That gift, but dout, ʒe gaue to me:
Tharefore sall now begin ʒour gloʒe,
Quhilk sall indure for euer moʒe.
Than sall he luke on his left hand,
And say vnto that bailfull band
Pas with my Maledictioun,
Till Eternall afflictioun,
In company with feindis fell,
In euerlasting fyʒe of hell,
Quhen I stude naikit at ʒour ʒet,
Hungrie, thʒistie, cauld and wet,
Richt febill, seik, and lyk to de,
I neuer gat of ʒow supple:
And quhen I lay in pʒisoun strang,
For ʒow I micht haue lyin full lang,
Without ʒour consolatioun,
Or ony suppoʒtatioyn.
Trymbling for dʒeid than sall thay say
With mony hydduous harmisay,
Allace gude Loʒde quhen saw we the,
Subiect to sic necessitie?
Quhen saw we the cum to our dure,

Hungre

Hungrie, thriſtie, naikit, pure?
Quhen ſaw we the in preſoun ly,
Or the refuſit herbery?
Than ſall that moſt precellent king,
To thoſe wretchis mak anſwering,
That tyme, quhen ʒe refuſit the puris,
Quhilkis neidfull cryit at ʒour duris,
And of ʒour ſuperfluitie,
For my ſaik maid thame na ſupplie,
Refuſand thame, ʒe me refuſit,
With wretchitnes ſo ʒe war abuſit:
Tharefor ʒe ſall haue to ʒour hyre,
The euerlaſting birnand fyre,
But grace, but pace, or conforting,
Than ſal thay cry full ſore weiping,
That we war maid, allace gude Lord,
Allace is thare nane miſericord,
But thus withouttin hope of grace,
Tyne preſence of thy pleſand face.
Allace for vs it had bene gude,
We had bene ſmorit in our cude.
Than with ane rair the eirth ſal rpue,
And ſwollie thame baith man and wyue
Than ſall thoſe Creaturis forlorne,
Warie the hour that thay war borne,
With mony ʒamer, ʒewt and ʒell,
From tyme thay feill the flammis fell,
Upon thair tender bodyis byte,
Quhoſe torment ſalbe infinyte.
The eirth ſall cloſe, and from thair ſicht,
Sal taikin be all kynd of licht,

     Thare

Thare salbe gowling and greiting,
But hope of ony conforting,
In that Inestimabill pane,
Eternallie thay sall remane,
Birnand in furious flammis reid,
Euer deand, bot neuer be deid,
That the small minute of ane hour,
To thame salbe sa greit dolour,
Thay sal think thay haue done remane
Ane thousand zeir into that pane,
Allace I trymmill to heir tell,
The terribill tormenting of hell:
That panefull pit, quha can deplore,
Quhilk mon indure for euer more?
Than sall those glorifyit Creaturis,
With mirth and infinyte plesuris,
Connoyit with Joy Angelicall
Pas to the Heuin Imperiall,
With Christ Jesu, our souerane king,
In glore Eternallie to ring,
Of man quhilk passis the Ingyne,
The thousand part for till defyne:
Illanerlie of the leist plesure,
Preordinat for ane Creature.
Than sall ane fyre, as Clarkis sane,
Mak all the hillis and valleyis plane,
From eirth vp to the Heuin Empyre,
All beis renewit be that fyre,
Purging all thing materiall,
Under the Heuin Imperiall:
Baith eirth and watter, fyre and air,

1.Pet.3.

Salbe

Salbe mair perfyte maid and fair,
The quhilk, afore had mixit bene,
Sall than be purifyit and maid clene,
The eirth lyke Christall salbe cleir,
And euerilk Planeit in his Spheir,
Sall rest withouttin mair mouing,
Baith sterny Heuin, and Cristalling:
The first and hyest Heuin Mouabill,
Sall stand but turning firme & stabill.
The Sonne into the Orient
Sall stand, and in the Occident,
Rest sall the Mone, and be mair cleir,
Nor now ben Phebus in his Spheir.
And als that Lantern of the Heuin,
Sall geif mair licht, be Greis seuin,
Nor it gaif, sen the warld began,
The Heuin renewit salbe than,
Richt sa the eirth, with sic deuyse,
Compair till Heuinlie Paradyse.
Sa Heuin and eirth, salbe all one,
Is menith the Apostill Jhone.
The greit sey sall na mair appeir,
Bot lyke the Cristall pure and cleir,
Passing Imaginatioun,
Of Man to mak Narratioun,
Of gloze quhilk God, hes done prepair,
Till euery ane that cummis thair,
The quhilk with eiris nor with ene,
Of man may nocht be hard nor sene,
With hart it is vnthinkabill,
And with toungis Inpronunciabill:

Apoc. 21

1. Cor. 2.

Quhose

Quhose plesouris salbe sa perfyte,
Hauing in God sa greit delyte,
The space now of ane thousand zeir,

1.Pet.3.
That tyme sal nocht ane hour appeir,
Quhilk can nocht comprehendit be,
Till we that plesand sicht sall se.

1.Cor.12
Quhen Paule was reuischit in þ̄ spreit
Till the thrid heuin of glore repleit,
He saith, the Secreitis quhilk he saw,
Thay wer nocht leifsum for till schaw,
To na man on the eirth leuand:
Quharefor preis nocht till vnderstand
Howbeit thare to thow haue desyre,
The Secretis of the Heuin Empyre:
The mair men luik on Phebus bricht,
The mair febill salbe thair sicht,
Richt sa lat na man set thair cure,
To serche the hich deuyne Nature.
The more men studie, I suppose,
Salbe the more from thair purpose,
To knaw, quhare to sulde men inteud,
Quhilk Angellis can nocht comprehend
Bot efter this greit Jugement,
All think till vs salbe patent.
Lat vs with Paule, our mynd addres,
He beand full of heuinlines,
Full humlie he teichit vs,
Nocht for to be to curious.
Howbeit men be of greit Ingyne,
To seik the hiche Secretis Deuyne,
Quhose Jugementis ar vnsercheabill,

His wayis

His wayis ſtrange and Inueſtigabill,
(That is to ſay)paſt out finding,
Of quhome na man may find ending,
It ſufficis vs foz till imploze,
Greit God,to bzing vs to his gloze.

❧ Of certane Pleſuris of the   VII.
glorifyit bodyis.

En thare is none in eirth may com‑
pzehend,
The heuinlie gloze , and pleſouris
infinyte,
Quharefoz,my ſone,I pzay the not
pzetend ,
Ouerfar to ſeik that matter of delyte,
Quhilk paſſit Naturall reſoun till indyte,
That God afoze that he the warld creat,
Pzeparit to thame quhilk ar pzedeſtinat.

All moztall men ſalbe maid Immoztall,
(That is to ſay)neuer to de agane,
Impaſſibill, and ſo Celeſtiall
That fyze noz ſwozd, may do to thame na pane,
Noz heit,noz cald,noz froſt, noz wind,noz rane,
Thocht ſic thing wer , may do to thame na deir
Thoſe Creaturis richt ſa ſalbe als cleir,

Is flammand Phebus in his Manſioun,
Conſidder than gif thare ſalbe greit licht,
Quhen

Quhen euery ane in that Regioun,
Sall schyne lyke to the Sonne, & be als bricht
Lat vs with Paull desyre to se that sicht:

Philip.1. To be dissoluit, Paull had ane greit desyre,
With Christ to be in till the Heuin Empyre.

And moreatour, as Clarkis can descryue,
Thir maruellous mirthis beis incomparabill,
Amang the rest in all thair wyttis fyue,
Thay sall haue sensuall plesuris delectabill,
The heuinlie sound, quhilk salbe inenarrabill,
In thair eiris continuallie sall ring,
And als the sicht of Christ Jesus our King.

In his tryumphand Throne Imperiall,
With his mother the Uirgine Quene of quenis
Thare salbe sene the Court Celestiall,
Apostolis, Martyris, Confessouris & Uirgenis,
Brichter than Phebus, in his spheir þ schynis.
The Patriarkis and Prophetis Uenerabill,
Thare salbe sene with glore Inestimabill.

And with thair Spirituall Eis salbe sene,
That sicht quhilk bene most superexcelland,
God as he, and euermore hes bene,
Continuallie that sicht contempland.
Augustine sayis, he had leuer tak on hand,
To be in Hell, he seing the essence,
Of God, nor be in Heuin, but his presence.

Quha seis God, in his Diuinitie,
He seis in him, all vther plesand thingis,
The quhilk with toung, can not pronuncit be,
noflus.   Quhat

Quhat plesour bene, to se that King of kingis,
The gretest pane, ȝ damnit folk doun thringis,
And to the Deuillis,the most punitioun,
It is of God,to want fruitioun.

And mairattouer,thay sall feill sic ane smell,
Surmonting far,ȝ flewour of eirdly flouris,
And in thare mouth,ane taist as I here tell,
Of sweit, and Supernaturall Sapouris,
Als thay sall se,the Heuinlie bricht colouris,
Schyning amang those Creaturis Deuyne,
Quhilk til descryue,trascendis mannis Ingyne

And als thay sall haue sic Agilitie,
In ane Instant, to pas for thair plesour,
Ten thousand mylis, in twinkling of ane Ee:
So thair Ioyis,salbe without mesour,
Thay sall reioyse to se the greit dolour,
Of dampnit folk in hell,and thair tormeut,
Because of God, it is the Iuste Iugement.

Subtilitie thay sall haue maruellouslie,
Supponing that thair war ane wall of bras,
Ane glorifyit body,may richt haistelie,
Out throw that wall without impediment pas
Siclyke as dois ȝ Sonne beme throw ȝ glas,
As Christ till his Discipulis did appeir,
All entres clois,and none of thame did steir.   Ioan.20.

Howbeit in Heuin,thocht euerilk Creature,
Haue nocht alyke felicitie nor glore,
Zit euerilk ane sall haue sa greit plesure,
And sa content thay sall desyre no more: 1.Cor.15
                          To haue

To haue mair Joy,thay fall na way imploꝛe,
Bot thay falbe all fatiffyit and content,
Lyke to this rude exempill fubfequent.

Take ane Crowat,ane pynt ſtop,ꝛ ane quart
Ane galoun pitchair,ane punſion, ꝛ ane tun,
Of wyne oꝛ balme,geue euerilk ane thair part,
And fill thame full,till that thay be ouer run,
The lytill Crowat in Comparifoun,
Salbe ſa full,that it may hald no moꝛe,
Of ſic meſuris thocht thare be twentie fcoꝛe.

Into the Tun,oꝛ in the Punſioun,
So all thoſe veſchellis in ane qualitie,
May hald na mair,without thay be ouer run,
Ʒit haue thay nocht alyke in quantitie.
Sa be this rude exempill thow may ſe,
Thocht euerilk ane be nocht alyke in gloꝛe,
Ar fatiffyit ſa, that thay defyꝛe no moꝛe.

Thocht pꝛeſentlie be Goddis puruyance,
Beiſtis , Fowlis, and Fiſchis in the Seis,
Ar neceſſair now foꝛ mennis ſuſtinance:
With coꝛnis,herbis,flouris,ꝛ fructfull treis.
Than fall thare be nane ſic commoditeis.
The eirth fall beir na plant,noꝛ beiſt bꝛutall,
Bot as the Heuinnis bꝛicht lyke burall.

Suppone ſum be on eirth,walkãd heir doun,
Oꝛ hiche abone , quhare euer thay pleis to go,
Of God thay haue ay cleir fruitioun,
Baith Eiſt oꝛ Weſt,vp doun,oꝛ to oꝛ fro,
Clarkis declaris pleſouris mony mo,

　　　　　　　　　　　　　　　Quhilk

Quhilk dois trâste̅d al moztall mennis Jngyne
The thousand part of those plesouris Deupne.

Into the Heuin thay sall persytlie knaw,
Thair tender freindȝ thair fader ꝫ thair moder,
Thair predecessouris, quhilkȝ thay neuer saw,
Thair spousis, barnis, sister, and thair brother,
And euerilk ane, sall haue sic lufe till vther,
Of vtheris gloze and Joy, thay sall reiose,
As of thair awin, as Clarkis doeth suppose.

Than salbe sene that bricht Jerusalem,
Quhilk Jhone saw in his Reuelatioun,
We moztall men, allace ar far to blame,
That will nocht haue Consideratioun,
And ane continuall Contemplatioun,
With hote desyre to cum vnto that Gloze,
Quhilk plesour sall indure foz euer moze.

O Lozd our God, and King Omnipotent,
Quhilk knew oz thou the heuin ꝫ eirth create,
Quha wald to the be Jnobedient,
And sa deserue foz to be reprobate.
Thow knew the noumer of predestinate,
Quhome thow did call, ꝫ hes thame Justifyit,
And sall in Heuin with the be glozifyit.

Grant vs to be, Lozd, of that chosin sozt,
Quhame of thy Mercy superexcellent,
Did purifie, as Scripture doith repozt,
With the blude of that holy Innocent,
Jesu quhilk maid him self Odebient,
Vnto the deith, and steruit on the Rude,

                    P   Lat vȝ

Lat vs O Lord, be purgit with that blude.

Rom. 8.
All Creature, that euer God create,
As wrytt is Paull, thay wis to se that day,

1.Cor. 15 Quhen the childzen of God predestinate,
Sall do appeir in thair new fresche array,
Quhen corruptioun beis clengit clene away,
And changit beis, thair moztall qualitie,
In the greit gloze of Immortalitie,

And mairattour, all deid thingis corporall,
Under the concaue of the Heuin Empyre,
That now to laubour, subiect ar and thrall,
Sonne, mone, & sterris, eirth, watter, air, & fyre,
In ane maner, thay haue ane hote desyre,
Wissing that day, that thay may be at rest,
As Erasmus exponeth manifest.

We se the greit Globe of the Firmement,
Continuallie, in mouing maruellous,
The seuin Planetis, contrary thair intent,
Ar rest about, with cours contrarious,
The Wynd, and Sey with stormes furious,
The troublit air, with frostis, snaw, and rane.
Unto that day, thay trauell euer in pane.

And all the Angellis of the Ordouris nyne,
Hauand compassioun of our Misereis,
Thay wis efter that day, and to that fyne,
To se vs fred, from our Infirmiteis,
And clengit from thir greit Calamiteis,
And troublous lyfe, quhilk neuer sall haue end,
Unto that day, I mak it to the kend.

Ane

Ane Exhortatioun geuin be VIII. Father Experience vnto his Sone the Courteour.

Y Sone, now mark weill in thy
memory,
Of this fals warld the troublous
tranſitorie,
Quhoſe dreidfull dayſ drawis neir
ane end:
Tharefore call to God to be thy adiutorie,
And euery day, my Sone, memento mori:
And wat not quhē, nor quhare þ thou ſall wend
Heir to remane, I pray the, nocht pretend,
And ſen thow knawis, the tyme is bery ſchort,
In Chriſtis blude, ſet all thy haill confort.

Be not to muche ſolyſt in temporall thingis, Matt. 6.
Sen thou perſauis Pape, Empriour nor Kingſ
Into the eirth, haith na place permanent,
Thou ſeis þ deith, thame dulfully doun thringis
And rauis thame from thair rent, riches & ringſ
Tharefor on Chriſt confirme thyne haill intent,
And of thy calling be richt weill content,
Than God, that feidis the fowlis of the air
All neidfull thing for the, he ſall prepair.

Conſidder in thy contemplatioun,   Iob. 14.
Ay ſen the warldis firſt Creatioun,
                    P ii   Mankynd

Mankynd hes tholit this Miserie mortall,
Ay torment with tribulatioun,
With dolour, dreid and desolatioun:
Gentiles, and chosin pepill of Israell,
To this vnhap, all subiect ar and thrall,
Quhilk misery but dout sall euer indure,
Till the last day, my Sone, thare of be sure.

That day, as I haue maid Narratioun,
Salbe the day of Consolatioun,
Till all the Childzen of the chosin noumer,
Thare endit beis thair desolatioun.
And als I mak the Supplicatioun,
In eirthlie materis, tak the na mair cummer.
Dzeid not to de, for deith is bot ane summer,
Leue ane Just lyfe, a with ane Joyous hart,
Aud of thy gudis take plesandlie thy part.

Of our talking, now lat vs mak ane end,
Behald how Phebus dounwart dois discend,
Towart his Palice, in the Occident.
Dame Cynthia I se scho dois pretend,
In till hir wattrie Regioun till ascend,
With vissage paill vp from the Orient.
The dew now donkis the Rosis redolent.
The Mariguldis, that all day war reiosit,
Of Phebus heit now craftily ar closit.

The blysfull Birdis bownis to the treis,
And ceissis of thair Heuinlie Harmoneis.
The Cornecraik in the croft I here hir cry,
The Bak, the Howlat, febill of thair eis,

Fo'

For thair paſtyme now in the euinning ſkis.
The Nichtingaill with myrthfull melody,
Hir Naturall notis, peirſit throuch the ſky,
Till Cynthia, makand hir obſeruance,
Quhilk on the nicht dois tak hir dalyance.

I ſe Pole artick in the North appeir,
And Uenus ryſing with hir bemis cleir,
Quharefor my Sone, I hald it tyme to go.
Wald God (ſaid I) ʒe did remane all ʒeir,
That I micht of ʒour heuinlie Leſſonis leir,
Of ʒour departing, I am wounder wo,
Tak pacience (ſaid he) it mon be ſo.
Perchance I ſall returne with diligence,
Thus I departit from Experience.

And ſped me home, with hart ſiching full ſore,
And enterit in my quyet Oritore,
I tuke paper, and thare began to wryte,
This Miſerie, as ʒe haue hard afore.
All gentill Redarʒ, hartlie I Implore,
For till excuſe my rurall rude Indyte,
Thocht Phariſeis will haue at me deſpyte,
Quhilk wald not þ thair craftines war kend,
Lat God be Iuge, and ſo I mak ane end.

FINIS

QVOD DAVID LYN-
DESAY.

P iij

¶ The Testament &

Complaint of our souerane Lordis
Papingo, king James the Fyst: Lyand sore
woundit, and may nocht de, till euery
man haue hard quhat scho sayis:
Quharefor, gentill Redaris,
haist zow that scho wer
out of pane.

(***)

¶ Compylit be Schir Dauid Lyndesay of the Mont
Knicht , Alias , Lyoun King of Armes.

Liuor post fata quiescit.

❧ THE PROLOG.

Uppose J had Jngyne Angelicall,
with Sapience mair than Sala-
monicall,
J not quhat mater put in memorie
The Poeitz auld in style Heroicall,
In breue subtell termes Rethoricall,
Of euerilk mater , Tragedie, and Storie,
Sa ornatlie to thair hiche laud and glorie,
Haith done indyte, quhose supreme Sapience,
Transcendith far the dull Jntelligence.

P iiij   Of Poeit,

Of Poeitƶ now,in til our vulgar toung,
(foƶ quhy?)the bell of Rethoƶick bene roung,
Be Chawcer,Gower,and Lidgate laureat.
Quha dar pƶesume,thir Poeitƶ till impugn?
Quhose sweit sentēce thƶouch Albion ben soung
Oƶ quha can now the woƶkis contrcfait,
Oƶ of Kennedie,with termes aureait?
Of Dunbar quha language had at large,
As may be sene, in till his goldin Targe.

Quitin Merser,Rowl,Hēdersō,Hay ҄ Hollād
Thocht thay be deid, thair libellis bene leuand,
Quhilkis to reherse,makis Reidarƶ to reiose,
Allace,foƶ ane, quhilk Lamp was in this land,
Of Eloquence the flowand balmy strand:
And in our Inglis Rethoƶick the Rose,
As of Rubeis, the Carbunckle bene chose:
And as Phebus dois Cynthia pƶecell,
Sa Gawin Dowglas, Bischop of Dunkell.

Had,quhen he was into this land on lyue,
Abuse vulgar Poeitƶ Pƶerogatyue,
Baith in Pƶactick,and Speculationn.
I say na mair, gude Reidarƶ may discryue,
His woƶthy woƶkis,in noumer mo than fyue.
And speciallie, the trew Translatioun
Of Uirgill, quhilk bene Consolatioun
To cunning men, to knaw his greit Ingyne,
Als weill in Naturall Science,as Deuyne.

And in the Court bene pƶesent in thir dayis,
That Ballatis bƶeuis, lustellie and layis,
                                        Quhilkƶ

Quhilkis to our Prince daylie thay do present.
Quha cã say mair, thã schir James Inglis sayͅ
In Ballatis, Farsis, and in plesand Playis?
Bot Culrose hes his pen maid Impotent.
Kid in cunning and practik richt prudent.
And Steward, quhilk defyzith ane staitlie style
Full oznate warkis daylie doith compyle.

Stewart of Lozne, will carp richt curiouslie
Galbzaith, kinloich, quhẽ thay list thame applie
Into that Art, ar craftie of Ingyne:
Bot now of late, is start vp haistelie,
Ane cunning Clark, quhilk wzytith craftelie,
Ane plant of Poeitis, callit Ballendyne,
Quhose oznat warkis, my wit can nocht defyne
Get he into the Court auctozitie,
He will pzecell Quintyn and Kennedie.

Sa thocht I had Ingyne, as I haue none,
I wat nocht quhat to wzyt be sweit sáct Jhone
(Foz quhy?)in all the garth of Eloquence,
Is na thing left, bot barrane stok and stone,
The Polite termes ar pullit euerilk one,
Be thir fozenaimit Poetis of Pzudence,
And sen I find, none vther new Sentence,
I sall declare, oz I depart zow fro,
The Complaynt of ane woundit Papingo.

Quharefoz, beeause myne mater bene sa rude
Of Sentence, and of Rethozick denude,
To rurall folk, myne Dyting bene directit,
Far fleinit from the sicht of men of gude,

Foꝛ cunning men, J knaw wyll fone conclude,
Jt dow na thing, bot foꝛ to be deiectit:
And quhen J heir myne mater bene detrectit,
Than fall J fweir, J maid it bot in mowis,
To landwart laſſis, quhilkꝭ keipith by ꝛ ʒowis.

I. The Complaint of
the Papingo.

Wha clymmis to hich, perfoꝛce his
feit mon faill,
Erpꝛeme J fall that be Experience
Gif that ʒow pleis to here ane pie-
teous raill,
How ane fair Bird be fatall violence,
Deuoꝛit was, and micht mak na defence,
Contrair the Deith, fa failʒeit Naturall ſtrenth
As efter J fall fchaw ʒow at mair lenth.

　Ane Papingo richt plefand and perfyte,
Pꝛefentit was till our moſt nobill king,
Of quhome his grace ane lang tyme had delyte
Mair fair of foꝛne, J wat flew neuer on wing:
This pꝛoper Bird he gaue in gouerning,
To me, quhilk was his fimpyll Seruiture,
On quhome J did my diligence and cure.

　　　　　　　　　　　To lerne

To lerne hir language Artificiall,
To play platfute, and quhissill sute before:
Bot of hir Inclinatioun Naturall,
Scho countrafaitit all fowlis les and more,
Of hir curage,scho wald without my lore,
Sing lyke the Merle,and craw lyke the Cok,
Pew lyke the Gled , & chant lyke the Laurok.

Bark lyke ane Dog,and kekill lyke ane Ka,
Blait lyke ane Hog,and bullet lyke ane Bull:
Gaill lyke ane Goik, & greit quhē scho wes wa.
Clym on ane Cord,syne lauch & play the fule,
Scho micht haue bene ane menstral agan̄ȝule
This blyssit bird was to me sa plesand,
Quhare euer J fure,J bure hir on me hand.

And sa befell,in till ane mirthfull morrow,
Into my garth,J past me to repose:
This Bird and J , as we war wount aforrow,
Amang the flowris fresche, fragrant,& formose:
My vitall Spreitis dewlie did reiose,
Quhen Phebus rose,and raue the cloudis sabill
Throuch brichtnes of his beimis amyabill.

Without vapour was weill purificate,
The temperate air, soft,sober,and serene:
The eirth be Nature sa edificate,
With holsum herbis,blew,quhyte,reid,& grene:
Quhilk eleuate my Spreitis from the splene,
That day Saturne nor Mars,durst not appeir
Nor Eole,of his Coue, he durst nocht steir.

That day perforce behuffit to be fair,
                                        Be In-

Be Influence ,and cours Celestiall.
Na Planeit preisit for to perturbe the air,
For Mercurius be mouing Naturall,
Exaltit was into the throne trvumphall,
Of his Mansioun vnto the fystene gre,
In his awin souerane Signe of Uirgine.

That day did Phebus plesandlie depart,
From Gemini , and enterit in Cancer:
That day Cupido did extend his dart,
Uenus that day coniunit with Iuppiter,
That day Neptunus hid hym lyke ane sker,
That day dame Nature with greit besines,
Fortherit Flora,to kith hir craftines.

And retrograde was Mars in Capricorne:
And Cynthia in Sagittar asseisit:
That day Dame Ceres,Goddes of the corne,
Full Joyfullie Jhone Uponland appleisit.
The bad Espect of Saturne was appeisit,
That day be Juno,of Iuppiter the Joy
Perturband spreitis causing to hald coy.

The sound of birdis, surmontit all the skyis,
With Melodie of notis Musicall.
The balmy droppis of dew Titan vpdryis,
Hingand vpon the tender twistis small,
The heuinlie hew,and sound Ingelicall,
Sic perfyte plesour, printit in my hart,
That w greit pyne, from thyne I micht depart.

So still amang those herbis amyabill,
I did remane ane space , for my pastance,

Bot

Bot warldlie plefour bene fa variabill,
Mixit with forrow, dreid and Inconftance,
That thair in till is na continuance.
Sa micht I fay my fchort folace allace,
Was dreuin in dolour,in ane lytill fpace.

For in that garth amãg thofe fragrãt flouris,
Walking allane,none bot my Bird and I.
Unto the tyme that I had faid myne houris:
This Bird I fet vpon ane branche me by:
Bot fcho began to fpeill richt fpedilie,
And in that tre fcho did fa hiche afcend,
That be na way I micht hir apprehend.

Sweit bird(faid I)bewar,mõt nocht ouer hie
Returne in tyme,perchance thy feit may failze,
Thow art richt fat,& nocht weill vfit to flie,
The gredie Sled, I dreid fcho the affailze,
I will(faid fcho)afcend,vailze quod vailze,
It is my kynd to clym ay to the hicht,
Of fether and bone, I wait weill I am wicht.

Sa on the hycheft lytill tender twift,
With wing difplayit, fcho fat full wantounlie,
Bot Boreas blew ane blaft,or euer fcho wift,
Quhilk brak the branche,& blew hir fuddandlie
Down to the ground, with mony carefull crie,
Upon ane ftob,fcho lichtit on hir breift,
The blude rufchit out,& fcho crpit for a preift.

God wait, gif than my hart wes wo begone,
To fe that fowll flichter amang the flouris,
Quhilk w greit murning,gan to mak hir mone
Now

Now cummin ar (said scho) the fatall houris,
Of bitter deith, now mon J thole the schouris:
O dame Nature, J pray the of thy grace,
Len me laiser, to speik ane lytill space,

For to complene my fate Infortunate,
And to dispone my geir, or J departe,
Sen of all confort J am desolate,
Allane, except the Deith heir with his dart,
With awfull cheir, reddy to perse myne hart:
And with that word, scho tuke ane passioun,
Syne flatlingis fell, and swappit into swoun.

With sory hart, persit with compassioun,
And salt teiris, distilling from myne Ene,
To here that Birdis lamentatioun:
J did approche, vnder ane Hauthorne grene,
Quhare J micht here and se, and be vnsene:
And quhē this bird had swounit twyse or thryse
Scho gan to speik, saying on this wyse.

O fals Fortune, quhy hes thow me begylit?
This day at morne quha knew this careful cace
Vane hope, in the my resoun haith exylit,
Hauing sic traist into thy fenzeit face,
That euer J was brocht into ẏ Court, allace.
Had J in forrest flowin amang me feiris,
J micht full weill haif leuit mony zeiris.

Prudent counsell allace J did refuse,
Agane resoun vsing myne appetyte:
Ambitioun did sa myne hart abuse,
That Eolus had me in greit dispyte:

                                    Poetis

Poeitis of me haith mater to indyte,
Quhilk clam sa hiche, & wo is me tharefoir,
Nocht douting that the deith durst me deuore.

This day at morne, my forme & feddrem fair,
Abufe the proude Pacok war precelland,
And now ane catyue carioun full of cair,
Bathand in blude, doun from my hart distellãd
And in myne eir, the bell of deith, bene knelland
O fals warld, fy on thy Felicitie,
Thy Pryde, Auarice, and Immundicitie.

In the Ise, na thing bene permanent,
Of thy schort solace, sorrow is the end:
Thy fals Infortunate giftis bene bot lent.
This day full proud, the morne na thing to spẽd
O ze that doith pretend, ay till ascend,
My fatall end, haue in remembrance,
And zow defend, from sic vnhappy chance.

Quhydder that I was strickin in extasie,
Or throuch ane stark Imaginatioun:
Bot it appeirit in myne fantasie,
I hard this dolent lamentatioun,
Thus dullit into desolatioun.
Me thocht this Bird, did breue in hir maneir,
Hir counsall to the King, as ze sall heir.

The First Epistill of the Papingo, II.
Directit to King Iames the Fyft.

Repotent Prence, peirles of pulchritude,
Gloze, honour, laud, tryumphe & victorie
Be to

Be to thy hich Excellend Celſitude,
With Martiall deidis, digne of memorie,
Sen Atropos conſumit haith my glorie,
And dolent deith allace mon vs depart,
I leue to the my trew vnfenzeit hart,

Togidder with this Cedull ſubſequent,
With maiſt reuerend Recommendatioun.
I grant thy grace, gettis mony ane document,
Be famous Fatheris predicatioun,
With mony notabill Narratioun,
Be pleſand Poeitis in ſtyle Heroicall,
How thow ſulde gyde thy Sait Imperiall.

Sum doith deplore the greit Calamiteis,
Of diuers Realmes Tranſmutatioun.
Sum pieteouſlie doith treit of Tragedeis,
All for thy graces informatioun.
So I intend, but adulatioun,
Into my barbour ruſticall indyte,
Amang the reſt, ſchir, ſum thing for to wryte.

Souerane conſaue this ſimpyll ſimilitude,
Of Officiaris, ſeruing thy Senzeorie.
Quha gydꝫ thame weil gettis of thy grace greit
Quha bene Iniuſt, degradit ar of glorie, (gude.
And Cancellat out of thy memorie,
Prouiding ſyne mair pleſand in thair place,
Beleue richt ſa ſall God do with thy grace.

Conſidder weill thow bene bot Officiare,
And waſſall, to that King Incomparabill.
Preis thow to pleis that puiſſant prince preclare
Thy

Thy riche reward salbe Inestimabill,
Exaltit hich in gloze Interminabill,
Abone Archangellis , Uirtues,Potestatis,
Plesandlie placit amang the Principatis.

Of thy Uertew, Poeit; perpetuallie,
Sall mak mentioun vnto the warld be endit:
So thow excers thyne office prudentlie:
In heuin and eirth, thy grace salbe commendit,
Quharefoz effeir,that he be nocht offendit,
Quhilk hes exaltit the to sic honour,
Of his pepill to be ane Gouernour.

And in the eirth haith maid sic Ozdinance,
Under thy feit all thing Terrestriall,
Ar subiect to thy plesour and pastance,
Baith fowll and fische,and beistis pastozall,
Men to thy seruice,and wemen thay ben thzall,
Halking,hunting,armes,and lefull amour,
Pzecozdinat ar be God, foz thy plesour.

Maisteris of Musike to recreat thy spzeit,
With dantit voce and plesand Instrument:
Thus thow may be of all plesouris repleit,
Sa in thyne office thow be diligent:
Bot be thou found sleuthfull,oz negligent,
Oz Jninst, in thyne Execution,
Thow sall nocht faill Deuine punition.

Quharetoz sen thow hes sic Capacitie,
To lerne to play so plesandlie,and sing,
Ryde hozs,ryn speiris,with greit audacitie,
Schut with hand bow,crosbow and culuering
                              O   Amang

Amang the reſt (Schir) lerne to be ane King,
Kyith on that craft, thy pregnant freſche ingyne
Grantit to the, be Influence Deuyne.

And ſen the Definitioun of ane King,
Is for to haue of pepill gouernance,
Addres the firſt, abuſe all vther thing,
Till put thy body till ſic Ordinance,
That thyne vertew, thyne honour may auance:
For how ſuld Princis gouerne greit Regionis,
That can not dewlie gyde thair awin perſonis.

And gif thy grace wald leif richt pleſandlie,
Call thy counſall, and caſt on thame the cure,
Thair Juſt Decreitis defend, and fortifie,
But gude counſall, may na Prince lang indure,
Wyrk with counſall, than ſall thy work be ſure.
Cheis thy counſall of the moſt Sapient,
Without regard to blude, ryches or rent.

Amang all vther paſtyme and pleſour,
Now in thy Adoleſcent zeiris zing,
Wald thow ilk day ſtudie bot half ane hour,
The regiment of Princely gouerning,
To thy pepill, it war ane pleſand thing,
Thare micht thow find thyne awin vocatioun,
How thou ſuld vſe thy ſceptour, ſword, & croun.

The Cronikillis to knaw I the exhort,
Quhilk may be Mirrour to thy Maieſtie,
Thare ſall thou find baith gude & euill report,
Of euerilk Prince efter his qualitie:
Thocht thay be deid, thair deidis ſall nocht de:

                                                    Traiſt

Traist weill thow salbe stylit in that storie,
As thow deseruis,put in memorie.

Requeist that Roy , quhilk rēt was on ÿ rude
The to defend from deidis of defame,
That na Poeit report of the bot gude,
For Princis dayis induris bot ane drame.
Sen first king Fergus bure ane Dyadame,
Thow art the last king of fyue score and fyue,
And all ar deid,and none bot thow on lyue.

Of quhose noumer fyftie and fyue bene flane,
And most part in thair awin misgouernance.
Quharefor I the beseik my Souerane,
Considder of thair lyuis the circumstance.
And quhen ÿ knawis ÿ cause of thair mischance
Of vertew than, exalt thy saillis on hie,
Traisting to chaip that fatall destenie.

Treit ilk trew Barron,as he war thy brother
Quhilk mon at neid, the and the realme defend,
Quhen suddandlie ane doeth oppres ane vther.
Lat Iustice myxit with mercy thame amend:
Haue thou thair hartis,thow hes yneuch to spēd
And be the contrair, thow art bot king of bone,
Frō tyme thyne heiris hartis bene frō the gone.

I haue na laiser for to wryte at lenth,
Myne haill intent,vntill thyne Excellence,
Decressit sa I am in wit and strenth,
My mortall wound doeth me sic violence,
Pepill of me may haue experience.
Because allace, I was Incounsolabill,
Now mon I de ane catyue miserabill.

Q ii   The

III. The secund Epistill of the Papingo,
Directit to hir Brether of Court.

BRether of Court, with mynd precordiall,
To the greit God, hartlie I comend zow
Imprent my fall, in zour memoriall,
Togidder with this Cedule, that I send zow,
To preis ouer hiche, I pray zow not preted zow
The vane ascens of court, quha will considder,
Quha sittith most hie, sal find ȝ sait most slidder.

Saȝe that now, be lansing vp the ledder,
Tak tent in tyme, festinning zour fingaris fast:
Quha climmȝ most hich, most dint hes of ȝ wed-
And leist defence aganis the bitter blast,   (der,
Of fals fortune, quhilk takith neuer rest,
Bot most redoutit daylie scho doun thringis,
Not sparing Paipis, Conquerouris, nor kingis

Thocht ȝe be montit vp aboue the skyis,
And hes baith king, and court in gouernance,
Su was als hich, quhilk now richt lawly lyis,
Complanyng sore the courtis variance.
Thare preterit tyme, may be experience,
Quhilk throw vane hope of court did clym so hie
Syne watit wingȝ, quhen thay wed best to flie.

Sen ilk court bene vntraist, and transitorie,
Changing als oft as weddercock in wind,
Sum makand glaid, and vther sum richt sorie,
Formaist this day, the morne may ga behynd,
Lat not vane hope of Court zour resone blynd.
                 Traist

Traist weill sum men wil geif ʒow laud as lordʒ
Quhilk wald be glaid,to se ʒow hang in cordis.

I durst declare the miserabilitie,
Of diuers courtʒ,war not my tyme bene schort,
The dreidfull change, vane gloʒe and vilitie:
The painfull plesour,as Poeitis doeth report,
Sum tyme in hope,sumtyme in disconfort:
And how sum mē dois spēd thair ʒoutheid haill,
In Court,syne endis in the hospitaill.

How sum in court bene quiet counsalouris,
Without regard to Commoun weill oʒ kingis,
Casting thair cure foʒ to be Conquerouris.
And quhen thay bene hich raisit in thair ringis,
How chāge of court thame dulfully doun thrigʒ
And quhen thay bene from thair estait deposit,
How mony of thair fall, bene richt reiosit.

And how fond fenʒeit fulis and flatteraris,
Foʒ small seruice obtenis greit rewardis.
Pandaris, pykthankis, custronis ⁊ clatteraris.
Loupis vp from laddis, syne lichtʒ amāg lardis,
Blasphematouris beggaris,⁊ commoun bairdis
Sum tyme in Court hes mair authoʒtie,
Noʒ deuote Doctouris in Diuinitie.

How in sum Countrie bene barnis of Beliall,
Full of dissimulit paintit flatterie,
Prouocand be Intoxicat counsall,
Princis till huredome and till hasardʒie.
Quha dois in Princis pʒent sic harlotrie,
I say foʒ me sic pert Prouocatouris,
	Q iij		Sulde

Suld punischit be abuſe all ſtrang tratouris.

Quhat trauers, troubill and Calamitie,
Haith bene in court within thir hundꝛeth ƺeiris?
Quhat moꝛtall changis, and quhat miſerie?
Quhat nobill men bene bꝛocht vpõ thair beiris?
Traiſt weil my freindƷ, follow ƺe mon ƺour feirƷ
Sa ſen in Court bene na tranquillitie,
Set nocht on it ƺour haill felicitie.

The Court chãgis ſumtyme with ſic outrage
That few oꝛ none, may makin reſiſtence,
And ſpairis not the Pꝛince mair than the page,
As weill appeirith be Experience:
The Duke of Rotheſay, micht mak na Defence,
Quhilk wes perteinand Roy of this Regioun,
Bot dulefully deuoꝛit in pꝛeſoun.

Quhat dꝛeid, quhat dolour, had ẏ nobill king
Robert the Thꝛid, from tyme he know the cace,
Of his twa Sonnis dolent departing?
Pꝛince Dauid deid, and James captyue allace,
Till trew ScottƷ mẽ, quhilk wes a careful cace.
Thus may ƺe knaw the Court bene variand,
Quhen blude royall, ẏ change may not gane ſtãd

Quha rang in Court, mair hie and triumphãd
Noꝛ dnke Murdok, quhyl that his day indurit:
Was he nocht greit Pꝛotectour of Scotland?
Ƶit of the Court, he was nocht weill aſſurit,
It changit ſa, his lang ſeruice was ſinurit:
He and his Sone, fair Walter but remeid,
Foꝛfaltit war, and put to dulefull deid.

King

King James the first, ꝑ patrone of vertu dēce,
Gem of Ingyne, and Perle of Policie,
Well of Justice, and flude of Eloquence,
Quhose vertew dois transcend my fantasie,
For till discryue, ȝit quhen he stude most hie,
Be fals exorbitant conspiracioun,
That prudent Prince, was pieteouslie put doun.

Als James the secund Roy of greit renoun,
Beand in his superexcellent gloꝛe,
Throuch rakles schutting of ane greit cannoun,
The dolent deith, allace did him deuoꝛe.
Ane thing thare bene, of quhilk I meruell moꝛe,
That foꝛtune had at him sic moꝛtall feid,
Throuch fiftie thousand, to waill him be ꝫ heid.

My hart is perst with painis foꝛ to pance,
Oꝛ wryte that Courtis variatioun,
Of James the Thꝛid, quhē he had gouernance,
The dolour, dꝛeid and desolatioun,
The change of Court and conspiratioun:
And how that Cochꝛane with his companie,
That tyme in Court clam sa pꝛesumptuouslie.

It had bene gude, ꝑai barnȝ had ben vnboꝛne
Be quhome that nobill Prince was sa abusit.
Thay grew as did the weid abuse the coꝛne,
That prudent Loꝛdis counsall was refusit.
And held him quiet, as he had bene inclusit,
Allace that Prince, be thair abusioun,
Was finallie bꝛocht to confusioun.

Thay clam so hich and gat sic audience,

And

And with thair Prince , grew sa familiar,
His Germane brother micht get na presence,
The Duke of Albanie, nor the Erle of Mar,
Lyke baneist men, was haldin at the bar,
Till in the King thare grew sic mortall feid,
He flemit the Duke, and pat the Erle to deid.

    Thus Cochrane with his catyue Companie,
Forsit schame to fle, bot zit thay wantit fedderis,
Abuse the hich Cederis of Libanie,
Thay clam so hie, till thay lap ouir thair leddarz
On Lawder brig, syne keippit wer in tedderis,
Stranglit to deith , thay gat nane vther grace,
Thair king captyve, quhilk wes ane careful cace

    Till put in forme, that fait Infortunate,
And mortall change perturbith myne Ingyne,
My wit bene waik, my fingeris fatigate,
To dyte or wryte the rancour and rewyne,
The Ciuill weir, the battell Intestyne:
How that the Sone, with baner braid displayit
Aganis the Father, in Battell come arrayit.

    Wald God ʒ prince had bene that day côfortit
With Sapience of the prudent Salomon:
And with ʒ strenth of strâg Sampson supportit
With the bauld Oste of the greit Agamemnon.
Quhat suld I wis, remedie was thare none,
At morne ane King, wᵗ Sceptour, sword & croun
At ewin ane deid deformit carioun.

    Allace quhare bene that richt redoutit Roy,
That potêt Prince, gentill King James ʒ feird
                         I pray

I pray to Chzist his Saull foz to conuoy,
Ane greiter nobill, rang nocht into the eird.
O Atropos warie we may thy weird:
Foz he was Mirrour of humilitie,
Lode Sterne, and Lamp of liberalitie.

During his tyme, sa Iustice did pzeuaill,
The Sauage Iles, trymblit foz terrour.
Eskdale, Euisdale, Liddisdale, & Annandaill,
Durst nocht rebell, douting his dyntis dour,
And of his Lozdis had sic perfyte fauour,
Sa foz to schaw, that he effeirit na fone,
Out throuch his reaime, he wald ryde him alone

And of his court throuch Europe spzāg ye fame
Of lustie Lozdis, and lusesum Ladyis zing,
Tryumphand toznapß, iusting, & knichtly game,
With all pastyme, accozding foz ane king:
He was the gloze of Pzincelie gouerning,
Quhilk throuch the ardēt lufe he had to France
Aganis Ingland did moue his Ozdinance.

Of Floddoun feild the rewyne to reuolue,
Oz that most dolent day foz till deploze,
I nyll foz dzeid, that dolour zow dissolue,
Schaw how that pzince in his triumphād gloze
Distroyit was, quhat neidith pzoces moze,
Nocht be the vertew of Inglis ozdinance,
Bot be his awin wilfull misgouernance.

Allace that day had he bene consolabill,
He had obteinit laud, gloze, and victozie:
Quhose pieteous pzoces bene sa lamentabill,

Q. v   I nyll at

I nyll at lenth , it put in memorie,
I neuer red, in Tragedie nor storie,
At one Iornay so mony Nobillis slane,
For the defence, and lufe of thair Souerane.

Now briether mark in zour remembrance,
Ane Mirrour of those mutabiliteis.
So may ze knaw, the Courtis inconstance,
Quhen Princis bene thus pullit from thair seis.
Efter quhose deith, quhat strange aduersiteis.
Quhat greit misrewill, into this Regioun rang,
Quhē our zōg prince could nother speik nor gāg

During his tender zouth & innocence,   (chāce!
Quhat stouth, quhat reif, quhat murther & mis-
Thare was not ellis bot wraking of vengeance
Into that Court thare rang sic variance.
Diuers Rewlaris, maid diuers Ordinance.
Sum tyme our Quene, rang in authoritie,
Sum tyme the prudent Duke of Albanie.

Sum tyme the Realme, was rewlit be regēt?
Sum tyme Lufetenentis, leidaris of the Law,
Than rang so mony Inobedientis,
That few or none, stude of ane vther aw.
Oppressioun did so lowd his Bugill blaw,
That none durst ryde, bot into feir of weir,
Iok vponland, that tyme did mys his meir.

Quha was more hich , in honour eleuate,
Nor was Margarete, our hich & michtie pricis?
Sic power was to hir appropriate,
Of king and Realme scho wes Gouernoures,
                                        Zit came

Zit came ane change,within ane schoꝛt pꝛoces,
That Perle pꝛeclare,that luſtie plꝭſand Quene,
Lang tyme durſt nocht into the Court be ſene.

The archebiſchop of ſanct Andꝛos James Be-
Chácellar,a pꝛimate in power Paſtoꝛall, (toun
Clam nyꝛt the king , moſt hich in his Regioun,
The ledder ſchuke, he lap and gat ane fall,
Authoꝛitie,noꝛ power Spirituall,
Ryches,freindſchip, micht not that tyme pꝛeuail
Quhen dame Curia began to ſteir hir taill.

His hich pꝛudence aualit him nocht ane myte,
That tyme the court bair him ſic moꝛtall feid,
As pꝛeſoneir thay keipt him in diſpyte,
And ſum tyme wiſt not,quhare to hide his heid,
Bot diſagyſit,lyke Jhoue the raif he zeid.
Had nocht bene hope bair him ſic companie,
He had bene ſtranglit be Melancholie.

Quhat cummer & care was in ẏ court of fráce,
Quhen king Francis was takin pꝛeſoneir?
The Duke of Burboun,amyd his Oꝛdinance,
Deid at ane ſtraik,richt bailfull bꝛocht on beir.
The Court of Rome,that tyme ran all areir,
Quhen Pape Clemét was put in ſtrang pꝛeſon,
The nobill Cietie put to confuſioun.

Ju Jngland quha had greiter gouernance,
Noꝛ thair triumphand courtly Cardinall,
The commoun weill, ſum ſayis he did auance,
Be equall Juſtice,baith to greit and ſmall,
Thare was na Pꝛelate to him peregall.
                                    Jngliſmen

Inglismen sayis,had he roung langer space,
He had deposit sanct Peter of his place.

His princely pompe,nor Papall grauitie,
His palice Royall,ryche,and radious:
Nor zit the flude of Superfluitie,
Of his ryches, nor trauell tedious,
From tyme Dame Curia held him odious,
Aualit him nocht,nor prudence most profound,
The ledder brak,and he fell to the ground.

Quhare bene ẏ douchtie Erlis of Dowglas,
Quhilkis Royallie,into this Regioun rang?
Forfalt and slane,quhat neidith mair proces?
The erle of marche,wes merschellit yame amag
Dame Curia thame dulfullie down thrang.
And now of late,quha claim more hich amāg vs,
Nor did Archebald vmquhyle the Erle of Ang?

Quha with his Prince wes mair familiar,
Nor of his grace had mair authoritie?
Was he nocht greit Wardain and Chancellar?
Zit quhen he stude vpon the hicheft gre,
Traisting na thing,bot perpetuitie,
Was suddandlie deposit from his place,
Forfalt and flemit, he gat nane vther grace.

Quharefor traist nocht in till auctoritie,
My deir Brether,I pray zow hartfullie,
Presume nocht in zour vane prosperitie,
Conforme zour traist in God alluterlie:
Syne serue zour prince with enteir hart trewlie
And quhen ze se the court bene at the best:
　　　　　　　　　　　　　I counsale

I counfall ʒow,than draw ʒow to ʒour reſt.

Quhare ben ẏ hich tryūphand court of Troẏ
Oꝛ Alexander with his twelf pꝛudent peiris,
Oꝛ Julius, that richt redoutit Roẏ?
Agamemnon,moſt woꝛthy in his weiris?
To ſchaw thair fyne,my frayit hart affeiris.
Sum murdꝛeſt war,ſum poyſonit pitecouſlie,
Thair carefull courtis diſperſit dulefullie.

Traiſt weill thare is na conſtãt court bot ane
Quhare Chꝛiſt ben King , quhoſe tyme intermi-
And hich triūphãd gloꝛe beis neuer gane. (nabil
That quiet court mirthfull and immutabill,
Bot variance ſtandith ay ferme and ſtabill.
Diſſimulance,flattrie noꝛ fals repoꝛt,
Into that Court ſal neuer get reſoꝛt.

Traiſt weill my freindꝛ, this is na fenʒeit fair
Foꝛ quha that bene,in the extreme of deid,
The veritie but dout,thay ſuld declair,
Without regarde, to fauour oꝛ to feid,
Quhyll ʒe haue tyme, deir bꝛether mak remeid,
Adew foꝛ euer,of me ʒe get no moꝛe.
Beſeikand God to bꝛing ʒow till his gloꝛe.

Adew Edinburgh,thou hich triumphãd toun
With quhoſe boundꝛ, richt blythful haue J bene
Of trew merchandis, the rute of this Regioun,
Moſt reddy to reſſaue, court,King,and Quene.
Thy Policie and Juſtice may be ſene,
War deuotioun,wyſedome, and honeſtie,
And credence tynt, thay micht be found in the.
                                                    Adew

Adew fair Snawdoun, with thy towris hie,
Thy Chapell royall, Park, and tabill round,
May, June, and July, wald I dwell in the,
War I ane man, to heir the birdis sound,
Quhilk dothe aganis thy royall roche redound,
Adew Lythquo, quhose Palice of plesance,
Micht be ane patrone, in Portugall or France.

Fare weill Falkland, the Fortres of Fyfe,
Thy polite Park, vnder the lowmound law:
Sum tyme in the, I led ane lustie lyfe,
The fallow Deir, to se thame raik and raw.
Court men to cum to the, thay stand greit aw,
Sayand thy burgh, bene of all burrowis baill,
Because in the, thay neuer gat gude aill.

IIII. The Commonning betuix the
Papingo, and hir holy Executouris.

THe Pye persauit the Papingo in pane,
He lichtit doun, & fenzeit him to greit.
Sister (said he) allace, quha hes zow slane.
I pray zow mak prouisioun for zour spreit,
Dispone zour geir, and zow confes compleit.
I haue power be zour contritioun,
Of all zour mys, to geue zow full remissioun.

I am (said he) ane Channoun Regulare,
And of my Brether Pryor principall:
My quhyte Rocket, my clene lyfe doeth declare,
The blak bene of the deith memoriall.

Quharefor

Quhairefor I think ʒour guddis naturall,
Sulde be submittit haill into my cure:
Ʒe knaw I am ane holy Creature.

The Rauin came rolpãd, quhẽ he hard ÿ rair,
Sa did the Gled, with mony pieteous pew,
And fenʒeitlie thay contrafait greit cair.
Sister (said thay) ʒour raklesnes we rew,
Now best it is, our Iust counsall ensew,
Sen we pretend to hich promotioun,
Religious men, of greit deuotioun.

I am ane blak Monk, said the ruttillãd rauin
Sa said the gled, I am ane holy Freir,
And hes power to bring ʒow quick to Heuin:
It is weill knawin my cõscience bene full cleir,
The blak Bybill pronunce I sall perqueir,
Sa till our Brether ʒe will geue sum gude,
God wait gif we haue neid of lyues fude.

The Papingo said, Father be the rude,
Howbeit ʒour rayment be Religious lyke,
Ʒour Conscience, I suspect be nocht gude,
I did persaue, quhen priuely ʒe did pyke,
Ane cheikin from ane hen, vnder ane dyke,
I grant (said he) that hen was my gude freind,
And I that cheikin tuke bot for my teind.

Ʒe knaw the faith be vs mon be susteind,
So be the Pope it is preordinate,
That spirituall men suld leif vpon thair teind,
Bot weill wait I, ʒe bene predestinate,
In ʒour extremis to be sa fortunate,

To haue

To haue sic haly consultatioun,
Quharefor we mak zow exhortatioun.

Sen Dame Nature hes grantit zow sic grace
Laiser to mak confessioun generall,
Schaw furth zour sin i haist,quhyl ze haif space
Syne of zour geir mak ane memoriall.
We thre sall mak zour feistis funerall:
And with greit blis, burie we sall zour bonis,
Syne Trentalis twentie,trattill all at onis.

The rukkis sall rair,ȝ men sall on thame rew,
Aud cry,Commemoratio Animarum.
We sall gar cheikinnis cheip,ꝗ gaislingis pew,
Suppose the geis and hennis,suld cry alarum,
And we sall serue secundum Vsum Sarum.
And mak zow saif, we find sanct Blase to broch
Cryand for zow,the carefull cozrinoch.

And we sall sing about zour Sepulture,
Sanct Mongois Matynis, ꝗ the mekle Creid:
And syne deuotelie say, I zow assure,
The auld Placebo bakwart,and the beid,
And we sall were for zow the murning weid,
And thocht zour spreit,with Pluto war profest,
Deuotelie sall zour Dirige be drest.

Father (said scho)zour facund wordis fair,
Full sore I dreid,be contrair to zour deidis.
The wyffis of the village,cryis ȝ cair, (meidis
Quhen thay persaue zow maw ouerthort thair
Zour fals consait,baith duke ꝗ draik sore dreid,
I maruell suithlie, ze be nocht eschamit.

f o?

Fo? ȝour defaltis,beyng sa defamit.

It dois abho?,my pure perturbit Sp?eit,
Till mak to ȝow ony Confeſſioun.
I heir men ſay,ȝe bene ane Hypocreit,
Exemptit from the ſeinȝe and ſeſſioun.
To put my geir in ȝour poſſeſſioun,
That will I nocht ſa help my Dame Nature,
No? of my Co?ps,I will ȝow geif na cure.

Bot had I heir,the nobill Nichtingall,
The gentill Ia,the Merle , and Turtur trew,
My obſequies and Feiſtis funerall,
O?dour thay wald, with Notis of the new,
The pleſand Powin,maiſt Angellyk of hew,
Wald God I war, this day with him confeſſ,
And my deuyſe dewlie be him add?eſt.

The mirthfull Maueis,w̃ the gay Goldſpink,
The luſtie Larke,wald God thay war p?eſent,
My Info?tune fo?ſuith, thay wald fo?think,
And confo?t me that bene ſa impotent.
The ſwift Swallow, in P?actik maiſt p?ud͂et,
I wait ſcho wald,my bleiding ſtem belyue,
With hir moſt vertuous ſtane reſtringityue.

Compt me the cace, vnder confeſſioun,
The Gled ſaid p?oudlie to the Papingo,
And we ſall ſweir be our P?ofeſſioun,
Counſall to keip,and ſchaw it to no mo.
We the beſeik,o? thow depart vs fro,
Declare to vs ſum cauſis reſonabill,
Quhy we bene haldin ſa abhominabill.

Be thy trauell thow hes Experience,
R   ſiꝛ

First beand bred into the Orient,
Syne be thy gude seruice and diligence,
To Princis maid heir in the Occident.
Thow knawis the vulgar pepillis Jugement,
Quhare thow transcurrit the hote Meridionall
Syne nixt the Pole, the plaig Septentrionall.

So be thyne hich Ingyne superlatyue,
Of all Cuntreis thow knawis the qualiteis:
Quharefor I the coniure be God of lyue,
The veritie declare withouttin leis,
Quhat thow hes yard, be landis or be seis,
Of vs Kirkmen, baith gude and euill report,
And how thay Iuge, schaw vs, we the exhort.

Father (said scho) I catyue Creature,
Dar nocht presume, with sic mater to mell,
Of zour caces ze knaw I haue na cure,
Demad thame quhilk in prudence doeth precell,
I may nocht pew, my panes bene sa fell.
And als perchance, ze will nocht stand content,
To knaw the vulgar pepillis Jugement.

Zit will the deith alyte withdraw his dart,
All thay. lyis in my Memoriall,
I sall declare with trew vnfeinzeit hart:
And first I say to zow in generall,
The commoun pepill saith, ze bene all,
Degenerit from zour holy Primityuis,
As testifyis the proces of zour lyuis.

Of zour peirles prudent Predecessouris,
The beginning, I grant wes berray gude:
Apostolis, Martyris, Uirginis, Confessouris,

The

The found of thair excellent Sanctitude,
was hard ouer all the warld be land and flude,
Planting the Faith,be Predicatioun,
As Chrift had maid to thame narratioun

To fortifie the faith thay tuke na feir,
Afore Princis preiching full prudentlie,
Of dolourous deith , thay doutit nocht the deir,
The veritie declaring feruentlie,
And Martyrdome thay fufferit pacientlie.
Thay tuke na cure of land,riches nor rent,
Doctryne and deid,war baith equiualent.

To fchaw at lēth thair wark,wer greit won-
Thair myraklis,thay war fa manifeſt,   (der,
In name of Chriſt, thay haillit mony honder,
Rafing the deid,and purging the poſſeſt,
With peruerſt fpreitis , quhilk had bene oppreſt
The crukit ran , the blind men gat thair Ene,
The deif men hard,the lipper war maid clene.

The Prelatis spoufit war,with pouertie,
Thoſe dayis,quhen fa thay flurifchit in fame,
And with hir generit Lady Chaiſtitie,
And dame Deuotioun,notabill of name.
Humill thay war , fimpell,and full of fchame.
Thus Chaiſtitie , and dame Deuotioun,
war principall caufe of thair promottoun.

Thus thay continewit,in this lyue deuyne,
Ay till thar range , in Romes greit Cietie,
Ane potent Prince,was namit Conſtantyne,
Perſauit the Kirk had fpoufit pouertie,
With gude intent,and mouit of pietie,

R ij   Caufe

Cause of Diuoꝛce he sand betuix thame two,
And partit thame, withouttin woꝛdis mo.

Syne schoꝛtlie with ane greit solempnitie,
withouttin ony Dispensatioun,
The Kirk he spousit with dame Pꝛopertie,
Quhilk haistely be Pꝛoclamatioun,
To pouertie gart mak narratioun,
Under the pane of persing hir ene,
That with the Kirk scho suld na mair be sene.

Sanct Siluester, ẏ tyme ꝵg Pope in Rome,
Quhilk first consent to the Mariage,
Of Pꝛopertie, the quhilk began to blome,
Taking on hir the cure, with hich curage.
Deuotioun dꝛew hir till ane Heremitage,
Quhen scho considerit Lady Pꝛopertie,
So hiche exaltit into Dignitie.

O Siluester, quhare was thy Discretioun?
Quhilk Peter did renunce, thow did ressaue.
Andꝛow and Jhone, did leue thair possessioun,
Thair schippis ꜩ nettis, lynis, and all the laif,
Of tempoꝛall substāce na thing wald thay haif,
Contrarious to thair contemplatioun,
Bot soberlie thair sustentatioun.

Jhone the Baptist, went to the wildernes,
Lazarus, Martha, and Marie Magdalane,
Left heritage, and gudis mair and les.
Pꝛudent sanct Paule, thotht pꝛopertie pꝛophane
From toun to toun, he ran in wynd and rane,
Upon his feit, teiching the woꝛd of grace,
And neuer was subiectit to ryches.

The

The Gled said,zit I here na thing bot gude,
Proceid schortlie, and thy mater auance.
The Papingo said, Father be the rude,
It wer to lang to schaw the circumstance,
How Propertie with hir new alliance,
Grew greit w̄ chyld, as trew men to me tald,
And bure twa dochteris gudlie to behald.

The eldest donchter namit was ryches,
The secund sister , Sensualitie,
Quhilk did incres, within ane schort proces,
Preplesand to the Spiritualtie,
In greit iubstance and excellent bewtie,
Thir Ladyis twa,grew sa within few zeiris,
That in ẏ warld,war none micht be thair peris

This Royall ryches,and Ladie Sensuall,
From that tyme furth,tuke haill the gouernāce,
Of the most part of the state Spirituall.
And thay agane with humill obseruance,
Amorouslie thair wittis did auance,
As trew luffaris,thair Ladyis for to pleis,
God wait,gif than thair hartis war at eis.

Sone thay forzet to studie,pray and preche,
Thay grew sa subiect to dame Sensuall,
And thoucht bot pane,pure pepill for to teche,
Zit thay decretit, in thair greit Counsall,
Thay wald na mair,to Mariage be thrall,
Traisting suerely, till obserue Chaistitie,
And all begylit,quod Sensualitie.

Apperandlie thay did expell thair wyffis,
That thay micht leif at large,without thirlage,
R iij   At

At libertie to leid thair lustie lyffis,
Thinkand men thrall,that bene in mariage,
For new saicis,prouokis new curage.
Thus Chaistitie thay turne into delyte,
Wanting of wyffis,bene cause of appetyte.

Dame Chaistitie did steill away for schame,
From tyme scho did persaue thair prouiance,
Dame Sensuall,ane letter gart proclame,
And hir exylit Italie,and France,
In Ingland,couth scho get none Ordinance,
Than to the King,and Court of Scotland,
Scho markit hir withouttin more demand.

Traisting into that Court,to get confort.
Scho maid hir humill Supplicatioun.
Schortlie thay said,scho sulde get na support,
Bot boistit hir with blasphematioun,
To Preistis ga mak zour protestatioun:
It is(said thay)mony ane hundreth zeir.
Sen Chaistitie,had ony entres heir.

Tyrit for trauell,scho to the Preistis past,
And to the Rewlaris of Religioun:
Of hir presence,schortlie thay war agast,
Sayand thay thocht it bot abusioun,
Hir to resaue,sa with conclusioun,
With ane auyce,decretit,and gaue dome,
Thay wald resset na rebell out of Rome.

Sulde we resaue that Romanis her refusit,
And banist Ingland,Italie,and France:
For zour flattrie,than war we weill abusit,
Pas hyne,said thay,and fast zour way auance,
Amang

Amang the Nonnis,ga seik zour Ozdinance,
Foz we haue maid aith of Fidelitie,
To dame Ryches and Sensualitie.

Than pacientlie scho maid pzogressioun,
Towart the Nonnis with hart siching full soze
Thay gaue hir pzesence,with pzocessioun,
Resaiuand hir with honour,laud and gloze,
Purposing to pzeserue hir euer moze.
Of that nouellis came to dame Pzopertie,
To Ryches,and to Sensualitie.

Quhilkis sped thame at the post richt spedilie,
And set ane sege,pzoudlie about the place:
The sillie Nonnis,did zeild thame haistelie,
And humillie of that gilt askit grace,
Syne gaif thair bandis of perpetuall pace:
Resaiuand thame thay kest vp wykketis wyde,
Than Chaistitie thare na langer wald abyde.

Sa foz refuge,fast to the freiris scho fled,
Quhilkis said , thay wald of ladyis tak na cure:
Quhare ben scho now, than said ỹ gredie Gled?
Nocht amang zow,said scho, I zow assure.
I traist scho bene,vpon the bozrow mure.
Besouth Edinburgh,& that richt mony menis,
Pzofest amang the Sisteris of the Senis.

Thare hes scho fund hir mother Pouertie,
And Deuotioun hir awin Sister Carnall:
Thare hes scho fund Faith, Hope,and Cheritie,
Togidder with the vertues Cardinall.
Thare hes scho fund ane Conuent zit vnthzall.
To dame Sensuall, noz with ryches abusit,

Sa quietlie thofe Ladyis bene inclufit.

The Pyot faid, J dreid be thay affailzeit,
Thay rander thame, as did the holy Nonnis.
Dout nocht(faid fcho)for thay bene fa artailzeit
Thay purpofe to defend thame w̄ thair gunnis,
Reddy to fchute, thay haue fex greit Cannonnis
Perfeuerance,Conftance and Confcience,
Jufteritie, Laubour and Abftinence.

To refift fubtell Senfualitie,
Strongly thay bene enarmit feit and handis,
Be Abftinence,and keipit pouertie,
Contrair ryches,and all hir fals feruandis.
Thay haue ane bumbard , braiffit vp in bandis,
To keip thair port,in middis of thair clois,
Quhilk is callit, Domine cuftodi nos.

Within quhofe fchot thair dar na Enemeis,
Approche thair place,for dreid of dyntis dour,
Boith nicht and day , thay werk lyke befie beis,
For thair defence,reddie to ftand in ftour,
And hes fic watchis,on thair vtter tour,
That dame Senfuall,w̄ feige dar not affailze,
Nor cum within the fchot of thair artailze.

The Pyot faid, quhareto fulde thay prefume
For to refift fweit Senfualitie,
Or dame Ryches quhilk[re wlaris ben in Rome
Ar thay more conftant in thair qualitie,
Nor the Princis of Spiritualitie,
Quhilkis pl̄fandlie withouttin obftaikle,
Haith thame reffauit, in thair habitakle.

How lang traift ze,thofe Ladyis fall remane,
Sa

Sa solitar in sic perfectioun?
The Papingo said, brother in certane,
Sa lang as thay obey correctioun,
Cheifing thair heidis be electioun,
Unthrall to riches, or to pouertie,
Bot as requyrith thair necessitie.

O prudēt prelatis, quhare was zour prescience
That tuke in hand till obserue Chaistitie,
But austeir lyfe, laubour and abstinence?
Persauit ze nocht the greit prosperitie,
Ipperandlie, to cum of propertie.
Ze knaw greit cheir, greit eis and Idilnes,
To Lecherie was mother and maistres.

Thou rauis bnrockit, ŷ Rauin said be ŷ rude,
So to reproue Ryches, or Propertie.
Ibraham and Isaac wer ryche & beray gude,
Jacob and Ioseph had prosperitie.
The Papingo said, that is beritie:
Ryches I grant, is nocht to be refusit,
Prouiding alwayis, that it be nocht abusit.

Than said the Rauin, ane replicatioun,
Syne said, thy reson is nocht worth ane myte,
Is I sall preue with protestatioun,
That na man tak my wordis in despyte,
I say, the Temporall Princis hes the wyte,
That in the Kirk sic Pastouris dois prouyde.
To gouerne saulis, ŷ nocht thame selfis cā gyde.

Lang tyme efter the Kirk tuke propertie,
The Prelatis leuit in greit perfectioun,
Unthrall to Ryches or Sensualitie,

Un-

Under the holy Spreitis protectioun,
Orderlie chosin be electioun,
As Gregore, Jerome, Ambrose, and Augustyne,
Benedict, Bernard, Clement, Cleit and Lyne.

Sic pacient Prelatis enterit be the port,
Plesand the pepill be predicatioun,
Now dyke lowparis, dois in the Kirk resort,
Be Symonie, and Supplicatioun,
Of Princis be thair presentatioun:
Ha sillie saulis that bene Christis scheip,
Ar geuin to hungrie gormand wolfis to keip,

Na maruell is, thocht we Religious men,
Degenerit be, and in our lyfe confusit.
Bot sing, and drink, nane vther craft we ken,
Our Spirituall Fatheris hes vs sa abusit,
Aganis our will, those trukouris bene intrusit:
Lawit men hes now Religious men in curis,
Profest Virginis, in keiping of strang huris,

Princis, princis quhare ben zour hich prudēs,
In dispositioun of zour Beneficeis?
The guerdoning of zour Courticiens,
Is sum caus of thir greit enormiteis,
Thare is ane sort, waitand lyke hungrie fleis,
For spirituall cure, thocht thay ben na thig abill.
Quhose gredie thristis bene insatiabill.

Princis, I pray zow be na mair abusit,
To verteous men hauing sa small regard?
Quhy sulde vertew throuch flatterie be refusit,
That men for couening can get na reward?
Allace that ane bragger, or ane baird,

                                        Ane

Ane hure maifter,oz commoun bafatture,
Suld in the kirk get ony kynd of cure.

War I ane man wozthy to weir ane Croun,
Ay quhen thair vaikit ony beneficeis,
I fulde gar call ane congregatioun.
The principall of all the Pzelaceis,
Moft cunning Clerkis of Uniuerfiteis,
Moft famous Fatheris of Religioun,
With thair aduyfe mak difpofitioun.

I fulde difpone,all offices Paftozaillis,
Till Doctouris of Diuinitie oz Jure.
And caufe dame Uertew pull vp all hir faillis,
Quhen cunning men had in the Kirk maift cure
Gar Lozdis fend thair Sonnis, I zow affure,
To feik fcience and famous fculis frequent,
Syne thame pzomoue , that war moft fapient.

Greit plefour war to here ane Bifchop pzeche
Ane Dane, oz Doctour in Diuinitie,
Ane Abbot,quhilk could weill his conuent teche
Ane Perfone,flowing in Philofophie.
I tyne my tyme, to wifs quhilk will nocht be:
War not the pzecheing of the begging freiris,
Tynt war the Faith amang the Seculeiris.

As foz thair pzeiching,quod the Papingo,
I thame excufe,foz quhy,thay bene fa thzall,
To Pzopertie,and hir Ding Dochteris twa,
Dame Ryches,and fair Lady Senfuall,
Thay may nocht vfe na paftyme Spirituall,
And in thair habitis thay tak fic Deiyte,
Thay haue renuncit ruffet, and reploch quhyte.

Clei-

Cleikand to thame Skarlot and Cramosie,
With Meneuer,martrik, gryce & ryche armyns
Thair lawe hartis, exaltit ar sa hie,
To se thair Papall pomp,it is ane pyne,
Mair riche array is now with freinȝeis fyne,
Upon the barding of ane Bischopis Mule,
Nor euer had Paule oꝛ Peter aganis Zule.

Syne fair ladyis,thair chene may not eschaip
Dame Sensuall sa, sic seid hes in thame sawin.
Les skaith it war with licence of the Paip,
That ilk Pꝛelate ane wyfe had of his awin,
Nor se thair bastardȝ ouirthoꝛt ẏ cuntrie blawin
Foꝛ now be thay, be weill cummin from ẏ sculis
Thay fall to woꝛk, as thay war cōmoun bullis.

'Ȝew (quod ẏ Gled) ẏ pꝛeichis al in vane,
Ze secular folkȝ hes of our cace na curis
I grant(said scho)ȝit men will speik agane,
How ȝe haue maid a hundꝛeth thousand huris,
Quhilkȝ neuer had bē,war not ȝour lecherꝰ lurȝ
And gif I lee,hartlie I me repent,
Was neuer Bird, I wait,mair penitent.

Than scho hir schꝛaue with deuote contenāce
To that fals gled, quhilk fenȝeit him ane freir.
And quhen scho had fulfillit hir pennance,
Full subtellie at hir he gan inqueir:
Cheis ȝow (said he(quhilk of vs Bꝛether heir,
Sall haue of all ȝour naturall geir the curis,
Ze knaw nane bene mair holy Creaturis.

I am content (quod the pure Papingo)
That ȝe freir Gled,& coꝛbie Monk ȝour bꝛother
Hawe

Haue cure of all my gudis and no mo.
Sen at this tyme freindſchip I fiud nane vther
We ſalbe to zow trew , as till our mother,
(Quod thay)and ſweir till fulfill hir intent.
Of that (ſaid ſcho) I tak ane Inſtrument.

The Pyot ſaid,quhat ſall myne office be?
Ouerman,ſaid ſcho,vnto the vther twa.
The rowpand Rauin,ſaid ſweit ſiſter lat ſe,
Zour holy intent, foz it is tyme to ga.
The gredie Gled ſaid, Bzother do nocht ſo,
We will remane , and haldin vp hir heid,
And neuer depart from hir till ſcho be deid.

The Papingo thame thankit tenderlie,
And ſaid,ſen ze haue tane on zow this cure,
Depart myne Naturall gudis equallie,
That euer I had,oz hes of Dame Nature.
Firſt to the Howlet, Indigent and pure,
Quhilk on the day foz ſchame dar nocht be ſene,
Till hir I leue my gay galbert of grene.

My bzicht depurit Ene,as cryſtall cleir,
Unto the Bak,ze ſall thame baith pzeſent.
In Phebus pzeſence, quhilk dar nocht appeir,
Of Naturall ſicht,ſcho bene ſa impotent,
My birneiſt beik,I leue with gude entent,
Unto the gentill,pieteous Pellicane,
To help to pers hir tender hart in twane.

I leue the Goik,quhilk hes na ſang bot ane,
My Muſike,with my voce Angelicall.
And to the Gouſe ze geif, quhen I am gane,
My Eloquence,and toung Rethozicall,

                        And

And tak and dry,my bonis greit and sman,
Syne clois thame in ane case of Ebure syne,
And thame present vnto the Phenix syne.

  To birne to hir , quhen scho hir lyfe renewis,
In Arabie,ze sall hir finde but weir,
And sal knaw hir, be hir most heuinlie hewis,
Gold, Asure,Gowles,Purpour & Synopeir,
Hir dait is for to leif fyue hundreth zeir:
Mak to that Bird my commendatioun,
And als I mak zow Supplicatioun.

  Sen of my corps, I haue zow geuin the cure
Ze speid zow to the Court but tarying,
And tak my hart of perfyte portrature,
And it present vnto my Souerane King,
I wait he will it close into ane ring,
Commend me to his grace,I zow exhort,
And of my passioun mak him trew report.

  Ze thre my tryppis sall haue for zour trauell,
With luffer & lowing,to part equall amang zow
Prayand Pluto ,the potent Prince of hell,
Gif ze failze,that in his feit he fang zow,
Be to me trew,thocht I na thing belang zow,
Sore I suspect zour Conscience be to large:
Dout nocht, said thay, we tak it with þ charge.

  Adew Brether, quod the pure Papingo,
To talkin mair,I haif na tyme to tarie:
Bot sen my spreit,mon fra my body go,
I recommend it to the Quene of Farie,
Eternallie,in till hir court to tarie,
In wyldernes, amang the holtis hore.
Than scho inclynit hir heid, and spak no more.
Pluu.

Plungit in till hir mortall paſſioun,
full greuouſlie ſcho grippit to the ground.
It war to lang to mak narratioun,
Of ſichis ſore with mony ſtang and ſtound,
Out of hir wound, the blude did ſa abound,
Ane compas round,was w̄ hir blude maid reid,
Without remeid,thare was na thing bot deid.

And be ſcho had In manus tuas ſaid,
Extinctit war hir naturall wittis fyue:
Hir heid full ſoftlie on hir ſchulder laid,
Syne zeild the ſpreit , with panes pungityue,
The Rauin began rudely to rug and ryue,
full gormoundlyke, his emptie throte to feid,
Eit ſoftlie Brother,ſaid the gredie Gled.

Quhyl ſcho is hote,depart hir euin amang vs
Tak thow ane half,and reik to me ane vther,
In till our richt I wait,na wicht dar wrang vs
The Pyot ſaid,the feind reſaue the fother,
Quhy mak ze me ſtepbarne, ꝗ I zour Brother?
Ze do me wrãg ſchir Gled,I ſchrew zour hart,
Tak thare(ſaid he)the pudding? for thy part.

Than wait ze weil,my hart was wonder ſair
for to behald that dolent departing,
Hir Angell fedderis fleing in the air,
Except the hart was left of hir na thing.
The Pyot ſaid,this pertenith to the King,
Quhilk till his grace I purpoſe to preſent,
Thow(quod the Gled)ſall faill of thyne intent.

The Rauin ſaid,God nor I rax in ane rape,
And thou get this till vther King or Duke:
The Pyot ſaid,plene I nocht to the Pape,
                                          Than

Than in ane smedie, I be smorit with smuke,
With that the Gled, the pece claucht in his cluke
And fled his way, the laue with all thair micht,
To chace the Gled, flew all out of my sicht.

Now haue ʒe hard, this lytill Tragedie,
The sore complaynt, the testament and mischāce
Of this pure Bird, quhilk did ascend so hie:
Beseikand ʒow, excuse myne Ignorance,
And rude indyte, quhilk is nocht till auance.
And to the quair, I geif commandement,
Mak na repair, quhare Poeitis bene present.

Because thow bene but Rethorike sa rude,
Be neuer sene, besyde none vther Buke,
With King nor Quene, w̄ Lord nor man of gude
With cote vnclene, clame kinrent to sum cuke.
Steill in ane nuke, quhen thay list on the Inke,
For smell of smuke, men will abhor to beir the
Heir I maneswetr þ, quharefor to lurk ga leir þ.

FINIS.

The Dreme of Schir

Dauid Lyndesay, of the Mont

Knicht: Familiar Seruitour, to our Souerane Lord, king James the fyft. &c.

* *
*

❧ THE EPISTILL TO the Kingis Grace.

Icht Potent Prince of hie Imperiall
blude,
Vnto thy Grace, I traist it be weill
knawin,
My seruice done vnto thy Celsitude,
Quhilk neidis nocht, at lenth for to be schawin:
And thocht my zoutheid, now be neir ouer blawi
Exercit in Seruice of thyne Excellence,
Hope hes my hecht ane gudlie Recompence.

Quhen thou wes zoung, I bure the i myne arme
Full tenderlie, till thow begouth to gang.
And in thy bed, oft happit the full warme,
VVith Lute in hand, syne sweitlie to the sang.

S   Sum

Sumtyme in danſing, feirelie I flan g:
And ſumtyme playand fairſis on th e flure,
And ſumtyme on myne office takand cure.

And ſumtyme lyke ane feind transfigurate,
And ſumtyme lyke the greiſlie gaiſt of Gy,
In diuers formis, oftymes diſſigurate,
And ſumtyme diſagyiſt full pleſandlie.
So ſen thy birth, I haue continuallie,
Bene occupyit, and ay to thy pleſour,
And ſnmtyme Stewar, Coppar, and Caruour.

Thy purs maiſter, and ſecreit Theſaurar,
Thy Iſchar ay ſen thy Natiuitie,
And of thy chalmer cheif Cubicular,
Quhilk to this hour, hes keipit me lawtie,
Louing be to the bleſſit Trinitie,
That ſic ane wrechit worme hes maid ſo able,
Till ſic ane Prince to be ſo agreable.

Bot now thow art be influence naturall,
Hie of Ingyne, and richt inquiſityue,
Of antike ſtoreis, and deidis Martiall,
More pleſandlie the tyme for till ouer dryue,
I haue at lenth the ſtoreis done diſcryue,
Of Hector, Arthur, and gentill Iulius,
Of Alexander and worthy Pompeius.

Of Iaſon and Medea, al at lenth,
Of Hercules the actis honorable,
And of Sampſon the ſupernaturall ſtrenth,
And of leil Luffaris ſtoreis amiable.
And oftymes haue I feinzeit mony fable,
                              Of Troylus

Of Troylus,the sorrow and the Ioy,
And Seigis all,of Tire Thebes and Troy.

The Prophecyis of Rymour, Beid and Marling,
And of mony vther plesand historie,
Of the reid Etin,and the gyir carling,
Confortand the , quhen that I saw the sorie,
Now with the support of the King of glorie,
I sall the schaw ane storie of the new,
The quhilk afore I neuer to the schew.

Bot humilie I beseik thyne Excellence,
VVith ornate termes , thocht I can nocht expres,
This sempyll mater for laik of eloquence,
Zit nochtwithstanding,all my besines.
VVith hart and hand my mynd I sall addres,
As I best can , and most compendious,
Now I begyn,the mater hapnit thus.

THE PROLOG

IN the kalendis of Ianuarie,
Quhen fresche Phebus be mouing
circulair,
from Capricorne was enterit in A-
quarie,
With blastis that the brancis maid full bair,
The snaw , and sleit perturbit all the air,
And flemit Flora,from euerie bank and bus,
Throuch support of the austeir Eolus.

Efter that I the lang wynteris night,
Had lyne walking, in my bed allone,

S ij   Throuch

Throuch heuy thocht,that na way sleip I micht
Remembring of diuers thingis gone:
Sa vp I rose,and cleithit me anone,
Be this fair Titan, with his lemis licht,
Ouer all the land had spred hir baner bricht.

With cloke and hude, I dressit me belyue,
With dowbill schone,& myttanis on my handis,
Howbeit the air , wes richt penetratyue,
Zit sure I furth, lansing ouerthort the landis,
Towart the Sey,to schort me on the sandis,
Because vnblomit was baith bank and bray.
And sa as I was passing be the way,

I met dame Flora, in dule weid disagysit,
Quhilk into May was dulce and delectabill,
With stalwart stormis,hir sweitnes wes suppraisit
Hir heuinlie hewis,war turnit into sabill,
Quhilkis vmquhyle war to Luffaris amyabill,
Fled from the Frost,the tender flouris I saw,
Under Dame Naturis mantill lurking law.

The small Fowlis,in flokkis saw I fle,
To Nature makand greit lamentatioun,
Thay lichtit doun besyde me on ane tre,
Of thair complaint, I had compassioun,
And with ane pieteous exclamatioun,
Thay said blissit be Somer with his flouris,
And waryit be thow wynter,with thy schouris.

Allace Aurora, the sillie Lark can cry,
Quhare hes thow left thy balmy liquour sweit,
That vs reiosit,we mounting in the sky?

                                             Thy

Thy siluer droppis ar turnit into sleit.
O fair Phebus, quhare is thy holsum heit?
Quhy tholis thow,thy heuinlie plesand face,
With mystie vapouris to be obscurit allace?

Quhare art ÿ May,& June thy sister schene,
Weill bordourit with dasyis of delyte?
And gentill Julie , with thy mantill grene,
Enamalit with Rosis,reid and quhyte?
Now auld and cauld Januar in dispyte,
Reiffis from vs,all pastyme and plesure.
Allace quhat gentill hart may this Indure?

Ouersylit ar with cloudis odious.
The goldin skyis of the Orient.
Changing in sorrow,our sang melodious;
Quhilk we had wount to sing with gude intent.
Resoundand to the Heuinnis firmament.
Bot now our day is changit into nicht,
With that thay rais, & slew furth of my sicht.

Pensyue in hart,passing full soberly,
Unto the Sey , fordwart I fure anone.
The Sey was furth,the sand was smoith & dry,
Than vp and down, I musit myne alone,
Till that I spyit,ane lytill Cane of stone,
Hich in ane craig,vp wart I did approche,
But tarying,and clam vp in the Roche.

And purposit,for passing of the tyme,
Me to defend from Ociositie,
With pen and paper to register in Ryme,
Sum mery mater of Antiquitie.

S iij   Bot

Bot Idelnes, ground of iniquitie,
Scho maid so dull my spreitis me within,
That I wist nocht at quhat end to begin.

Bot sat still in that coue, quhare I micht se,
The weltering of the wallis vp and doun,
And this fals warldis Instabilitie
Unto that sey makand comparisoun,
And of this warldis wrechit variatioun,
To thame that fixis all thair haill intent,
Considering quho most had, suld most repent.

So with my hude, my heid I happit warme,
And in my cloke, I fauldit boith my feit.
I thocht my corps, with cauld suld tak na harme
My mittanis held my handis weill in heit.
The skowland craig, me couerit from the sleit,
Thare still I sat, my bonis for to rest,
Till Morpheus with sleip my spreit opprest.

So throw the bousteous blastis of Eolus,
And throw my walking, on the nicht before,
And throuch the seyis mouing maruellous,
Be Neptunus, with mony rout and rore,
Constrainit I was to sleip withouttin more.
And quhat I dremit in conclusioun,
I sall zow tell ane maruellous visioun.

The

The Dreme of Schir
Dauid Lindesay.

Me thocht ane lady of poztratour per=
fyte,
Did falut me w bening contenance,
And J quhilk of hir prefens had de=
lyte,
Till hir agane maid humill reuerence,
And hir demandit fauing hir plefance,
Quhat was hir name? fcho anfwerit courteouffy
Dame Remembzance (fcho faid) callit am J.

Quhilk cummin is foz paftyme and plefour,
Of the, and foz to beir the companie,
Becaufe J fe thy fpzeit without mefour,
So foze perturbit be melancholie,
Caufing thy cozps, to waxin cauld and dzy,
Tharefoze get vp and gang anone with me,
So war we boith in twinkling of ane Ee,

Doun thzow the eirth, in middis of the Céter
Oz euer J wift into the laweft hell,
And to that carefull Coue, quhen we did enter,
Zowting and zowling we hard with mony zell
Ju flamme of fyze richt furious and fell,

S iiij   was

Was cryand mony carefull Creature,
Blasphemand God, and wariand Nature.

Thare sawe we diuers Paip;, and Empriour;
Without recouer mony carefull Kingis.
Thare sawe we mony wrangous Conquerour;,
Withouttin richt, reiffaris of vtheris ringis,
The men of Kirk, lay boundin into bingis,
Thare saw we mony carefull Cardinall,
And Archebischopis in thair Pontificall.

Proude and peruerst Prelatis, out of nummer
Pryouris, Abbattis, and fals flatterand Freiris:
To specifie thame all, it wer ane cummer,
Regular Chānon;, churle Monk; & Charterciris
Curious Clerkis, and Preistis Seculeiris.
Thare was sum part of ilk Religioun,
In holy Kirk, quhilk did abusioun.

Than J demandit dame Remembrance,
The cause of thir Prelatis punitioun.
Scho said the cause of thair vnhappy chance,
Was Couetyce, Lust, and ambitioun,
The quhilk now garris thame want fruitioun,
Of God, and heir eternallie mon dwell,
Into this painfull poisonit pit of hell.

Als thay did nocht instruct the Ignorent,
Prouocand thame to penitence be preiching,
Bot seruit warldlie Princis insolent,
And war promouit, be thair senzeit fleiching,
Nocht for thair science, wisdome nor teiching,
Be Symonie, was thair promotioun,

                                      More

Moze foz dauciris,noz foz deuotioun.

Ane vther cause of the punitioun.
Of thir vnhappy Prelatis Imprudent,
Thay maid nocht equall diſtributioun,
Of haly kirkis Patrimonie and rent,
Bot tempozallie, thay haue it all miſpent.
Quhilkis ſulde haue bene trypartit into thze,
firſt to vphauld the kirk in honeſtie.

The ſecund part to ſuſtene thair eſtaitis,
The thzid part,to be geuin to the puris,
Bot thay diſpone that geir all vther gaitis,
On cartis,and dyce,on harlotrie,and huris,
Thir Catyuis tuke na compt of thair awin curis
Thair kirkis reuin , thair Ladyis clenely cled,
And richelie rewlit baith at bꝛ— ꝟed.

Thair baſtard bairnis, pzoudely thay pzoupdit
The kirk geir largelie, thay did on thame ſpend,
In thair defaltis,thair ſubditis wer miſgydit,
And comptit nocht thair God foz till offend,
Quhilk gart thame wãt grace at thair latter end
Rewland that rout I ſaw in Caipis of Bzas,
Symon Magus,and Biſchop Caiphas.

Biſchop Annas,and the Tratour Judas,
Machomeit,that Propheit poyſonabill,
Choze, Dathan,and Abiron thare was,
Heretykis we ſaw innumerabill:
It was ane ſicht,richt wounderous lamentabill
How that thay lay into thay ſiammis ſleiting.
With carefull cryis, girning and greiting.
                    S v   Religious

Religious men war punischit panefullie,
For vane glorie als for Inobedience,
Brekand thair constitutionis wilfullie,
Nocht hauand thair ouermen in reuerence,
To knaw thair rewll thay maid na diligence,
Unleiffumlie thay vsit propertie,
Passing the boundis of wilfull pouertie.

Full sore weiping with vocis lamentabill,
Thay cryit loud, O Empriour Constantine
We may wryit thy possessioun poysonabill,
Of all our greit punitioun and pyne.
Howbeit thy purpose was till ane gude fyne,
Thow baneist from vs, trew deuotioun,
Hauand sic Ee till our promotioun.

Than we beheld ane den ful dolorous,
Quhare that Princis and Lordis Temporall,
War cruciate with penis rigorous.
Bot to expreme thair panis in speciall,
It dois exceid all my memoriall,
Importabill pane thay had but conforting,
Thair blude royall made thame na supporting.

Sum catiue kingis for cruell oppressioun,
And vther sum for thair wrangous conquest,
War condampnit, thay and their successioun,
Sum for publict Adulterie and Incest.
Sum leit thair pepill neuer leue in rest,
Delyting so in plesour sensuall,
Quharefore thair pane was thare perpetuall.

Thare was the cursit Empriour Nero,

Of

Of euerilk vice the horribill veschell,
Thare was Pharao, with diuers Princis mo,
Oppressouris of the bairnis of Israell,
Herode and mony mo, than I can tell,
Ponce Pylate was thare hangit be the hals,
With vniust Jugis, for thair sentence fals.

Dukis, Marquessis, Erlis, Barronis, knichtis,
With thay Princis war punist panefullie.
Participant thay war of thair vnrichtis,
Fordwart we went, and leit thair Lordisly,
And saw quhare Ladyis lamentabilly,
Lyke wod Lyonis war carefully cryand,
In flam of fyre, richt furiouslie fryand.

Emprices, Quenis, and Ladyis of honouris,
Mony Duches, and Countes, full of care:
Thay persit myne hart, thay tender Creaturis
So pynit in that pit full of dispare,
Plungit in pane, with mony reuthfull rair.
Sum for thair pryde, sum for adulterie,
Sum for thair tysting men to Lecherie.

Sum had bene cruell and malicious,
Sum for making of wrangous heritouris,
For to rehers their lyffis vitious,
It war bot tarie to the auditouris,
Of Lecherie thay war the verray luris,
With thair prouocatiue Impudicitie,
Brocht mony ane man to Infelicitie.

Sum wemen for thair pusillanimitie,
Ouerset w schame, thay did thame neuer schryue,
Of se-

Quhat
horribill
torment
of confci
ens was
this auri
cular có-
feſſioun.

Of ſecreit Synnis,done in quietie,
And ſum repentit neuer in thair lyue:
Quharefor but reuth thay ruffez did thaine ryue,
Rigozouſlie without compaſſioun.
Greit was thair dule,and lamentatioun.

That we war maid, thay cryit oft allace,
Thus tormentit with panis intollerabill,
We mendit nocht,quhen we had tyme and ſpace
Bot tuke in eirth our luſtis delectabill:
Quharefor with feindis vgly and horribill,
We ar condampnit for euer mair allace,
Eternallie,withouttin hope of grace.

Quhare is the meit and drink delicious,
With quhilk we fed our carefull carionis?
Gold,ſiluer,ſilk, with Perlis precious,
Our ryches,rentis,and our poſſeſſionis?
Withouttin hope of our Remiſſionis,
Allace our panis ar Inſufferabill,
And our tormentis to compt Innumerabill.

Than we beheld , quhare mony ane thouſand,
Commoun pepill lay ſlichterand in the fyre,
Of euerilk ſtait,thare was ane baiſfull band.
Thare micht be lene,mony ſorrowfull Syre,
Sum for Inny ſufferit,and ſum for Ire,
And ſum for laik of reſtitutioun,
Of wrangous geir without Remiſſioun.

Maneſworne Marchandis , for thair wran-
gous winning,
Hurdaris of gold and commoun Okkeraris,
Fals

fals men of Law,in Cautelis richt cunning,
Cheiffis,reuaris,and publyct oppreſſaris.
Sum part thare was of vnleill Labozaris,
Craftiſmen thare ſaw we out of nummer,
Of ilk ſtate to declare,it war ane cummer.

And als langſum to me,foz tyll Indyte,
Of this pzeſoun,the painis in ſpeciall.
The heit,the cauld,the Dolour and diſpyte,
Quharefoz I ſpeik of thame in generall:
That dully den,that furneis Jnfernall,
Quhoſe reward is,rew without remeid,
Euer deand,and neuer to be deid.

Hounger and thziſt, in ſteid of meit and dzink,
And foz thair cleithing , taidis and Scozpionis.
That mirk Manſioun is tapeſſit with ſtink:
Thay ſe na thing bot hozribill viſionis:
Thay here bot ſcozne and deriſionis,
Of foule feindis, and blaſphemationis,
Thair ſcilling is impoztabill paſſionis.

Foz melodie , miſerabill murning,
Thare is na ſolace , bot dolour infinyte,
In bailfull beddis,bitterlie burning,
With ſobbing,ſiching,ſozrow,and with ſyte,
Thair conſcience,thair hartſ ſa did byte,
To heir thame ſlyte,it was ane cace of cair,
So in diſpyte plungit into diſpair.

A lytill aboue that dolourous doungeoun,
We enterit in ane Cuntrie full of cair,
Quhare that we ſaw mony ane Legioun,
                              Greitand

Gretand and gowland,with mony ruthfull rair.
Quhat place is this(quod I)of blis so bair,
So answerit, and said,Purgatorie,
Quhilk purgis Soulis,or thay cum to glorie,

I se no plesour heir, bot mekle pane,
Quharefore (said I) leif we this sort in thrall,
I purpose neuer to cum heir agane.
Bot zit I do beleue and euer sall
That the true kirk can na way erre at all,
Sic thing to be,greit clerkis dois conclude,
Howbeit my hope,standis most in Christis blude

Abufe that in the thrid presoun anone,
We enterit in ane place of perditioun,
Quhare mony babbis war makand drery mone,
Because thay wantit the fruitioun
Of God,quhilk was ane greit punitioun,
Of Baptisme , thay wantit the Ansenze,
Upwart we went, and left that mithles menze.

Sic was the igno-rance of yai dayis that men euin of scharpest Iugemét cold not espy all abusis.

Intill ane Uolt,abone that place of pane,
Unto the quhilk but sudgeorne we ascendit,
That was the Lymb,in the quhilk did remane,
Our forefatheris , because Adam offendit,
Eitand the frute,the quhilk was defendit,
Mony ane zeir thay dwelt in that doungeoun,
In mirknes , and in desolatioun.

Than throuch the eirth, of nature cauld & dry,
Glaid to eschaip those places perrilous
We haistit vs richt wounder speidily .
Zit we beheld the Secretis maruellous,

          The

The Mynis of Gold and ſtonis precious,
Of Syluer, and of euerilk fyne mettell,
Quhilk to declare,it war ouer lang to dwell.

Up throuch the water ſchortlie we intendit,
Quhilk enuironnis the eirth,withouttin dout.
Syne throw the air,ſchortlie we aſcendit
His Regionis throuch,behalding in and out,
Quhilk eirth and water cloſis round about.
Syne ſchortly vpwart , throw the fyre we went
Quhilk wes the hieſt, and hoteſt Element.

Quhen we had all thir Elements ouerpaſt:
That is to ſay, Eirth, Water,Air,and Fyre,
Upwart we went,withouttin ony reſt,
To ſe the Heuinnis, was our maiſt deſyre.
Bot or we micht win to the heuin Empyre,
It behuffit vs to pas , the way full euin.
Up throuch the Spheiris of the Planetis ſeuin.

Firſt to the Moone,and beſyit all hir Spheir
Quene of the Sey,and bewtie of the nicht,
Of nature wak and cauld,and na thing cleir,
For of her ſelf , ſcho hes none vther licht,
Bot the reflex of Phebus bemis bricht.
The twelf ſignis ſcho paſſis round about,
In aucht and twentie dayis , withouttin dout.

Than we aſcendit to Mercurious,
Quhilk Poetis callis God of Eloquence,
Richt Doctourlyke, with termes delicious,
In art expert , and full of Sapience:
It was pleſour to pans on his Prudence,

                                    Payn-

Payntouris, Poeitis, ar subiect to his cure,
And hote and dry, he is of his Nature.

And als as cunning Astrologis sayis,
He dois compleit his cours Naturallie,
In thre houndreth & aucht, and thretty Dayis,
Syne vpwart we ascendit haistelie,
To fair Uenus, quhare scho richt lustelie,
Wes set into ane sait, of syluer schene,
That fresche Goddes, that lustie luffis Quene.

Thy persit myne hart, hir blenkis amorous,
Howbeit that sumtyme scho is chengeabill,
With countenance and cheir full dolourous,
Quhylummis richt plesand, glaid & delectabill,
Sumtyme constant, and sumtyme variabill.
Zit hir bewtie, resplendent as the fyre,
Swagis the wraith of Mars, that God of Ire.

This plesand Planeit, gif I can richt descriue
Scho is baith hote and waik of hir Nature,
That is the cause, scho is prouocatiue,
Till all thame that ar subiectit to hir cure,
To Uenus werkis, till that thay may indure.
As scho completis hir coursis naturail,
In twelf Monethis, withouttin ony fail.

Than past we to the Spheir of Pheb° brycht,
That lustie Lamp & Lanterne of the Heuin,
And glaider of the Sterris with his licht:
And principall of all the Planeitis seuin,
And sat in myddis of thame all full euin,
As Roy Royall, rolling in his Spheir,

                                    Full

full plefandlie into his goldin Chair.

Quhofe Influence and vertew excellent,
Geuis the lyfe till euerilk eirthlie thing.
That Prince of euerilk Planeit precellent,
Dois fofter flouris, and garris herbis fpring,
Throuch the cauld eirth, and caufis birdis fing,
And als his regular mouing in the heuin,
Is iuft vnder the Zodiack full euin.

For to difcryue his Diademe Royall,
Bordourit about with ftonis fchyning bricht.
His goldin Cart, or throne Imperiall,
The foure fteidis, that drawis it full richt,
I leif to Poeitis, becaufe I haue na flicht,
Bot of his nature he is hote and dry,
Compleitand in ane zeir his cours trewly.

Than vp to Mars, in hy we haiftit vs,
Wounder hote, and dryer than the tounder
His face flammand, as fyre richt furious,
His boft and brag mair aufull than the thunder
Maid all y̌ heuin, moft lyke to fchaik in funder,
Quha wald behald his conntenance and feir,
Micht call him weill the God of men of weir.

With colour reid and luke malicious,
Richt Colerik of his complexioun,
Aufteir, angrie, fweir and feditious,
Principall caufe of the deftructioun,
Of mony gude and nobill Regioun:
War nocht Uenus, his Ire dois mitigate,
This warld of peace wald be full defolate.

T   This

This God of greif withouttin sudgeoꝛning,
In ȝeiris twa, his cours he doith compleit,
Than past we vp quhare Iuppiter the king,
Sat in his Spheir, richt amiabill and sweit,
Complexionate with waknes and with heit,
That plesand Pꝛince, fair, dulce and delicate,
Pꝛouokis peace and banissis debait.

The auld Poeitis be superstitioun,
Held Iuppiter the Father pꝛincipall,
Of all thair Goddis in conclusioun,
Foꝛ his pꝛerogatyuis in speciall,
Als be his vertew into generall,
To auld Saturne, he makis resistance,
Quhen in his malice he wald wirk vengeance.

This Iupiter withouttin sudgeoꝛning,
Passis thꝛow all the twelf Planeitis full euin,
In ȝeiris twelf, and than but tarying,
We past vnto the hyest of the seuin,
Till Saturnus, quhilk troublis all the heuin,
With heuy cheir, and colour paill as leid,
In him we saw bot dolour to the deid.

And cauld and dꝛy he is of his nature,
Foule lyke ane Oule, of euill conditioun,
Richt vnplesand he is of poꝛtrature,
His Intoxicate dispositioun,
It puttis all thing to perditioun,
Ground of seiknes, and melancholious,
Peruerst and pure baith fals and Inuyous.

His qualitie, I can nocht loue bot lack,

                                    As foꝛ

As for his mouing naturallie but weir,
About the signis of the Zodiack,
He dois compleit his cours, in thretty zeir,
And so we left him in his frosty Spheir,
Upwart we did ascend incontinent,
But rest, till we come to the Firmament.

The quhilk was firit full of sterris bricht,
Of figour round, richt plesand and perfyte,
Quhose influence and richt excellent licht,
And quhose nummer may nocht be put in wryte,
Zit cunning Clerkis dois naturallie indyte,
How that he dois compleit his cours but weir,
In space of seuin and thretty thousand zeir.

Than the nyne Spheir, and mouair principall
Of all the laif, we besyit all that heuin,
Quhose daylie motioun is continuall,
Baith firmament, and all the Planeitis seuin,
From Eist to West, garris thame full euin,
Into the space of foure and twenty zeiris,
Zit be the myndis of the Astronomeiris.

The seuin Planeitis, into thair proper spheiris
From West to Eist, thay moue naturallie:
Sum swift, sum slaw, as to thair kind effeiris,
As I haue schawin afore speciallie,
Quhose motioun causis continuallie,
Richt melodious, harmonie and sound,
And all throw mouing of this Planeitis round.

Than mountit we, with richt feruent desyre,
Up throw the heuin callit Crystaline,

And so we enterit into Heuin Empyre,
Quhilk to descryue, it passis myne Ingyne,
Quhar God into his holy throne deuyne
Regnis into his glorie Inestimabill,
With Angellis cleir, quhilkis ar innumerabill.

In Ordouris nyne, thir spreitis glorious.
Ar deuydit, the quhilkis excellentlie,
Makis louyng with sound melodious,
Singand Sanctus, richt wounder feruentlie.
Thir ordouris nyne thay ar full plesandlie,
Deuydit into Hierarchies thre,
And thre Ordouris in euerilk Hierarchie,

The lawest Ordour is the Angellis bricht,
As Messingeris send to this lawe Regioun,
The secund Ordour Archangellis full of micht,
Uirtues, Potestatis, Principatis of renoun.
The sext is callit Dominationn.
The seuint Thronus, the auchtin Cherubin,
The nynt and hyest, callit Seraphin.

And nixt vnto the blissit Trinitie,
In his tryumphand throne Imperiall,
Thre in till ane, and ane substance in thre,
Quhose indiuisibill Essence eternall,
The rude Ingyne of mankynd is to small,
Till comprehend, quhose power infinyte,
And deuyne nature na creature can wryte.

So myne Ingyne is nocht sufficient,
For to treit of his hich Diuinitie,
All mortall men ar insufficient,

Till

Till confidder thay thre in vnitie,
Sic subtell mater I mon on neid lat be,
To studie on my Creid, it war full fair,
And lat Doctouris of sic hie materis declair.

Than we beheld the blissit Humanitie,
Of Chrift, sittand into his Sege Royall,
At the richt hand of the Diuinitie,
With ane excelland Court Celestiall,
Quhose exercitioun continuall,
Was in louyng thair Prince, with reuerence,
And on this wyse thay keipit Ordinance.

Nixt to the throne, we saw þ Quene of Quenis
Weill companyit with Ladyis of delyte,
Sweit was the sang of those blyssit Uirginnis,
Na mortall man thair solace may indyte,
The Angellis bricht, in nummer infinyte,
Euerilk Ordour in thair awin degre,
War Officiaris vnto the Deitie.

Patriarkis and Propheitis, honorabill,
Collaterall Counsalouris in his consistorie,
Euangelistis, Apostolis venerabill,
War Capitanis vnto the King of Glorie,
Quhilk Chiftane lyke had wyn the victorie,
Of that tryumphand Court Celestiall,
Sanct Peter was Lieutenand generall.

The Martyris war as nobill stalwart knichtis
Disconfitouris of cruell battellis thre,
The flesche, the warld, the feind & all his michtis,
Confessouris, Doctouris in Diuinitie,

T iij   As

As Chapell Clerkis vnto his Deitie,
And laſt we ſawe infinyte multitude,
Makand ſeruice vnto his Celſitude.

Quhilkis be the hie diuyne permiſſioun,
Felicitie thay had inuariabill,
And of his Godheid cleir cognitioun,
And compleit peace thay had interminabill,
Thair gloꝛie and honour was inſeparabill,
That pleſand place repleit of pulchꝛitude,
Unmeſurabill it was of magnitude.

Thare is plentie of all pleſouris perfyte,
Euydent bꝛichtnes, but obſcuritie.
Withouttin dolour, dulcoꝛe and delyte,
Withouttin rancour perfyte Cheritie,
Withouttin hounger, ſatiabilitie,
O happy ar the Saulis pꝛedeſtinate,
Quhen Saule and body ſalbe gloꝛificate.

Thir maruellous mirthis foꝛ to declare,
Be Arithmetike, thay ar innumerabill,
The poꝛtratour of that place pꝛeclare,
By Geometrie, it is inmeſurabill,
By Rethoꝛike als Inpꝛonunciable:
Thare is naue eiris may here, noꝛ ene may ſie,
Noꝛ hart may think, this thair felicit ie.

Quhare to ſulde I pꝛeſume foꝛ till indyte,
The quhilk Sanct Paule, that Doctour ſapient
Can nocht expꝛes, noꝛ into paper wꝛyte,
The hie excellent woꝛk indeficient,
And perfyte pleſour euer permanent,

                                    In pꝛe

In presence of that michtie king of glore,
Quhilk was, and is,and salbe euer more.

At Remembrance , humilitie I did inquyre,
Gif I micht in that plesour still remane.
(Scho said) aganis resoun is thy desyre:
Quharefor,my freind,thow mon returne agane,
Into the warld, quhare thow sall suffer pane,
And thole the deith with cruell panis sore,
Or thow be digne,to regne with him in glore.

Than we returnit sore aganis my will,
Doum throw Spheiris of the heuinnis cleir,
Hir commandement behuiffit I fulfill,
With sorie hart,wit ze withouttin weir:
I wald full faine haif taryit thare all zeir:
Bot scho said to me, thare is na remeid,
Or thow remane heir,first thow mon be deid.

Quod I,I pray zow hartfully madame,
Sen we haue had sic Contemplatioun,
Of heuinlie plesouris , zit or we pas hame,
Lat vs haue sum consideratioun,
Of eirth,and of his situatioun.
Scho answerit,and said,that salbe done,
So wer we boith brocht in the air full sone.

Quhare we micht se the eirth all at ane sicht,
Bot lyke ane moit,as it appeirit to me,
In the respect of the heuinnis bricht:
I haue maruell(quod I)how this may be,
The eirth semis of so small quantitie.
The leist sterne fixit the Firmament,

T. iiij	Is mair

Is mair than all the eirth be my Jugement.

Scho sayis Sone , ẏ hes schawin the veritie,
The smallest sterne fixit in the firmament,
In deid it is of greiter quantitie,
Than all the eirth, efter the intent,
Of wise and cunning Clerkis sapient,
Quhat quantitie is than the eirth (quod I)
That sall I schaw (quod scho) to the schortly.

Efter the myndis of the Astronomouris,
And speciallie the Authoz of the Spheir,
And vther diuers greit Philosophouris,
The quantitie of the eirth Circuleir,
Is fiftie thousand liggis, withouttin weir,
Seuin houndzeth, and fiftie and no mo,
Deuyding ay ane leig, in mylis two.

And euerilk myle, in aucht staidis deuyde,
Ilk staid, ane houndzeth pais, twenty and fyue,
Ane pais fyue fute , quha wald than richt decyde
Ane fute four palmes, gif I can richt descryue,
Ane palme four Inche, and quha sa wald belyue
The circuite of the eirth, pas round about,
Mon be considderit on this wise but dout.

Suppone that thare war none Impediment,
Bot that the eirth but perrell war and plane,
Syne that the person war richt diligent,
And zeid ilk day, ten leiggis in certane,
He micht pas round about, and cum agane,
In four zeiris, sertene Oulkis, and dayis two,
Ga reid the Auctour, and thou sall find it so.

                                    The

✠The Diuisioun of the Eirth.   II.

Then certanlie scho tuke me be the hand,
And said,my sone,cum on thy wayis ẃ me
And so scho gart me cleirly vnderstand,
How that the eirth tripartit was in thre:
In Aphrike,Europe and in Asie:
Efter the myndis of the Cosmographouris,
That is to say .)e warldis Descriptouris.

First Asia contenit is in the Orient,
And is weill more,than baith the vther twane,
Aphrik,and Europe in the Occident,
And ar deuydit in ane sey certane,
And that is callit te Sey Mediterrane,
Quhilk at the strait of Marrok hes entrie,
That is betuix Spanze and Barbarie.

Towart the Southwest lyis Aphrica,
And in the Northwest Europa doith stand,
And all the Eist conteinis Asia.
On this wyse , is deuydit the ferme land,
It war mekle to me,to tak on hand,
Thir Regionis,to declare in speciall.
Zit sall I schaw thair names in generall.

In mony diuers famous Regionis,
Is deuydit this part of Asia,
Weill plenisch it with Cieteis, Towris ⁊ townis
The greit Inde,and Mesopotamia,
Penthapolis,Egypt and Syria,
Cappadocia,Seres and Armenie,
                    T v   Babilon,

Babilon, Chaldea, Parth and Jrabie.

Sidon, Judea, and Palestina,
Upper Scithia, Tire and Galilie,
Hiberia, Bactria and Philestina,
Hircania, Compagena, and Samarie.
Jn lytill Asia standis Galathie,
Pamphilia, Jsauria and Leid,
Rhegia, Arethusa, Assyria and Meid.

Secundlie we considderit Aphrica,
With mony freuctfull famous Regioun,
As Ethiopie and Tripolitana,
Zewges, quhare standis the tryumphand toun,
Of nobill Carthage, that cietie of renoun.
Garamantes, Nadabar, Libia,
Getulia and Mauritania.

Fezensis, Numidie and Thingitane:
Of Affricke thir ar the principall.
Than Europe we considderit in certane,
Quhose Regionis schortlie reherse I sall:
Four principallis I find abone thame all,
Quhilkis ar Spanze Jtalie and France,
Quhose Subregionis wer mekle till auance.

Nether Scithia, Thrace and Carmanie,
Thusia, Histria, and Pannonia,
Denmark, Gotland, Grundland, and Almauie,
Pole, Hungarie, Boeme, Norica, Rethia,
Teutonica, and mony diuers ma,
And was in four deuydit Jtalie,
Tuscane, Hethzuria, Naplis, and Champanie.

Jnd

And subdeuydit sindry vther wayis,
As Lumbardie, Ueneis, and vther ma,
Calaber, Romanie, and Genowayis.
In Grece, Epyrus and Dalmatia,
Thessalie, Attica, and Illyria,
Achaya, Beotia and Macedone,
Archadie, Pierie and Lacedemone.

And France we sawe deuydit into thre,
Belgica, Celtica, and Aquitane.
And subdeuydit in Flanderis, Picardie,
Normandie, Gasconze, Burgunze and Britane,
And vtheris diuers Duchereis in certane,
The quhilkis wer to lang for to declair,
Quharefore of thame as now I speik na mair.

In Spanze lyis Castillie and Arragone:
Nauarre, Galice, Portugall and Granate,
Than sawe we famous Ilis mony one,
Quhilkis in the Occeane sey was situate,
Thame to discriue, my wit was desolate,
Of Cosmographie I am nocht expart
For I did neuer studie in that art,

Zit I sal sum of thair names declare,
As Madagascar, Gades, and Taprobane,
And vther diuers Ilis gude and fair,
Situate into the sey Mediterrane,
As Cyper, Candie, Corsica and Sardane,
Crete, Abydos, Thoes, Sicilia,
Tapsus, Eolie, and mony vther ma.

Quha wald at lenth here the descriptioun,
Of

Of euerilk Jle, als weill as the ferme land,
And properteis of euerilk Regioun,
To study and to reid mon tak on hand,
And the attentike werkis vnderstand,
Of Plinius and worthy Ptholomie,
Quhilkis war expert into Cosmographie.

Thare sall thay find the namis and properteis
Of euerie Jle and of ilk Regioun.
Than J inquirit of eirthly Paradeis,
Of the quhilk Adam tynt possessioun.
Than schew scho me the situatioun,
Of that precelland place of delyte,
Quhose properteis wer lang for to Jndyte:

III. Of Paradyse.

This Paradise, of all plesont repleit,
Situate J saw to the Orient
That glorious gairth of euery flouris did fleit,
The lustie lillyis, the rosis redolent,
Fresche hailsum fructis indeficient,
Baith herbe and tre, thare growis euer grene,
Throw vertew of the temperate air serene.

The sweit hailsum Aromatike odouris,
Proceiding from the herbis Medicinall,
The heuinlie hewis of the fragrant flouris,
It was ane sicht wounder celestiall,
The perfectioun to schaw in speciall,
And Joyis of the Regioun diuine,
Of mankynde, it exceidis the Ingyne.

And

And als so hie in situatioun,
Surmounting the myd Regioun of the air,
Quhare na maner of perturbatioun,
Of wedder may ascend so hie as thair:
Four fludis flowing from ane fontane fair,
As Tigris, Ganges, Euphrates and Nyle.
Quhilk in the Eist, transcurris mony ane myle.

The Cuntrie closit is about full richt,
With wallis hie, of hote and birning fyre,
And straitly keipit be ane Angell bricht,
Sen the departing of Adam our Grandschyre
Quhilk throw his cryme incurrit Goddis Ire,
And of that place tynt the possessioun,
Baith from him self, and his successioun.

Quhen this lufesum lady Remembrance,
All this forsaid had gart me understand,
I prayit hir of hir beneuolence,
To schaw to me the Cuntric of Scotland,
Weill sone (scho said) that sall I take on hand,
So suddandlie, scho brocht me in certane,
Euin iust abone the braid Ile of Britane.

Quhilk standis Northwest in the Occeane sey
And deuydit in famous Regionis two.
The South part Inglad, ane ful riche countrey,
Scotland be North, with mony Ilis mo.
Be West Ingland, Ireland doith stand also:
Quhose properteis I will nocht take on hand,
To schaw at lenth, bot onelie of Schotland,

Of

IIII. &Of the Realme of Scotland.

QUhilk efter my sempyl Intendement,
And as Remembrance did to me report,
I fall declare the suith and verrayment,
As I best can, and into termes schort,
Quharefor effecteouslie, I zow exhort,
Howbeit my wryting be nocht till auance,
Zit quhare I faill, excuse myne Ignorance.

Quhen that I had ouersene this Regioun,
The quhilk of Nature is boith gude and faire,
I did propone, ane litill questioun,
Beseikand hir, the same for to declare.
Quhat is the cause our boundis bene so bare?
(Quod I)or quhat dois moue our miserie,
Or quhareof dois proceid our pouertie?

For throw the support of zour hie prudence,
Of Scotland I persaue the properteis.
And als considderis be experience,
Of this countrie the greit commoditeis.
First the aboundance of fischis in our seis,
And fructuall montanis for our bestiall,
And for our cornis, mony lusty vaill.

The riche ryueris, plesand and proffitabill,
The lustie lochis, with fische of sindry kyndis,
Hounting, halking, for nobillis conuenabill,
Forrestis full of Da, Ra, Hartis and Hyndis,
The fresche fontanis, quhose halsum cristal strā-
Refreschis so the flurischit grene meidis,   (dis,
                                            So laik

So laik we na thing that to nature neidis,

Of euerilk mettell we haue the riche mynis,
Baith gold, siluer, and stonis precious.
Howbeit we want the Spyeis and the Wynis,
Or vther strange fructis delicious,
We haue als gude, & more neidfull for vs,
Meit, drink, fyre, claith, pair micht be gart abound
Quhilkis ellis is nocht in the Mapamound.

More fairer, nor of greiter ingyne,
Nor of mair strenth, greit deidis till indure,
Quharefore I pray zow, that ze wald defyne,
The principall cause quharefore we ar so pure,
For I maruell greitlie, I zow assure,
Consdderand the pepill, and the ground,
That riches sulde nocht in this realme redound.

My Sone (scho said) be my discretioun,
I sall mak answeir, as I vnderstand,
I say to the vnder confessioun,
The falt is nocht, I dar weill take on hand,
Nother into the pepill nor the land,
As for the land, it laikis na vther thing,
Bot laubour and the pepillis gouerning.

Than quharein lyis our inprosperitie,
(Quod I) I pray zow hartfullie Madame,
Ze wald declare to me the veritie,
Or quha sall beir of our barrat the blame?
For be my treuth to se, I think greit schame,
So plesand pepill and sa fair ane land,
And so few verteous deidis tane on hand.

Quod

Quod scho, I sall efter my Iugement,
Declare sum causis into generall,
And into termes schozt schaw myne intent:
And syne transcend into moze speciall.
So this is myne conclusioun finall:
Wanting of Iustice , Policie and Peace,
Ar cause of thir vnhappines allace.

It is difficill,riches till incres,
Quhare Polycie makith na residence.
And Policie may neuer haue entres,
Bot quhare that Iustice dois diligence,
To puneis quhare thare may be found offence,
Iustice may nocht haue Dominatioun,
Bot quhare peace makis habitatioun.

Quhat is the cause that wald I vnderstand,
That we suld want Iustice and policie,
Mair than dois France, Italie,oz Ingland,
Madame (quod I)schaw me the veritie?
Sen we haue Lawis in this Cuntrie,
Quhy want we Lawis exercitioun,
Quha suld put Iustice till executioun.

Quhare in dois stand our pzincipall remeid,
Oz quha may mak amendis of this mischeif?
(Quod scho)I find the falt into the heid,
Foz thay,in quhome dois ly our haill releif,
I find thame rute, and ground of all our greif,
Foz quhen the heidis ar nocht diligent,
The membzis moz on neid be negligent.

So I conclude the causis pzincipall,

Of all

Of all the trubill of this Natioun,
Ar into Princis into speciall,
The quhilkis hes the Gouernatioun,
And of the pepill Dominatioun.
Quhose contynuall exercitioun,
Sulde be in Justice Execucioun.

For quhen the sleuthfull hird dois sloug & sleip,
Taking na cure, in keiping of his flok,
Quha will ga serche almang sic hirdis scheip,
May able find mony pure scabbit crok,
And goyng wyld at large withouttin lok,
Than Lupus cummis & Lowrence in ane ling,
And dois but reuth, the sely scheip dounthring.

Bot the gude hird , walkryfe and diligent,
Doith so, that all his flockis ar rewlit richt,
To quhose quhissell all ar obedient,
And gif the wolfis cummis day or nicht,
Thame to deuore, than ar thay put to flicht,
Houndit and slane be thair weill dantit doggis,
So ar thay sure, baith rowis, lambis, & hoggis.

So I conclude that throw the negligence,
Of our infatuate heidis insolent,
Is cause of all this Realmes indigence,
Quhilkis in Justice hes nocht bene diligent,
Bot to gude counsaill inobedient,
Hauand small Ee vnto the commoun weill,
Bot to thair singular profyte euerilk deill.

For quhen thir wolfis be oppressioun,
The pure peple but pietie doith oppres,

U   Than

Than sulde the princis mak punitioun,
And cause thay Rebaldis for to mak redres,
That ryches micht be, and Policie incres,
Bot richt difficill it is to mak remeid,
Quhen that the falt is sa into the heid.

V.   The complaint of the Common weill of Scotland.

And thus as we wer talking to and fro,
we saw a busteous berne cum ouir ỹ bent,
But hors on fute als fast as he micht go,
Quhose rayment wes all raggit, reuin and rent,
with visage lene, as he had fastit Lent:
And fordwart fast his wayis he did aduance,
with ane richt melancholious countenance.

with scrip on hip, and pykstaff in his hand,
As he had bene purposit to pas fra hame,
(Quod I) gude man, I wald fane vnderstand,
Gif that ze pleisit, to wit quhat wer zour name,
(Quod he) my sone, of that I think greit schame:
Bot sen thow wald of my name haue ane feill,
Forsuith thay call me Jhone the Comoun weill.

Schir Comoun weil, quha hes zow sa dilgysit
(Quod I) or quhat makis zow sa miserabill?
I haue maruell, to se zow sa supprysit,
The quhilk that I haue sene so honorabill,
To all the warld ze haue bene proffitabill,
And weil honorit in euerilk Natioun,

                       How

How happinnis now your tribulatioun?

Allace(quod he) thow seis how it dois stand,
With me, and how J am dishcrisit,
Of all my grace,and mon pas of Scotland,
And ga afore,quhare J was cherisit,
Remane J heir,J am bot perischit,
For thare is few to me,that takis tent,
That garris me ga, sa raggit,reuin and rent.

My tender freindis ar all put to the flicht,
For Policie is fled agane in France,
My syster Justice almaist haith tynt hir sicht,
That scho can nocht hald euinly hir ballance,
Plane wrang is plane Capitane of Ordinance,
The quhilk debarris Lawte and resoun,
And small remeid is found for oppin tresoun.

Into the South allace,J was neir slane,
Ouer all the land J culde find na releif,
Almost betuir the Mers, and Loichmabane,
J culde nocht knaw ane leill man be ane theif,
To schaw thair reif, thift, murthour, & mischeif,
And vicious workis, it wald infect the air,
And als langsum to me for till declair.

Into the hie land,J could find na remeid,
Bot suddandlie J was put to exile,
Thay sweir swingeouris yai tuke of me none heid
Nor amangis thame, lat me remane ane quhyle:
Als in the out Ilis,and in Argyle,
Unthrift,sweirnes,falset,pouertie and stryfe,
Pat Policie in danger of hir lyfe.

U ij   Inthe

In the lawe land I come to seik refuge,
And purposit thare to mak my residence,
Bot singulare proffect gart me sone disluge,
And did me greit iniuris and offence,
And said to me, swyith harlote, hy the hence,
And in this countrie se thow tak na curis,
So lang as my authoritie induris.

And now I may mak na langer debait,
Nor I wait nocht, quhome to I sulde me mene,
For I haue socht throw all the Spirituall stait,
Quhilkis tuke na compt for to heir me complene
Thare officiaris thay held me at disdane,
For Symonie, he rewlis vp all that rout,
And Couetice that Carle gart tar me out.

Pryde haith chaist from thame humilitie,
Deuotioun is fled vnto the freiris,
Sensual plesour hes bancist chaistitie,
Lordis of Raligioun thay go lyke Sculeiris,
Taking mair compt in telling thair deneiris,
Nor thay do of thair constitutioun,
Thus ar thay blyndit be ambitioun.

Our gentill men ar all degenerate,
Liberalitie and Lawtie, baith ar lost,
And Cowardice with Lordis is laureate,
And knichtlie curage turnit in brag and boist,
The Ciuill weir misgydis euerilk oist,
Thare is nocht ellis bot ilk man for him self,
That garris me ga thus bancist lyke ane elf.

Tharefor adew, I may na langer tarie,

Fare

Fare weil (quod J)⁊ to ſanct Johne to boꝛow
Bot wit ʒe weil,my hart was wounder ſarie,
Quhen comoun weill ſo ſopit was in ſoꝛrow,
Ʒit efter the nicht,cummis the glaid moꝛrow:
Quharefoꝛe J pꝛay ʒo w,ſchaw me in certane,
Quhen that ʒe purpoſe foꝛ to cum agane.

That queſtioun it ſalbe ſone decydit,
(Quod he)thare ſall na Scot haue confoꝛting,
Of me till that J ſe the Countrie gydit,
Be wyſedome of ane gude auld pꝛudent king,
Quhilk ſall delyte him maiſt aboue all thing,
To put Juſtice till execution,
And on ſtrang tratouris make punition.

Als ʒit to the J ſay ane vther thing,
J ſe richt weill that Pꝛouerbe is full trew,
Wo to the Realme,that hes ouer ʒoung ane king
With that he turnit his back,and ſaid Adew,
Ouer firth and fell,richt faſt fra me he flew:
Quhoſe departing to me was diſpleſand,
With that Remembꝛance tuke me be the hand.

And ſone me thocht ſcho bꝛocht me to þ roche,
And to the Coue, quhare J began to ſleip,
With that ane ſchip did ſpeidily appꝛoche,
Full pleſandly ſailling vpon the deip,
And ſyne did ſlak hir ſaillis,and gon to creip,
Towart the land,anent quhare that J lay:
Bot wit ʒe weill,J gat ane fellown fray.

All hir Cannounis,ſche leit crak atonis,
Down ſchuke the ſtremaris,frome the topcaſtell

Thay spairit nocht the poulder nor the stonis,
Thay schot thair boittis, & doun thair ankers fell,
The Marinaris, thay did so zout and zell,
That haistelie I stert out of my Dreme,
Half in ane fray, and speidilie past hame.

And lychtlie dynit, with lift and appetyte,
Syne efter past in till ane Oritore,
And tuke my pen, and thare began to wryte,
All the visioun that I haue schawin afore.
Schir of my dreme, as now thou gettis no more
Bot I beseik God, for to send the grace,
To rewle thy Realme in vnitie and pace.

VI. THE EXHORTATION
to the Kingis Grace.

Schir sen that God of his preordinance,
Haith grantit the, to haue the gouernance
Of his peple, and create the ane King,
Faill nocht to prent in thy remembrance,
That he will nocht excuse thyne Ignorance,
Gif thow be rekles in thy gouerning.
Quhairfor dres the abone all vther thing,
Of his lawis to keip the obseruance,
And thow schaip lang in Royaltie to ring.

Thank him, that hes commandit Dame Nature
To prent the of sa plesand portrature,
Hir giftis may be cleirly on the knawin,
Till Dame Fortune thow neidis na procurature,
For scho hes largelie kyith on the hir cure,

Hir

þir gratitude ſcho hes vnto the ſchawin.
And ſen that thou mon ſcheir as thou hes ſawin,
Haue all thy hope in God thy Creatour,
And aſk him grace, that thow may be his awin.

And ſyne conſidder thy vocatioun,
That for to haue the gubernatioun,
Of this kynrik, thow art predeſtinate,
Thow may weill wit be trew narratioun,
Quhat ſorrow and quhat tribulationn,
Hes bene in this pure Realme infortunate,
Now comforte thame, that hes bene deſolate,
And of thy pepill haue compaſſioun,
Sen thow be God art ſo preordinate.

Tak manlie curage, and leif thyne Inſolence,
And vſe counſaill of nobill dame Prudence,
Founde the ſermelie on Faith and Fortitude.
Draw to thy court Juſtice and Temperance.
And to the Commoun weill haue attendance,
And alſo J beſeik thy Celſitude,
Hait vicious men, and lufe thame that ar gude,
And ilk flatterar thow fleme frome thy preſence,
And fals report out of thy Court exclude.

Do equall Juſtice, baith to greit and ſmall,
And be exempill to thy pepill all,
Exercing vertuous deidis honorabill,
Be nocht ane wretche, for oucht that may befall,
To that vnhappy vice and thow be thrall,
Till all men thow ſa be abhominabill,
Kingis nor knichtis ar neuer conuenabill,
                        V iiij   To rewle

To rewle pepill, be thay nocht liberall,
was neuer zit na wreche to honour abill.

And take exemple of the wrechit ending,
Quhilk maid Mydas, of Thrace the michty king
That to his Goddis maid Jnuocatioun,
Throw gredines that all substantiall thing,
That euer he twichit, suld turne but tarying,
Into fyne golde, he gat his supplicatioun,
All that he twichit but dilatioun,
Turnit in golde, boith meit, drink and cleithing,
And deid for hounger but recreatioun,

Als J beseik thy Maiestie serene,
From Lecherie thow keip thy body clene,
Taist neuer that intoxicat poysoun,
From that vnhappy sensuall sin abstene,
Till that thow get ane lustie plesand Quene,
Than tak thy plesour with my benissoun.
Tak tent how prideful Tarquine tynt his croun
For the deforsing of Lucrece the schene,
And was depryuit, and baneist Romes toun.

And in dispite of his lecherous leuing,
The Romainis wald be subiect to na king,
Mony lang zeir, as storyis doith record,
Till Julius, throw verteous gouerning,
And Princely curage gan on thame to ring,
And chosin of Romanis, Emproiur and Lord,
Quharefor my Souerane into thy mynd remord
That vicious lyfe, makis oft ane euill ending,
without it be throw speciall grace restord.

And

And gif thou wald thy fame and honour grew
Use counsall of thy prudent Lordis trew,
And se thow nocht presumptuouslie pretend,
Thy awin particular weill for till ensew,
Wirck with consall, so sall thow neuer rew,
Remember of thy freindis the fatall end,
Quhilkis to gude counsall wald not condiscend,
Till bitter deith (allace) did thame persew,
Frome sic vnhap I pray God the defend.

And finallie, remember thow mon de,
And suddandlie pas of this mortall se,
And art nocht sicker of thy lyfe twa houris,
Sen thare is nane from that sentence may flie,
King, Quene, nor knicht of lawe estait nor hie,
Bot all mon thole of deith, the bitter schouris.
Quhare ben thay gane, thir Paipis & Empriouris
Bene thay nocht dede, so sall it fare on the:
Is na remeid, strenth, riches, nor honouris.

And so for conclusioun,
Mak our prouisioun,
To get the infusioun,
   Of his hie grace:

Quhilk bled with effusioun,
With scorne and derisioun,
And deit with confusioun,
   Confirmand our peace. AMEN.

FINIS.

VII· THE COMPLAYNT

of Schir Dauid Lindesay, of the
Mont knicht, &c. directit to the
Kingis Grace.

* *
*

Schir I beseik thyne Excellence,
Here my complaint with pacience,
My dolent hart dois me constraine,
Of my Infortune to complaine,
Howbeit I stand in greit doutance,
Quhome I sall wyte of my mischance.
Quhidder Saturnus crueltie,
Regnand in my Natiuitie,
Be bad aspect, quhilk wirkis vengeance
Or vtheris heuinlie Influence.
Or gif I be predestinate,
In Court to be Infortunate,
Quhilk hes so lang in seruice bene,
Continually with King and Quene,
And enterit to thy Maiestie,
The day of thy Natiuitie,
Quharethrow my freind is bene eschamit
And with my face I am defamit,
Seand that I am nocht regardit,
Nor with my brether in court rewardit,
Blamand my sleuthfull negligence,
That seikis nocht sum recompence,
Quhen diuers men dois me demand,
Quhy gettis thou nocht sum pece of land,

As

As weill as vther men hes gottin,
Than wis I to be deid and rottin,
With sic extreme discomforting,
That I can mak na answering.
I wald sum wise man did me teche,
Quhidder that I suld flatter or fleche,
I will nocht flyte, that I conclude,
For crabing of thy Celsitude:
And to flatter I am defamit,
Want I reward, than am I schamit:
Bot I hope, thow sall do als weill,
As did the Father of Fameill,
Of quhome Christ makis mentioun,
Quhilk for ane certane pensioun,
Feit men to wirk in his wyne zaird,
Bot quha came last, gat first rewaird,
Quharethrow þ first men wer displeisit,
Bot he thame prudentlie ameisit:
For thocht the last men, first wer seruit,
Zit gat the first that day deseruit.
So am I sure thy Maiestie,
Sal ainis reward me or I die,
And rub the roust of my Ingyne,
Quhilk bene for langour lyke to tyne:
Althocht I beir nocht lyke ane baird,
Lang seruice zairnis ay rewaird.
I can nocht blame thyne Excellence,
That I sa lang want recompence,
Had I solystit lyke the laue
My reward had nocht bene to craue,
Bot now I may weill vnderstand,

An

Ane dum man 3it wan neuer land.
And in the Court men gettis na thing,
Without inopportune asking,
Allace my sleuth and schamefulnes,
Debarrit fra me all gredines.
Gredie men that ar diligent,
Richt oft obtenis thair intent,
And failzeis nocht to conqueis landis,
And namelie at zoung Princis handis.
Bot J tuke neuer none vther cure,
In speciall bot for thy plesure,
Bot now J am na mair dispaird,
Bot J sall get Princely rewaird,
The quhilk to me salbe mair glore,
Nor thame thow did reward afore:
Quhen men dois aske ocht at ane King,
Sulde ask his grace ane nobill thing,
To his Excellence honorabill,
And to the asker profitabill,
Thocht J be in my asking lidder,
J pray thy grace for to considder.
Thow hes maid baith lordis ʒ lairdis,
And hes geuin mony riche rewairdis,
To thame that was full far to seik,
Quhen J lay nichtly be thy cheik.

    J tak the Quenis grace thy mother,
My Lord Chancellar and mony vther,
Thy Nuris and thy auld Maistres,
J tak thame all to beir witnes.
Auld Willie Dillie, wer he on lyue,
My lyfe full weill he could discryue.

                              How

How as ane chapman beiris his pak,
I bure thy grace vpon my bak.
And sumtymes striblingis on my nek,
Dansand with mony bend and bek.
The first sillabis that thow did mute,
was pa,da lyn vpon the lute.
Than playit I twentie springis perqueir,
Quhilk was greit pietie for to heir.
Fra play thow leit me neuer rest,
Bot gynkertoun thow luiffit ay best.
And ay quhen thow come frome the scule,
Than I behuiffit to play the fule:
As I at lenth into my Dreme,
My sindry serupce did expreme.
Thocht it bene better (as sayis the wise)
Hap to the Court, nor gude seruise:
I wait thow luiffit me better than,
Nor now sum wife dois hir gude man.
Than men till vther did record,
Said Lyndesay, wald be maid ane Lord,
Thow hes maid lordis (Schir) be sanct Geill,
Of sum, that hes nocht seruit so weill.
    To zow my Lordis that standis by,
I sall zow schaw the causis quhy,
Gif ze list tary, I sall tell,
How my Infortune first befell.
I prayit daylie on my kne,
My zoung maister that I micht se,
Of eild in his Estait Royall.
Hauand power Imperiall.
Than traistit I without demand,

To be

To be promouit to sum land,
Bot my asking I gat ouer sone,
Because ane Clips fell in the Mone,
The quhilk all Scotland maid on steir,
Than did my purpose ryn arreir,
The quhilk war langsum till declair,
And als my hart is wounder sair,
Quhen I haue in remembrance,
The suddand change to my myschance.
The king was bot twelf zeiris of age,
Quhen new rewlaris came in thir rage
For commoun weill makand na cair,
Bot for thair profyte singulair.
¶ Imprudently lyke witles fulis,
Thay tuke ẏ zoung Prince from ẏ sculis
Quhare he vnder Obedience,
Was leirnand Uertew and Science,
And haistely plat in his hand,
The gouernance of all Scotland,
As quha wald in ane stormie blast,
Quhen Marinaris bene all agast,
Throw danger of the seis rage,
Wald take ane chylde of tender age,
Quhilk neuer had bene vpon the sey,
And to his bidding all obey,
Geuing him haill the gouernall,
Of Schip, Marchand and Marinall,
For dreid of rockis and foreland,
To put the Ruther in his hand,
Without Goddis grace is na refuge,
Gif thare be danger, ze may Iuge,

I gene

I geue thame to the Deuill of Hell,
Quhilk first deuysit that counsell.
I will nocht say that it was tresoun,
Bot I dar sweir it was na trsoun:
I pray God, lat me neuer se ring,
Into this Realme so zoung ane King.
¶ I may nocht tary to decrybit,
How than þ court ane quhile was gydit
Be thame that partlie tuke on hand,
To gyde the King and all Scotland,
And als langsum for to declair,
Thair facund flattering wordis fair.
　Schir, sum wald say, zour Maiestie,
Sall now ga to zour libertie,
Ze sall to na man be coactit,
Nor to the scule na mair subiectit.
We think thame verray naturall fulis,
That leirnis ouer mekle at the sculis.
Schir, ze mon lerne to ryn ane speir,
And gyde zow lyke ane man of weir,
For we sal put sic men about zow,
That all þ warld, and mo sall dout zow,
Than to his grace thay put ane gaird,
Quhilk haistely gat thair rewaird:
Ilk man efter thair qualitie,
Thay did solist his Maiestie,
Sum gart him rauell at the rakket,
Sum harlit him to the hurly hakket.
And sum to schaw thair courtlie corsis,
Wald ryd to leith, and ryn thair horsis,
And wichtly wallop ouer the sandis:

Ze no-

The Complaint

Ze nother spairit spurris nor wandis,
Castand galmoundis with bendis and beckis,
For wantones , sum brak thair neckis.
Thare was na play bot cartis and dyce,
And ay schir flatterie bure the pryce.
Roundand and rowkand ane till ane vther,
Tak thow my part (quod he) my bruther,
And mak betuix vs sicker bandis,
Quhen ocht sall baik amangis our handis,
That ilk man stand to help his fallow:
I hald thareto mon be alhallow,
Swa thow fische nocht within my boundis,
That sall I nocht by Goddis woundis,
(Quod he) but eirar tak thy part.
Swa sall I thyne be Goddis hart.
And gif the Thesaurar be our freind,
Than sall we get baith tak and teind,
Tak he our part , than quha dar wrang vs?
Bot we sall part the pelf amang vs.
Bot haist vs quhile the King is zoung,
And lat ilk man keip weill ane toung,
And in ilk quarter haue ane spy,
Ustill aduertis haistely,
Quhen ony casualiteis,
Sall happin in till our countreis,
Lat vs mak sure prouisioun,
Or he cum to discrecioun.
Na mair he wait nor dois ane sanct,
Quhat thing it bene to haue or want.
So or he be of perfyte age
we salbe sicker of our wage,

                                          And

And syne lat ilk ane carll craue vther,
That mouth speik mair (quod he) my brother,
For God nor I rar in ane raip,
Thow micht giue counsall to the Paip:
Thus lauborit thay within few zeiris,
That thay became no paigis peiris,
Swa haistelie thay maid ane hand:
Sum gadderit gold, sum conqueist land.
(Schir) sum wald say be sanct Dionis,
Geue me sum fat Benefyis,
And all the proffyt ze sall haue,
Geue me the name, tak zow the laue,
Bot be his bowis war weill cummit hame,
To mak seruice he wald think schame:
Syne slip away withouttin more,
Quhen he had gottin that he sank fore,
Me thocht it was ane pieteous thing,
To se that fair zoung tender King,
Of quhome thair gallandis stude none aw,
To play with him pluk at the craw,
Thay become riche I zow assure,
Bot ay the Prince remanit pure,
Thare was few of that garnisoun,
That leirnit him ane gude lessoun.
Bot sum to crak, and sum to clatter,
Sum maid the fule, and sum did flatter.
(Quod ane) the Deuill stik me with ane knife.
Bot schir, I knaw ane maide in fyfe,
Ane of the lustiest wantoun lassis,
Quhareto schir be goddis blude scho passis,
Hald thy toung brother (quod ane vther)

X   I knaw

I knaw ane fairer be fyftene futher,
(Schir) quhen ʒe pleis to Linlithgow pas,
Thare fall ʒe fe ane luſtie las,
Now trittell trattill trow low,
(Quod the thrid man)thow dois bot mow,
Quhen his grace cummis to fair Stirling,
Thare fall he fe ane dayis darling.
Schir(quod the fourt) tak my counfell,
And go all to the hie bordell,
Thare may we lowp at libertie,
Withouttin ony grauitie.
Thus euery man faid for him felf,
And did amang thame part the pelf,
Bot I (allace)or euer I wyſt,
Was trampit doun into the duſt,
With heuy charge,withouttin more,
Bot I wiſt neuer ʒit quharefore,
And haiſtelie before my face,
Ane vther ſlippit in my place,
Quhilk lichtelie gat his rewaird,
And ſtylit was the auncient laird.
That tyme I micht mak na defence,
Bot tuke perforce in pacience:
Prayand to fend thame ane miſchance,
That had the Court in gouernance,
The quhilkis aganis me did maling,
Contrair the plefour of the king,
For weill I knew his Gracis mynd,
Was euer to me trew and kynd:
And contrair thair Intentioun,
Gart pay me weill my penſioun,

Thocht

Thocht I ane quhyle wantit prefence,
He leit me haue na Indigence,
Quhen I durft nother peip nor luke,
Zit wald I hyde me in ane nuke,
To fe thofe vncouth vaniteis,
How thay lyke ony befie beis,
Did occupy thir goldin houris,
With help of thair new gouernouris,
Bot my complaint for to compleit,
I gat the four, and thay the fweit.
As Ihone Makrery the kingis fule,
Gat dowbill garmentis agane the zule,
Zit in his maift tryumphand gloze,
For his reward he gat the grand gloze.
Now in the Court feindill he gois,
In dreid men ftramp vpon his tois:
As I that tyme durft nocht be fene,
In oppin Court for baith my ene.
℀Allace I haue na tyme to tarie,
To fchaw zow all the ferie farie.
How thofe that had the gouernance,
Amangis thame felfis raift variance,
And quha maift to my fkaith confentit,
Within few zeiris full fore repentit,
Quhen thay culd mak me na remeid,
For thay wer harlit out be the heid,
And vtheris tuke the gouerning,
Weill wors than thay in all kin thing.
Thay Lordis tuke no more regaird,
Bot quha micht purches beft rewaird.
Sum to thair freindis gat Beneficeis,

X ü   Ind

And vther sum gat Bischopreis,
For euery lord, as he thocht best,
Brocht in ane bird to fill the nest,
To be ane wacheman to his marrow,
Thay gan to draw at the cat harrow,
The proudest Prelatis of the kirk,
Was fane to hyde thame in the mirk,
That tyme so failzeit was thare sicht.
Sen syne thay may nocht thole the licht
Of Christis trew Gospell to be sene,
So blyndit is thair corporall Ene,
With warldlie lustis sensuall,
Taking in Realmes the gouernall,
Baith gyding Court and sessioun,
Contrair to thair professioun,
Quhareof I think thay sulde haue schame,
Of Spirituall Preistis to tak the name,
For Esayas into his wark,
Callis thame lyke doggis that can nocht bark,
That callit ar preistis, and can nocht preche,
Nor Christis law to the pepill teche.
Gif for to preche, bene thair professioun,
Quhy suld thay meill with Court or Sessioun?
Except it war in Spirituall thingis,
Referring vnto Lordis and kingis,
Temporall causis to be decydit.
Gif thay thair Spirituall office gydit,
Ilk man micht say, thay did thair pairtis,
Bot gif thay can play at the cairtis,
And mollet moylie on ane Mule,
Thocht thay had neuer sene the scule,

Zit

Zit at this day,als weill as than,
Wil be maid sic ane Spiritual man,
Princis that sic Prelatis promouis,
Accompt thareof to geue behouis,
Quhilk sall nocht pas but punischement
Without thay mend,and sore repent,
And with dew ministratioun,
Wyrk efter thair vocatioun,
I wis that think quhilk will nocht be,
Thir peruerst Prelatis ar so hie,
From tyme that thay bene callit Lordis
Thay ar occasioun of discordis,
And largelie will propynis hecht,
To gar ilk Lord with vther fecht,
Gif for thair part it may auaill,
Swa to the purpose of my taill,
That tyme in Court rais greit debait,
And etterilk Lord did stryue for stait,
That all the Realme micht mak na redding,
Quhill on ilk syde thare was blude schedding,
And feildit vther in land and burgh,
At Linlithgow,Melros,and Edinburgh,
Bot to deplore I think greit pane,
Of nobill men,that thare was slane,
And als langsum to be reportit,
Of thame quhilk to the Court resortit,
As tyrannis tratouris and transgressouris,
And commoun publict plane oppressouris,
Men murdricisaris,and commoun theiffis,
Into that court gat all releiffis:
Thair was few Lordis in all thair landis,

X iij   Bot till

Bot till new Regentis maid thair bandis,
Than rais ane reik or euer I wist,
The quhilk gart all thair bandis brist,
Than thay allane, quhilk had the gyding,
Thay could nocht keip thair feit from flyding:
Bot of thair lyffis thay had sic dreid,
That thay war fane till trot ouer Tweid.

   ¶ Now potent Prince I say to the,
I thank the haly Trinitie,
That I haue leiuit to se this day,
That all that warld is went away,
And thow to na man art subiectit,
Nor to sic Counsalouris coactit,
The four greit Uertues Cardinallis,
I se thame with the principallis,
For Justice haldis hir sweird on hie,
With hir ballance of Equitie,
And in this Realme hes maid sic ordour
Baith throw the hie land & the bordour,
That oppressioun and all his fallowis,
Ar hangit hich vpon the gallowis,
Dame Prudence hes the be the heid,
And Temporance dois thy brydill leid,
I se Dame Force mak assistance
Beirand thy Targe of assurance,
And lusty Lady Chaistitie,
Hes banischit Sensualitie.
Dame Ryches takis on the sic cure,
I pray God that scho lang indure,
That Pouertie dar nocht be sene,
Into thy hous, for baith hir Ene,

                                      Bot fre

Bot fra thy grace fled mony mylis,
Amangis the Hountaris in the Ilis,
Diſſimulance dar nocht ſchaw hir face,
Quhilk wount was to begyle thy grace
Foly is fled out of the toun,
Quhilk ay was contrair to reſoun.
Policie and peice beginnis to plant,
That vertuous men can na thing want
And as foꝛ ſleuthfull Idle lownis,
Sall fetterit be in the Gailȝownis,
Ihone Uponland ben ful blyith I trow
Becauſe the ryſche bus, keipis his kow.
Swa is thare nocht, I vnderſtand,
Without gude oꝛdour in this land,
Except the Spiritualitie,
Pꝛayand thy grace, thareto haue Ee,
Cauſe thame mak miniſtratioun,
Confoꝛme to thair vocatioun,
To pꝛeche with vnfeinȝeit intentis,
And trewlie vſe the Sacramentis,
Efter Chꝛiſtis Inſtitutionis,
Laiuing thair vane Traditionis,
Quhilk dois the ſillie ſcheip illude,
Quham foꝛ Chꝛiſt Ieſus ſched his blude
As ſuperſtitious pilgramagis,
Pꝛayand to grauin Imagis,
Expꝛes aganis the Loꝛdis command,
I do thy grace till vnderſtand:
Gif thow to mennis Lawis aſſent
Aganis the Loꝛdis Commandement,
As Ieroboam, and mony mo,

                    X iiii   Pꝛincis

Princis of Iſraell alſo,
Aſſentaris to Idolatrie,
Quhilkis puniſt war richt piteouſlie,
And from thair realmes wer rutit out,
So ſall thow be withouttin dout,
Baith heir and hyne withouttin moꝛe,
And want the euerlaſting gloꝛe,
Bot gif thow will thyne hart inclyne,
And keip his bleſſit Law Diuyne,
As did the faithfull Patriarkis,
Baith in thair woꝛdis, & in thair warkis
And as did mony faithfull Kingis
Of Iſraell during thair ringis,
As king Dauid and Salomone,
Quha Imagis wald ſuffer none,
In thair riche Tempillis foꝛ to ſtand,
Becaus it was nocht Goddis command
Bot diſtroyit all Idolatrie,
As in the Scripture thow may ſie,
Quhoſe richereward was heuinlie bliſſ,
Quhilk ſalbe thyne, thow doand this.
Sen thow hes choſin ſic ane gaird,
Now am I ſure to get rewaird,
And ſen thow art the rycheſt King,
That euer in this Realme did ring,
Of gold and ſtonis pꝛecious,
Maiſt pꝛudent and Ingenious,
And hes thy honour done auance,
In Scotland, Ingland and in France
Be Martiall deidis honoꝛabill,
And art till euery vertew abill,

　　　　　　　　　I wait

I wait thy grace will nocht misken me,
Bot thow will other geue oz len me.
Wald thy grace,len me to ane day,
Of gold ane thousand pound oz tway,
And I sall fir with gude intent,
Thy grace ane day of payment,
With scillit Obligatioun,
Under this protestatioun,
Quhen the Bas and the Ile of May,
Beis set vpon the Mont Sinay:
Quhen the Lowmound beside Falklad,
Beis liftit to Northumberland:
Quhen kirkmen zairnis na dignitie,
Noz wyffis no Soueranitie,
Winter but frost, snaw, wynd oz rane,
Than sal I geue thy gold agane,
Oz I sall mak the payment,
Efter that day of Jugement,
Within ane Moneth at the leist,
Quhen Sanct Peter sall mak ane feist,
To all the Fischaris of Aberladie,
Swa thou haue myne acquittas reddie
Failzeand thareof be sanct Phillane,
Thy grace gettis neuer ane grote agane
Gif thou be nocht content of this,
I mon requeist the King of blis,
That he to me haue sum regaird,
And cause thy grace me to rewaird.
Foz Dauid King of Israell,
Quhilk was the greit Propheit Royall,
Sayis, God hes haill at his command,

The

The hartis of Princis in his hand,
Euin as he list thame for to turne,
That mon thay do without sudgeorne,
Sum till exalt to dignitie,
And sum to depryue in pouertie.
Sum tyme of layit men to mak Lordis,
And sum tyme Lordis to bind in cordis,
And thame alluterlie distroy,
As pleisis God that Royall Roy,
For thow art bot ane instrument,
To that greit King Omnipotent:
So quhen it pleisis his Excellence,
Thy grace sall mak me recompence,
Or he sall cause me stand content,
Of qnyet lyfe and sober rent,
And tak me in my latter age,
Unto my sempyl Hermitage,
And spend that my Eldaris woun,
As did Diogenes in his toun,
Of this Complant with mynd ful meik,
Thy gracis answeir (Schir) I beseik.

FINIS

QVOD DAVID LYNDESAY

TO THE KING.

The Tragedie of the

vmquhyle maist Reuerend Father
Dauid, be the Mercy of God, Cardinall,
& Archebischop of Sanctandrois &c.
**Compylit be Schir Dauid Lyndesay,
of the Mont Knicht, Alias
Lyoun, King of
Armes.**

Mortales cùm nati sitis, ne supra Deum
vos erexeritis.

THE PROLOG

Ocht lang ago, efter þ hour of prime
Secreitlie sitting in myne Oratorie
I tuke ane buke til occupy the time,
Quhare I fand mony tragedie and
storie,
Quhilk Jhone Boccace had put in memorie,
How mony Princis, Conquerouris and Kingis,
War dulefullie deposit, frome thair ringis.

How Alexander the potent Conquerour,
In Babilon was poysonit pieteouslie,
And Julius the michtie Emperour,
Murdreist at Rome, causles and cruellie,
Prudent Pompey, in Egypt schamefullie,
He murdreist was, quhat neidith proces more?
Quhose

Quhose Tragedyis wer pietie till deploze.

I sitting so, vpon my Buke reiding
Richt suddandlie afoze me did appeir,
Ane woundit man aboundantlie bleiding,
With visage paill, and with ane deidlie cheir,
Semand ane man of twa and fyftie zeir,
In Rayment reid, clothit full courteouslie,
Of veluoit and of Satyn Crammosie.

With febill voice, as man opprest with pane,
Softlie he maid me supplicatioun,
Sayand, my freind, go reid, and reid agane,
Gif thou can find be trew Narratioun,
Of ony pane lyke to me passioun.
Richt sure I am, war Jhone Boccace on lyue,
My Tragedie at lenth he wald descryue.

Sen he is gone, I pray the till indyte,
Of my Infortune sum Remembzance,
Oz at the leist my Tragedie to wzyte,
As I to the sall schaw the circumstance,
In termis bzeue of my vnhappy chance,
Sen my beginning till my fatall end,
Quhilk I wald till all creature war kend.

I not said I, mak sic memoziall,
But of thy name I had Intelligence,
I am Dauid that carefull Cardinall,
Quhilk doith appeir (said he) to thy pzesence,
That vinquhyle had sa greit pzeeminence,
Than he began his deidis till indyte,
As ze sall heir, and I began to wzyte.

¶ Th

⸿ The Tragedie of
the Cardinall.

 Dauid Betoun vmquhyl Cardinal
Of nobil blude be lyne I did disced
During my tyme I had na peregal
Bot now is cum allace my fatal end
Ay gre be gre bywart I did ascend
Swa that into this Realme did neuer ring,
Sa greit ane man as I, vnder ane King.

Quhen I was ane zoung Ioly gentill man,
Princis to serue I set my haill Intent,
First till ascend, at Arbroith I began
Ane Abbacie of greit ryches and rent.
Of that estait zit was I nocht content,
To get mair ryches, dignitie and gloze,
My hart was set, allace, allacs, tharefoze.

I maid sic seruice till our souerane King,
He did promoue me till moze hie estate.
Ane Prince abuse all Preistis for till ring,
Archebischop of Sanctandzois consecrate:
Till that honour quhen I was eleuate,
My prydefull hart was nocht content at all,
Till that I creat was ane Cardinall.

Zit preissit I till haue mair auctozitie,
And finallie was chosin Chancellair,
And foz vphalding of my dignitie,
Was maid Legate, than had I na compair,
                              I purchest

I purchest my proffyt singulair,
My Boxis, and my Thresure till auance,
The Bischoprik of Merepois in France.

Of Scotland I had the gouernall,
Bot my aduyse concludit was na thing,
Abbot, Bischop, Archebischop, Cardinall,
Into this Realme, na hiear culd I ring,
Bot I had bene Pape, Empriour, or King,
For schortnes of the tyme I am nocht abill,
At lenth to schaw my actis honorabill.

For my most Princely prodigalitie,
Amang Prelatis in France I bure the pryce,
I schew my Lordlie liberalitie,
In banketting, playing, at cairtis and dyce,
Into sic wisedome, I was haldin wyse,
And spairit nocht to play with king nor knicht,
Thre thousand crownis of golde vpon ane nicht,

In France I maid fair honest voyagis,
Quhare I did actis digne of remembrance,
Throuch me wer maid tryumphand mariagis,
Till our Souerane baith proffyt and plesance,
Quene Magdalene, the first Dochter of France,
With greit ryches was into Scotland brocht,
That mariage throch my wisedō it was wrocht.

Efter quhose deith in France I past agane,
The secund Quene hamewart I did conuoy,
That lustie Princes, Marie de Lorane,
Quhilk was resaiuit with greit tryumphs ⁊ Joy
So seruit I our richt redoutit Roy,

　　　　　　　　　　　　　　　Sone

Sone efter that, Henry of Ingland King,
Of our Souerane desyrit ane commoning.

Of that meting, our King was weill content,
So that in York was set baith tyme and place,
Bot our Prelatis, nor I wald neuer consent,
That he suld se king Henry in the face,
Bot we wer weill content, howbeit his grace,
Had saillit the Sey, to speik with ony vther,
Except that king, quhilk was his mother brother

Quhairthroch yair rose greit weir & mortal strife
Greit heirschips, hunger, deirth, and desolatioun,
On ather syde, did mony lose thair lyfe,
Gif I wald mak ane trew narratioun,
I causit all that tribulatioun,
For till take peace, I neuer wald consent,
Without the king of France had bene content.

During this weir, war taking preisoneiris,
Of nobill men fechting full furiouslie,
Mony ane Lord, Barroun and Bacheleiris,
Quhare throuch our king tuke sic melancholie,
Quhilk draue him to the deith richt dulefullie,
Extreme doulour ouerset did so his hart,
That from this lyfe allace, he did depart.

Bot efter that baith strenth & speiche was leisit
Ane paper blank, his grace I gart subscryue,
Into the quhilk, I wrait all that I pleisit,
Efter his deith, quhilk lang war till descryue,
Throuch that wryting, I purposit belyue,
With support of sum Lordis beneuolence,

In this

In this Regioun till haue preeminence.

As for my Lord our richteous gouernour,
Gif I wald schortlie schaw the veritie,
Till him I had na maner of fauour,
During that tyme I purposit that he
Sulde neuer cum to nane auctoritie,
For his support tharefor he brocht amang vs,
Furth of Ingland, the nobill Erle of Angus.

Than was I put abak from my purpose,
And suddandlie cast in Captiuitie,
My prydefull hart to dant, as I suppose,
Deuysit be the hich Diuinitie,
Zit in my hart sprang na humilitie,
Bot now the word of God full weill I knaw,
Quha dois exalt him self, God sall him law.

In the mene tyme, quhen I was so subiectit,
Ambassadouris war send into England,
Quhare thay boith peice & mariage contractit,
And mair surely for till obserue that band,
war promeist diuers pledgis of Scotland.
Of that contract I was na way content,
Nor neuer wald thareto geue my consent.

Till Capitanis, that keipit me in waird,
Giftis of gold, I gaue thame greit plentie,
Rewlaris of Court, I rychelie did rewaird,
Quhare throuch I chaipit from captiuitie:
Bot quhen I was fre at my libertie,
Than lyke ane Lyoun, lowsit of his cage,
Out throuch this Realme, I gan to reill & rage.
　　　　　　　　　　　　　　　　Contrair

Contrair the Gouernour and his cōmpanie,
Oft tymes maid I Insurrectioun,
Purposing foʒ till haue him haistelie,
Subduit vnto my coʒrectioun,
Oʒ put him till extreme subiectioun,
During this tyme,gif it war weill decydit,
This Realme be me was vtterlie deuydit,

The Gouernour purposing to subdew,
I rasit ane oist of mony bald Barroun,
And maid ane raid quhilk Lithgow ʒit may rew
Foʒ we distroyit ane myle about the toun,
Foʒ that I gat mony blak malisoun.
Zit contrair the Gouernouris intent,
With our ʒoung Pʒinces we to Striuiling wēt.

Foʒ hich contemptioun of the Gouernour,
I bʒocht the Erle of Lennox furth of France,
That lustie Loʒd,leuand in greit pleisour,
Did lose that land and honest Oʒdinance,
Bot he and I fell sone at variance,
And thʒoch my counsell was within schoʒt space,
Foʒfaltit and flemit,he gat nane vther grace.

Than thʒouch my pʒudence,pʒactik and ingyne
Our gouernour I causit to consent,
Full quyetlie to my counsall inclyne,
Quhare of his nobillis wer nocht weill content,
Foʒ quhy? I gart dissolue in plane Parlyament,
The band of peice contractit with Ingland,
Quharthʒoch come harme & heirschip to Scotlād

That peice bʒokin,arose new moʒtall weiris,
P   Be

Be ſey, and land, ſic reif, without releif,
Quhilk to repoꝛt my frayit hart effeiris,
The veritie to ſchaw in termis bꝛeif,
I was the rute, of all that greit miſcheif.
The South Cuntrie may ſay, it had bene gude
That my Nuriſche had ſmoꝛit me in my cude.

　I was the cauſe of mekle mair miſchance,
foꝛ vphalde of my gloꝛe and dignitie,
And pleſour of the potent King of France,
With Ingland wald I haue na vnitie:
Bot quha conſydder wald the veritie,
We micht full weill haue leiuit in peice and reſt,
Nine oꝛ ten ȝeiris, and than playit louſe oꝛ faſt.

　Had we with Ingland keipit our contrackis,
Our nobill men had leiuit in peice and reſt.
Our Merchandſ had nocht loſt ſo mony packis,
Our commoun pepill had nocht bene oppꝛeſt:
On ather ſyde all wꝛangis had bene redꝛeſt.
Bot Edinburgh ſen ſyne, Leith, and Kingoꝛne,
The day and hour may ban that I was boꝛne.

　Our Gouernour to mak him to me ſure,
With ſweit and ſubtell woꝛdis, I did him ſyle,
Tyll I his Sone and Air, gat in my cure,
To that effect I fand that craftie wyle,
That he na maner of way micht me begyle,
Than leuch I quhen his liegis did alledge,
How I his Sone had gottin into pledge.

　The Erle of Angus and his Germane bꝛother
I purpoſit to gar thame loſe thair lyfe,

Richt ſo

Richt so till haue distroyit mony vther,
Sum with the fyre, sum with the swozd & knyfe,
In speciall mony gentill men of fyfe,
And purposit till put to greit tozment,
All fauozeris of the auld and new Testament.

Than euerie man thay tuke of me sic feir,
That tyme quhen I had so greit gouernance,
Greit Lozdis dzeiding, I sulde do thame deir,
Thay durst nocht cum till court but assurance,
Sen syne thare hes nocht bene sic variance,
Now till our Prince Barronis obedientlie,
But assurance thay cum full courteslie.

My hope was most into the King of france,
To gidder with the Popis holynes,
Mare than in God, my wozschip till auance,
I traistit so into thair gentilnes,
That na man durst presume, me till oppzes,
Bot quhen the day came of my fatall hour,
far was from me, thair suppozt and succour.

Than to prescrue my ryches and my lyfe,
I maid ane strenth of wallis hich and bzaid,
Sic ane fortres was neuer found in fyfe,
Beleiuand thare durst na man me inuaid.
Now fynd I trew the law quylk Dauid said:
Without God of ane hous, be maister of wark,
He wirkis in vane, thocht it be neuer so stark.

foz I was throuch the hie power Diuine,
Richt dulefullie doung doun amang the as,
Quhilk culd not be throch moztall mānis ingyne
          P ij   Bot as

Bot as Dauid did slay the greit Golyas,
Or Holopherne, be Judith keillit was,
In myd amang his tryumphand Armie,
So was I slane into my cheif Cietie.

Quhen I had greitest dominatioun,
As Lucifer had in the heuin Empyre,
Came suddandlie my Depriuatioun,
Be thame quhilk did my dolent deith conspire,
So cruell was thair furious birnand Ire,
I gat na tyme, layser nor libertie,
To say, In manus tuas Domine.

Behald my fatall Infelicitie,
I beand in my strenth, incomparabill.
That dreidsull Dungeoun maid me na supple,
My greit ryches, nor rentis proffitabill,
My syluer work, Iowellis inestimabill,
My Papall pompe, of golde my ryche thresour,
My lyfe and all I lost in half ane hour.

To the peple wes maid ane Spectakle,
Of my deid and deformit carioun.
Sum said it was ane manifest mirakle:
Sum said it was Diuine punitioun,
So to be slane, into my strang Dungeoun,
Quhen euery man had iudgit as him list,
Thay saltit me, syne closit me in ane kist.

I lay vnburyit seuin Monethis and more,
Or I was borne to closter, kirk or queir,
In ane midding quhilk pane bene till deplore,
Without suffrage of Chanoun, Monk or Freir,
                                        All proude

All proude Prelatis at me may Lessonis leir,
Quhilk rang so lang and so tryumphantlie,
Syne in the dust doung doun so dulefullie.

To the Prelatis. II.

O Ze my Brether, Princis of the Preistis,
I mak zow hartlie Supplicatioun:
Boith nicht and day reuolue into zour breistis,
The Proces of my Depriuatioun,
Consiooer quhat bene zour Uocatioun,
To follow me, I pray zow, nocht pretend zow,
Bot reid at lenth this Cedull, that I send zow.

Ze knaw how Jesus his Discipulis sent,
Ambassadouris till euerie Natioun,
To schaw his Law and his commandement,
To all pepill by Predicatioun,
Tharefore I mak to zow narratioun,
Sen ze to thame ar berray Successouris,
Ze aucht to do as did zour Predecessouris.

How dar ze be so bauld till tak on hand,
For to be Heraldis to so greit ane King,
To beir his message boith to burgh and land,
Ze beand dum, and can pronunce na thing,
Lyke Menitrans, that can nocht play nor sing.
Or quhy suld men geue to sic Hirdis hyre,
Quhilk can not gyde thair scheip about þ myre.

Eschame ze nocht to be Christis Seruitouris,
And for zour fee, hes greit temporall landis?
Syne of zour office can nocht tak the curis,

V iij Is

As Cannone Law, ⁊ Scripture ʒow cōmandis
Ʒe will nocht want teind scheif,nor offerandis,
Teind woll,teind lamb,teind calf , teind gryce ⁊
To mak seruice ʒe ar all out of vse.   (guse.

My deir brother do nocht as ʒe war wount,
Amend ʒour lyfe now, quhile ʒour day Induris,
Traist weill,ʒe salbe callit to ʒour count,
Of euerilk thing belanging to ʒour curis.
Leue ʒalartrie,ʒour harlotrie,and huris,
Remembring on my vnprouisit deid ,
For efter deith may na man mak remeid.

Ʒe Prelatis quhilk hes thousandis for to sped
Ʒe send ane sempyll freir, for ʒow to preche,
It is ʒour craft,I mak it to ʒow kend,
Ʒour selfis in ʒour templis for to preche,
Bot ferlie nocht,thocht sillie freiris sleche:
For and thay planelie schaw the veritie,
Than will thay want the Bischopis cheritie.

Quharefor bene geuin ʒow sic Royall rent?
Bot for till fynd the peple Spirituall fude,
Prechand to thame the auld ⁊ new Testament,
The Law of God doith planely so conclude,
Put nocht ʒour hope into na warldlie gude,
As I haue done,behald my greit thresour,
Maio me na help at my vnhappy hour.

That day quhen I was Bischop consecrait,
The greit Byble was bound vpon my bak
Quhat was thare in , lytill I knew, God wait,
Mair than ane beist berand ane precious pak,
                                        Bot

Bot haiſtely my conuenant J bꝛak,
Foꝛ J wes obliſſit with my awin conſent,
The law of God to pꝛeche with gude intent.

Bꝛether richt ſo quhen ʒe wer conſecrait,
Ʒe obliſſit ʒow all on the ſamin wyſe,
Ʒe may be callit Biſchoppis countrefait,
As Gallandis buſkit foꝛ to mak ane gyſe,
Now think J, Pꝛincis ar na thing to pꝛyſe,
Till geue ane famous office till ane fule,
As quha wald put ane Myter on ane Mule.

Allace, and ʒe that ſoꝛowfull ſicht had ſene,
How J lay bullerand, baithit in my blude,
To mend ʒour lyfe, it had occaſioun bene,
And leaue ʒour auld coꝛruptit conſwetude,
Failʒeing thareof than ſchoꝛtlie J conclude,
Without ʒe from ʒour ribaldꝛie aryſe,
Ʒe ſalbe ſeruit, on the ſamyn wyſe.

To the Princis. III.

J Mypꝛudent Pꝛincis but diſcrecioun,
Hauing in eirth power Jmperiall,
Ʒe bene the cauſe of this tranſgreſſioun:
J ſpeik to ʒow all into generall,
Quhilk doith diſpone all office Spirituall,
Geuand the ſaulis, quhilkis bene Chꝛiſtis ſcheip,
To blynd Paſtouris but conſcience to keip.

Quhen ʒe Pꝛincis doith laik ane Officiar,
Ane Barter, Bꝛowſter, oꝛ ane maiſter Cuke,
Ane trym Tailʒeour, ane cunning Coꝛdynat,

Ouer all the land at lenth, ʒe will gar luke,
Most abill men sic officis till bʒuke.
Ane Bʒowster quhilk can bʒew most hailsum aill
Ane cunning Cuke quhilk best can sessoun caill.

Ane Tailʒour quhilk hes fosterit bene in Fråce
That can mak garmentis on the gayest gyse.
Ze Pʒincis bene the cause of this mischance,
That quhen thare doith vaik ony Benesyse,
Ze aucht to do vpon the samin wyse.
Gar serche and seik boith into burgh and land,
The Law of God quha best can vnderstand.

Mak hum Bischop that pʒudentlie can pʒeche,
As dois pertene till his vocatioun .
Ane Persone quhilk his parischoun can teche,
Gar Uicaris mak dew Ministratioun.
And als J mak ʒow Supplicátioun,
Mak ʒour Abbottis of richt Religious men,
Quhilk to the peple Chʒistis Law can ken.

Bot not to rebaldis, new cum from the rost,
Noʒ of ane stuffat stollin out of ane stabill,
The quhilk into the scule maid neuer na cost,
Noʒ neuer was til Spirituall science abill,
Except the cairtis, the dyce, the ches and tabill,
Of Rome raikeris, noʒ of rude Ruffianis,
Of calsay Paikeris, noʒ of Publicanis.

Noʒ of fantastik feinʒeit flatteraris,
Most meit to gather mussillis into May.
Of cowhubeis, noʒ ʒit of clatteraris,
That in the kirk can nother sing noʒ say,

                               Thocht

Thocht thay be clokit vp in Clerkis array,
Lyke doitit Doctouris new cum out of Athenis
And mummill ouer ane pair of maiglit Matenis

Nocht qualyfyit to bruke ane Benefyis,
Bot throuch schir Symonis solistatioun,
I was promouit on the sampyn wyis,
Illace throuch Princis supplicatioun,
And maid at Rome throuch fals narratioun,
Bischop, Abbot, bot na Religious man,
Quha me promouit , I now thare banis ban.

Howbeit I was Legate and Cardinall,
Lytill I knew tharein quhat sulde be done,
I vnderstude na science Spirituall,
No moze than did blynd Alane of the Mone,
I dreid the king that sittith hich abone,
On zow Princis sall mak soze punischement,
Richt so on vs throuch richteous Jugement.

On zow Princis foz vndiscreit geuing,
Till Ignozantis sic officis till vse,
And we foz our Jnopoztune asking,
Quhilk suld haue done sic dignitie refuse,
Our Ignozance hes done the warld abuse,
Throuch Couetice of ryches and of rent,
That euer I was ane Prelate I repent.

¶ O Kingis mak ze na cair to geue in cure,
Uirginis profest into Religioun,
In till the keiping of ane commoun hure?
To mak think ze nocht greit derisioun,
Ane woman Persone of ane Parischoun?
        P v   Quhare

Quhare thare bene twa thousand saulis to gyde,
That frome harlottis can not hir hippis hyde.

Quhat and King Dauid leiuit in thir dayis,
Or out of heuin quhat and he lukit down,
The quhilk did found so mony fair Abbayis?
Seand the greit abhominatioun,
In mony Abbayis of this Natioun,
He wald repent that narrowit so his boundis,
Of zeirly rent , thre scoze of thousand poundis.

Quharefoze I counsall euerilk Christiane king
Within this Realme mak reformatioun,
And suffer no mo rebaldis foz to ring,
Abuse Christis trew Congregatioun.
Failzeing thareof I mak narratioun.
That ze Princis and Prelatis all at onis,
Sall bureit be in hell,saule, blude,and bonis.

That euer I bzukit Benefice I rew,
Oz to sic hicht so proudelie did pretend.
I mon depart, tharefoze my freindis adew.
Quhare euer it plesith God,now mon I wend,
I pray the till my freindis me recommend,
And failze noche at lenth to put in wryte,
My Tragedie,as I haue done indyte.

FINIS.

¶ The Deploratioun

II

of the Deith of Quene
Magdalene.

Cruell deith, to greit is thy puissāce,
Deuorar of all eirthly lyuing thingſ
Adã, we may þ wyit of this miſchāce
In thy defalt this cruel tyrane ringſ
And ſpairis nother emprior nor kigſ
And now allace hes reſt furth of this land,
The flour of France, and comfort of Scotland.

Father Adam allace, that thow abuſit,
Thy fre will being Inobedient,
Thow cheiſit Deith, and laſting lyfe refuſit,
Thy ſucceſſioun allace, that may repent,
That thow hes maid mankynd ſo Impotent,
That it may mak to Deith, na reſiſtance,
Exemple of our Quene, the flour of France.

O dreidfull Dragoun, with thy dulefull dart,
Quhilk did not ſpair of Feminine the Flour,
Bot cruellie did perſe hir throuch the hart,
And wald nocht geue hir reſpite for ane hour,
To remane with hir Prince, and Paramour,
That ſcho at laiſer, micht haue tane licence,
Scotland on the, may cry ane lowd vengeance,

Thow leit Mathuſalē leif nine hundreth ʒeir,
Thre

Thre score and nyne , bot in thy furious rage.
Thow did deuore this zoung Princes but peir,
Or scho was compleit seuintene zeir of age.
Gredie gorman,quhy did thow nocht assuage,
Thy furious rage, contrair that lustie Quene,
Till we sum fruct had of hir bodie sene?

O Dame Nature,thow did na diligence,
Cōtrair this theif quhilk all the warld cōfoundis
Had thow with naturall targis maid defence,
That brybour had nocht cummit win hir boundz
And had bene sauit from sic mortall stoundis,
This mony ane zeir,bot quhair was thy discretiō
That leit hir pas,till we had sene succession.

O Venus with thy blynd sone Cupido,
Fy on zow baith , that maid na resistance,
Into zour Court,ze neuer had sic twa .
So leill Luiffaris without dissimulance,
As James the Fyft, and Magdalene of France,
Discending baith of blude Imperiall,
To quhome in lufe, I find na perigall.

For as Leander swame outtrow the flude,
To his fair Lady Hero,mony nichtis,
So did this prince,throw bulring streinis wode
With Erlis,Baronis,Squyarz & with knichtis
Contrair Neptune,and Goll & thair michtis,
And left his Realme in greit disesperance,
To seik his Lufe,the first Dochter of France.

And scho lyke prudent Quene Penelope,
Ful constantlie wald change him for none vther,
And

And for his plesour left hir awin Cuntrie,
Without regard,to Father or to Mother,
Taking na cure of Sister nor of Brother,
Bot schortlie tuke hir leaue,and left thame all,
For lufe of him to quhome lufe maid hir thrall.

O Dame Fortune quhare was thy greit cōfort
Till hir to quhome thow was so fauorable,
Thy slyding giftis,maid hir na support,
Hir hie lynage,nor Riches intellible,
I se thy puissance bene bot variable,
Quhen hir father the most hie cristinit King,
Till his deir Chyld,micht mak na supporting.

The potent Prince hir lustie lufe and knicht,
With his most hardie Noblis of Scotland,
Contrair that baitfull bribour had na micht,
Thocht all the men had bene at his command,
Of France, Flanderis,Italie,and Jngland,
With fiftie thousand Millioun of tresour,
Micht nocht prolong that Ladyis lyfe ane hour.

O Paris of all Citeis principall,
Quhilk did resaue our Prince with laud & glorie
Solempnitie throw Arkis triumphall,
Quhilk day bene digne to put in memorie,
For as Pompey efter his victorie,
we as into Rome resauit with greit Joy,
So thow resauit,our richt redoutit Roy.

Bot at his Mariage maid vpon the morne,
Sic solace , and Solempnizatioun,
was neuer sene afore,sen Christ was borne,
                                    Nor to

Nor to Scotland sic consolatioun,
Thare stilit was the confirmatioun,
Of the weill keipit ancient alliance,
Maid betuix Scotland, & the Realme of France

I neuer did se ane day mair glorious,
So mony in so ryche abilzementis,
Of silk and gold with stonis precious,
Sic banketting, sic sound of Instrumentis,
With sang and dance, & Martiall tormentis,
Bot lyke ane, storme, efter ane plesand morrow,
Sone was our solace changit into sorrow.

O traitour deith quhome none may contramad
Thow micht haue sene the preparatioun,
Maid be the thre Estaitis of Scotland,
With greit comfort and consolatioun,
In euerilk Cietie, Castell, Towre and Town,
And how ilk nobill set his haill intent,
To be excellent in habilzement.

Theif saw thow nocht the greit preparatyuis,
Of Edinburgh the nobill famous toun,
Thow saw the pepill laubouring for thair lyuis,
To mak tryumphe, with trump and Clarioun,
Sic plesour was neuer into this Regioun,
As suld haue bene the day of hir entrace,
With greit proppynis geuin till hir grace.

Thow saw makand richt costlie scaffalding,
Depaintit weill with gold and asure fyne,
Reddie prepairit for the vpsetting,
With fontanis flowing water cleir and wyne,
Disagysit

Difagyfit folkis, lyke Creaturis Brutyne,
On ilk fcaffold to play ane fyndzie ftonie,
Bot all in greiting turnit thow that glozie.

Thow faw mony ane luftie frefche galland,
Weill ozdourit foz refaiuing of thair Quene,
Ilk Craftifman with bent bow in his hand,
Full gailзeartlie in fchozt cleithing of grene.
The honeft Burges, cled thow fuld haue fene,
Sum in fcarlot, and fum in claith of grane,
Foz till haue met thair Lady fouerane.

Proueft, Baillies, and Lozdis of the town,
The Senatouris in ozdour confequent,
Cled into filk of purpure blak and brown,
Syne the greit Lozdis of the Parliament,
With mony knichtlie Barroun and baurent,
In filk and gold, in colouris confortabill,
Bot thow allace, all turnit into fabill.

Syne all the Lozdis of Religioun,
And Princis of the Preiftis venerabill,
Full plefandlie in thair Proceffioun,
With all the cunning Clerkis honozabill,
Bot thiftuouflie thow tyrane trefourabill,
All thair greit folace and Solempniteis,
Thow turnit in till duleful Dirigeis.

Syne nyrt in Ozdour paffing throw the toun,
Thow fuld haue hard the din of Inftrumentis,
Of Tabzone, Trumpet, Schelme, & Clarioun,
With reird redoundand throw the Elementis,
The Herauldis, with thair awful veftimentis,
                                        With

With Maseris vpon ather of thair handis,
To rewle the preis, with burneist siluer wandis.

Syne last of all in ordour tryumphall,
That most illuster Princes honorabill,
With hir the lustie Ladyis of Scotland,
Quhilk sulde haue bene, ane sicht most delectabll
Hir rayment to rehers, I am nocht abill,
Of gold and perle, and precious stonis bricht,
Twinkling lyke sterris in ane frostie nicht.

Under ane pale of golde, scho suld haue past,
Be Burgesis borne, clothit in silkis fyne,
The greit maister of housholde, all thair last,
With him in ordour all the Kingis tryne,
Quhais ordinance war langsum to defyne,
On this maner, scho passing throw the toun,
Suld haue resauit mony benisoun.

Of Virginis, and of lustie burgeis wyffis,
Quhilk suld haue bene ane sicht Celestiall,
Viue la Royne, cryand for thair lyffis,
With ane Harmonious sound Angelicall,
In euerilk corner, myrthis Musicall,
Bot thow tyrane in quhome is found na grace,
Our Alleluya hes turnit in allace.

Thou sulde haue hard the ornate Oratouris,
Makand hir hienes Salutatioun,
Baith of the Clergy, Town and Counsalouris,
With mony notabill Narratioun,
Thow sulde haue sene hir Coronatioun,
In the fair Abbay of the holy rude,

In pre

In præfence of ane myrthfull multitude.

Sic Banketting, Sic awfull tornamentis,
On hors & fute, that tyme quhilk fuld haue bene,
Sic Chapell Royall, with fic Inftrumentis,
And craftie Mufick, finging from the fplene,
In this cuntrie, was neuer hard nor fene,
Bot all this greit folempnitie and gam,
Turnit thow hes in Requiem æternam.

Inconftant warld, thy freindfchip I defy,
Sen ftrenth nor wifedome, ryches nor honour,
Uertew nor bewtie, none may certify,
Within thy boundis for to remane ane hour,
Quhat bailith to the King or Emprtour,
Sen Princely puiffance may nocht be exeimit,
Frō Deith, quhofe dolour can nocht be exprimit.

Sen man in eirth hes na place permanent,
Bot all mon pas be that horribill port,
Lat vs pray to the Lord Omnipotent,
That dulefull Day to be our greit comfort,
That in his Realme, we may with him refort,
Quhilk from the hell, w his blude ranfonit bene,
With Magdalene, vmquhyl of Scotlād Quene.

O deith, thocht thow the bodie may deuore,
Of euery man, zit hes thow na puiffance,
Of thair vertew for to confume the glore,
As falbe fene, of Magdalene of France,
Vmquhile our Quene, quhome Poëtis fal aūce
And put hir in perpetuall memorie,
So fall hir fame of the haue Uictorie.
                    Z   Thocht

Thocht thow hes slane ẏ heuinlie flour of Fráce
Quhilk Impit was, into the Thrissill kene,
Quhairein all Scotland saw thair haill plesance,
And maid the Lyon reioysit from the splene,
Thocht rute be pullit from the leuis grene,
The smell of it, sall in despyte of the,
Keip ay twa Realmes in peice and amitie.

QVOD LYNDESAY.

IIII. The Answer quhilk
Schir Dauid Lindesay maid to
the Kingis Flyting.

Edoutit roy zour ragmét J haif red
Quhilk dois pturb my dul intédemét
frô zour Kitig wald god ẏ J wer fred
Orellis su tygerris, toug wer to me lét
Schir, pdone me, thocht J be impa-
Quhilk ben so w̄ zour prinzeád pé detrectit (ciét
And rude repozt frome Uenus Court deiectit.

Lustie Ladyis, that zour Libellis luikis,
My cumpaniedois halb abhominable,
Commandand me beir cumpanie to the Cuikis,
Woist lyke ane Deuill thay hald me detestable,
Thay baneis me, sayand, J am nocht able,
Thaine to compleis, oz preis to thair presence,
Jpon zour pen, J cry ane loud vengeance.

War J

Wer I ane Poeit, I suld preis with my pen,
To wreik me on zour wennemous wryting:
Bot I mon do, as dog dois in his den,
Fald baith my feit, or else fast frome zour flyting,
The mekle Deuil may nocht indure zour Dyting
Quharefor Cor mundum crea in me, I cry,
Proclamand zow the Prince of Poetry.

Schir w my Prince, perteinit me nocht to pley
Bot sen zour grace, hes geuin me sic command,
To mak answer, it must neidis me obey,
Thocht ze be now strang lyke ane Elephand,
And in till Uenus werkis maist bailzeand,
The day will cum, and that within few zeiris,
That ze will draw at laiser with zour seiris,

Quhat can ze say further, bot I am failzeit,
In Uenus werkis I grant schir, that is trew,
The tyme hes bene, I was better artailzeit,
Nor I am now, bot zit full sair I rew,
That euer I did mouth thankles so persew,
Quharefor tak tent, and zour syne powder spair
And waist it nocht, bot gif ze wit weill quhair.

Thocht ze rin rudelie, lyke ane restles Ram,
Schutand zour bolt, at mony sindrie schellis,
Beleif richt weill, it is ane bydand gam,
Quharefor bewar, with dowbling of the bellis,
For mony ane dois haist thair awin saule knellis
And specially, quhen that the wall gois dry,
Syne can nocht get agane, sic stufe to by.

I giue zour counsale, to the feynd of hell,
That wald nocht of ane Princes zow proupde,
                    Z ij   Tholand

Tholand 30w rin schutand from schell to schell,
Waistar'd 3our corps,lettand the tyme ouerslyde
For lyke ane boisteous bull,3e rin and ryde,
Ropatouslie lyke ane rude Rubeatour,
Ipsukkand lyke ane furious fornicatour.

    On Ladronis for to loip,3e will nocht lat,
Howbeit the Caribaldis cry,the cozinoch.
Remember how besyde the masking fat,
3e caist ane Quene ouerthort ane stinkig troch
That feind with fuffilling of hir roistit hoch,
Caist doun þ fat,quharethrow drink draf & inggz
Come rudely rinnand doun about 3our luggis.

    Wald God the Lady that luffit 3ow best
Had sene 3ow thare ly swetterãd like twa swyne
Bot to indyte how that duddroun was drest,
Drowkit wt dreggz quhimperãd wt mony quhryne
That proces to report, it war ane pyne.
On 3our behalf, I thank God tymes ten score,
That 3ow preseruit,from gut,& from grandgore.

    Now schir fairweill because I can nocht flyte,
And thocht I could, I war nocht till auance,
Aganis 3our ornate Meter to indyte:
Bot 3it be war, with laubouring of 3our lance,
Sũ sayis,thair cũmis ane bukler furth of Frãce,
Quhilk wil indure 3our dintz,thocht 3ai be dour
Fare weill of flowand Rethorik the flour.

    Quod Lyndesay in his flyting,
    Aganis the Kingis dyting.

FINIS.

ℭThe Complaynt & v.

publict Confessioun of the Kingis
auld Hound, callit Bagsche, directit to Bawtie,
the Kingis best belouit dog, & his companzeonis.
Maid at command of King James the Fyst,
Be Schir Dauid Lyndesay, of the Mount
Knicht, aliàs Lyoun King
of Armes.

Allace quhome to suld I complaine,
In my extreme necessitie:
Or quhame to sall I mak my maine
In court na Dog will do for me,
Beseikand sum for Cheritie,
To beir my Supplicatioun,
To Scudlar, Luffra and Bawtie,
Now or the King pas to the town.

I haue followit the Court so lang,
Quhyll in gude faith, I may na mair,
The cuntrie knawis, I may nocht gang
I am so crukit, auld and sair,
That I wait nocht quhare to repair,
For quhen I had auctoritie,
I thocht me so familiar,
I neuer dred necessitie.

Frew the race that Geordie Steill,
Brocht Bawtie to the Kingis presence,

Z iij   I pray

I pray God lat him neuer do weill,
Sen syne I gat na audience,
For Bawtie now gettis sic credence,
That he lyis on the Kingis nicht gown,
Quhare I perforce for my offence,
Mon in the clois ly lyke ane lown.

For I haue bene ay to this hour,
Ane wirrear of lamb and hog,
Ane tyrane and ane Tulȝeour,
Ane murdriciſſar of mony dog,
Fyue foullȝ I chaiſt outthroch ane ſcrog
Quharefor thair motheris did me warie
For thay war drownit all in ane bog,
Speir at Jhone Gordoun of Pittarie.

Quhilk in his hous did bryng me vp,
And vſit me to ſlay the deir,
Sweit milk and meill he gart me ſup,
That craft I leirnit ſone perqueir,
All vther vertew ran arreir,
Quhen I began to bark and ſkyte,
For thair was nother Monk nor Freir,
Nor wyfe,nor barne,bot I wald byte.

Quhen to the king þ cace was knawin
Of my vnhappy hardines,
And all the ſuith vnto him ſchawin,
How euerilk dog I did oppres,
Than gaif his Grace command expres,
I ſuld be brocht to his preſence,
Notwithſtanding my wickitnes,

                              In Court

In Court I gat greit audience.

I schew my greit Ingratitude,
To the Capitane of Badzeno,
Quhilk in his hous did find me fude,
Twa zeir, with vther houndis mo.
Bot quhen I saw that it was so,
That I grew hich into the Court,
For his reward I wrocht him wo,
And cruellie I did him hurt.

So thay that gaue me to the King,
I was thair mortall enemie,
I tuke cure of na kynd of thing,
Bot pleis the Kingis Maiestie,
Bot quhen he knew my crueltie,
My falset and my plane oppressioun,
He gaue command that I suld be
Hangit without confessioun.

And zit because that I was auld,
His grace thocht pietie for to hang me,
Bot leit me wander quhare I wald,
Than set my fais for to fang me,
And euery bouchour dog doun dang me
Quhen I trowit best to be ane laird,
Than in y court sik wicht did wrang me
And this I gat for my rewaird,

I had wirreit blak Makesoun,
War nocht that rebaldis come and reb,
Bot he was flemit of the toun,
From tyme the king saw how I bled,
    ຠ   Z iiij   He gatt

He gart lay me vpon ane bed,
For with ane knyfe I was miſcheiuit,
This Makeſoun for feir he fled,
Ane lang tyme or he was releiuit.

And Patrik Striuiling in Ergyle,
I bure him bakwart to the ground,
And had him ſlane within ane quhyle,
War nocht the helping of ane hound.
Zit gat he mony bludie wound,
As zit his ſkin will ſchaw the markis,
Find me ane dog quhare euer ze found,
Hes maid ſo mony bludie ſarkis.

Gude brother lanceman, Lindeſayꝭ dog
Quhilk ay hes keipit thy lawtie,
And neuer wirryit lamb nor hog,
Pray Luffra, Scudlar and Bawtie,
Of me Bagſche to haue pietie,
And prouide me ane portioun,
In Dumfermeling, quhare I may dre,
Peunance for my extortioun.

Get be thare Soliſtatioun,
Ane letter from the kingis grace,
That I may haue Collatioun,
With fyre and candill in the place,
Bot I will leif ſchort tyme allace,
Want I gude freſche fleſche for my gammis,
Betuir Aſwedniſday and Pace,
I mon haue leif to wirrie Lambis.

Bawtie conſidder weill this bill,

And

And reid this Cedull that I send zow,
And euerilk point thareof fulfill.
And now in tyme of mys amend zow,
I pray zow, that ze nocht pretend zow,
To clym ouer hie, nor do na wrang,
Bot from zour faig,ts eicht defend zow,
And tak example how I gang.

I was that na man durst cum neir me
Nor put me furth of my ludgeing,
Na dog durst fra my denner sher me,
Quhen I was tender with the king,
Now euerilk tyke dois me doun thring,
The quhilk before be me war wrangit,
And sweiris I serue na vther thing,
Bot in ane helter to be hangit.

Thocht ze be hamelie with the King,
Ze Luffra, Scudlar, and Bawtie,
Be war that ze do nocht doun thring,
Zour nychtbouris throw auctoritie:
And zour exempill mak be me,
And beleue weill ze ar bot doggis,
Thocht ze stand in the hyest gre,
Se ze byte nother lambs nor hoggis.

Thocht ze haue now greit audience,
Se that be zow be nane opprest,
Ze will be punischit for zour offence,
From tyme the King be weill confest,
Thare is na dog that hes transgrest,
Throw crueltie, and he may fang hym,

Z v

Dis

His Maiestie will tak na rest,
Till on ane gallous he gar hang him,

I was anis als far ben as ʒe ar,
And had in court als greit credence,
And ay pretendit to be hiar.
Bot quhen the Kingis Excellence,
Did knaw my falset and offence,
And my prydefull presumptioun,
I gat nane vther recompence,
Bot hoyit, and houndit of the town.

Was neuer sa vnkynd ane corce,
As quhen I had auctoritie.
Of my freindis I tuke na force,
The quhilkis afore had done for me,
This Prouerb, it is of veritie,
Quhilk I hard red in till ane letter,
Hiest in Court, nyrt the weddie,
Without he gyde him all the better.

I tuke na mair compt of ane Lord,
Nor I did of ane keitching knaif,
Thocht euerilk day I maid discord,
I was set vp abone the laif,
The gentill hound was to me slaif,
And with the Kingis awin fingeris fed,
The sillie ratchis wald I raif,
Thus for me euill deidis was I dred.

Tharefor Bawtie luke best about,
Quhen thow art hiest with the King,
For than thou standis in greitest dout,

Be thow

Be thow nocht gude of gouerning,
Put na pure tyke frome his steiding,
Nor zit na sillie Ratchis reif,
He sittis abone that seis all thing,
And of ane Knicht can mak ane knaif.

  Quhen I cum steppand ben the flure,
All Raichis greit roume to me red,
I of na creature tuke cure,
Bot lap vpon the Kingis bed,
With claith of gold, thocht it war spred,
For feir ilk freik wald stand on far,
With euerilk dog I was so dred,
Thay trimblit quhen thay hard me nar,

  Gude brother Bawtie beir the tuin,
Thocht with thy Prince thou be potent,
It crys ane vengeance from the heuin,
For till oppres ane Innocent:
In weilth be than maist vigilent,
And do na wrang to dog nor betche,
As I haue, quhilk I now repent,
Na Messane reif to mak the retche.

  Nor for augmenting of thy boundis,
Ask na reward schir at the King,
Quhilk may do hurt to vther houndis,
Expres aganis Goddis bidding,
Chais na pure tyke from his midding,
Throw cast of court, or Kingis requeist
And of thy self presume na thing,
Except thow art ane brutall beist.

           Traist

Traist weill thare is nane oppressour,
Nor boucheour dog, drawer of blude,
Ane tyrane nor ane transgressour,
That sall now of the King get gude,
From tyme furth that his Celsitude,
Dois cleirlie knaw the veritie,
Bot he is demit for to conclude,
Or hangit hich vpon ane tre.

Thocht ze be cuplit all to gidder,
With silk and swoulis, of siluer fyne,
Ane dog may cum furth of Balquhidder
And gar zow leid ane lawer tryne,
Than sall zour plesour turne in pyne,
Quhen ane strange hounter blawis his horne,
And all zour treddingis gar zow tyne,
Than sall zour laubour be forlorne.

I say no more, gude freindis, adew,
In dreid we neuer meit agane.
That euer I kend the Court, I rew,
Was neuer wicht so will of wane,
Lat na dog now serue our Souerane,
Without he be of gude conditioun,
Be he peruerst, I tell zow plane,
He hes neid of ane gude remissioun.

That I am on this way mischeiuit,
The Erle of Hountlie I may warie,
He wend I had bene weill releiuit
Quhen to the Court he gart me carie,
Wald God I war now in Pittarie,

Wald

Becauſe I haue bene ſo euil deidie,
Adew, I dar no langer tarie.
In dreid, I waif in til ane wyddie,

FINIS.

¶Ane Supplication VI.
directit from Schir Dauid Linde-
ſay knicht, to the kingis grace, in
Contemptioun of ſyde
Taillis.

Chir, thocht your grace hes put greit
ordour,
Baith in the hicland & the Bordour
Zit mak I Supplicatioun,
Till haue ſum Reformatioun,
Of ane ſmall falt, quhilk is nocht Treſſoun,
Thocht it be contrarie to Reſſoun:
Becauſe the mater bene ſo vyle,
It may nocht haue ane ornate ſtyle:
Quharefor I pray your Excellence,
To heir me with greit Patience,
Of ſtinkand weidis maculate,
Na man may mak ane Rois Chaiplate.
Souerane I mene of thir Syde Taillis,

Quhill

Quhilk throw the dust and dubbis traillis,
Thre quarteris lang behynd thair heillis,
Expres agane all Commoun weillis.
Thocht Bischoppis in thair Pontificallis,
Haue men for to beir vp thair Taillis,
For dignitie of thair office.
Richtso ane Quene or ane Emprice,
Howbeit thay vse sic grauitie,
Conformand to thair Maiestie,
Thocht thair re b Royallis be vpborne,
I think it is ane verray scorne,
That euery Lady of the land
Suld haue hir taill so syde trailland.
Howbeit thay bene of hie estait,
The Quene thay suld nocht counterfait,
Quhare euer thay go, it may be sene,
How Kirk and calsay thay soup clene,
The Imagis into the Kirk,
May think of thair syde taillis Irk,
For quhen the wedder bene most fair,
The dust fleis, hiest in the air,
And all thair facis dois begarie,
Gif thay culd speik, thay wald thame warie,
To se I think ane plesand sicht,
Of Italie the Ladyis bricht,
In thair cleithing most tryumphand,
Aboue all vther Christin land.
Zit quhen thay trauell throw ẏ townis
Men seis thair feit beneth thair gownis
Four inche abone thair proper heillis,
Circulat about als round as quheillis,

Quhare

Quhare throw thare dois na poulder ryis,
Thair fair quhyte lymmis to ſupprryis,
Bot I think maiſt abuſioun,
To ſe men of Religioun,
Gar beir thair taillis throw the ſtreit,
That folkis may behald thair feit,
I trow ſanct Bernard nor ſanct Blais,
Gart neuer man beir vp thair clais,
Peter nor Paule, nor ſanct Androw,
Gart neuer beir vp thair taylis, I trow,
Bot I lauch beſt to ſe ane Nwn,
Gar beir hir taill abone his bwn,
For nothing ellis, as I ſuppois,
Bot for to ſchaw hir lillie quhyte hois,
In all thair rewlis, thay will nocht find
Quha ſuld beir vp thair taillis behind,
Bot I haue maiſt into deſpyte,
Pure Claggokis cled in roiploch quhyte
Quhilk hes ſkant twa markis for thair ſeis,
Will haue twa ellis beneth thair kneis,
Kittok that clekkit was ȝiſtrene,
The morne will counterfute the Quene.
Ane mureland Meg that mylkit the ȝowis,
Claggit with clay abone the howis,
In barn, nor byir, ſcho will nocht byde,
Without hir kirtill taill be ſyde,
In Burrowis wantoun Burges wyiffis,
Quha may haue ſydeſt taillis ſtryiffis,
Weill bordourit with veluoit fyne,
Bot following thame it is ane pyne:
In Somer quhen the ſtreittis dryis,

                              Thay

Thay rais the dust abone the skyis,
Nane may ga neir thame at thair eis
Without thay couer mouth and neis,
Frome the powder to keip thair ene,
Considder gif thair cloiffis bene clene.
Betuixt thair cleiuing, and thair kneis,
Quha micht behald thair sweitie theis,
Begairit all with dirt and dust,
That war aneuch to stanche the lust,
Of ony man that saw thame naikit,
I think sic giglottis ar bot glaikit:
Without proffite to haue sic pryde,
Harland thair claggit taillis so syde:
I wald thay borrowstounis barnis had breikkis
To keip sic mist fra Malkinnis cheikkis.
I dreid rouch Malkin de for drouth,
Quhen sic dry dust blawis in hir mouth.
I think maist pane efter ane rane,
To se thaine tukit vp agane.
Than quhen thay step furth throw the streit,
Thair faldingis flappis about thair feit,
Thair laithlie lyuing furthwart flypit,
Quhilk hes the muk and midding wypit.
Thay waist mair claith within few zeiris,
Nor wald cleith fyftie score of freiris
Quhen Marioun frome the midding gois,
Frome hir morne turne, scho strypit the nois,
And all the day quhare euer scho go,
Sic liquour scho likkith vp also.
The Tutcunnis of hir taill I trow,
Micht be ane supper till ane sow.

                                  I ken

I ken ane man,quhilk swoir greit aithis,
How he did lift ane kittokis claithis,
And wald haue done, I wait nocht quhat.
Bot sone remeid of lufe he gat.
He thocht na schame to mak it wittin,
How hir syde tayle was all beschittin,
Of filth sic flewer straik till his hart,
That he behouit for till depart.
(Quod scho)gude schir,me think ze rew,
(Quod he)zour taill makis sic ane stew,
That be sanct Bryde , I may nocht byde it,
Ze war nocht wyse,that wald nocht hyde it.
Of taylis I will no more indyte,
For dreid sum duddroun me dispyte:
Nochtwithstanding,I will conclude,
That of syde taylis can cum na gude,
Spder nor may thare hanclethis hyde,
The remanent proceidis of pryde ,
And pryde proceidis of the Deuill,
Thus alway thay proceid of euill.

  ¶ Ane vther fault schir may be sene,
Thay hyde thair face all bot the ene,
Quhen gentill men biddis thame gude day,
Without reuerence thay slyde away,
That none may knaw I zow assure,
Ane honest woman be ane hure,
Without thair naikit face I se,
Thay get no mo gude dayis of me,
Hals ane Frence lady quhen ze pleis,
Scho wil discouer mouth and neis.
And with ane humill countenance,

With Uisage bair mak reuerence.
Quhen our Ladyis dois ryde in rane,
Suld no man haue thame at disdane,
Thocht thay be couerit mouth and neis.
In that cace thay wyll nane displeis,
Nor quhen thay go to quiet places.
I thame excuse to hyde thair faces,
Quhen thay wald mak collatioun,
With ony lustie companzeoun,
Thocht thay be hid than to the ene,
Ze may considder quhat I mene,
Bot in the kirk and market placis,
I think thay suld nocht hide thair facis,
Without thir faltis be sone amendit,
My flyting, schir, sall neuer be endit,
Bot wald zour grace my counsall tak,
Ane Proclamatioun ze suld mak,
Baith throw the land & Borrowstounis
To schaw thair face, & cut thair gounis,
Nane suld fra that exemptit be,
Except the Queinis Maiestie,
Because this mater is nocht fair,
Of Rethorik it mon be bair,
Wemen will say this is na bourdis,
To wryte sic vyle and fylhtie wordis,
Bot wald thay clenge thair filthy taylis
Quhilk ouir the myris & middingis traylis,
Than suld my wryting clengit be,
None vther mendis thay get of me,
The suith suld nocht be haldin clos,
Veritas non querit angulos.

                                    I wait

I wait gude wemen that bene wyse,
This rurall Ryme will nocht dispryse.
None will me blame, I zow assure,
Except ane wanton glorious hure,
Quhais flyting I feir nocht ane fle,
Fair weill, ze get no more of me.

Quod Lindesay in contempt of the syde taylis,
That duddrounis & duntibouris throw the dubbis traylis.

Kitteis Confession VII.

Compylit (as is beleiuit) be Schir David Lindesay of the Mount Knicht &c.

The Curate, and Kittie.

The Curate Kitte culd confesse,
And scho tald on baith mair & lesse,
Quhen scho was telland as scho wist,
The Curate Kitte wald haue kist,
Bot zit ane countenance he bure,
Degeist, deuote, daine, and demure,
And syne began hir to exame,
He was best at the efter game.
(Quod he) haue ze na wrangous geir?
(Quod scho) I staw ane pek of beir,
(Quod he) that sulde restorit be,
Tharefore delyuerit to me,

Tibbe and Peter bad me speir,
Be my Conscience thay sall it heir.
(Quod he) leue ȝe in lecherie?
(Quod scho) Wyll Leno mouit me,
(Quod he) his wyfe that sall I tell,
To mak hir acquentance with my sell.
(Quod he) Ken ȝe na heresie?
I wait nocht quhat that is (quod sche)
(Quod he) hard ȝe na Inglische buikis?
(Quod scho) my maister on thame luikis
(Quod he) the Bischop that sall knaw,
For I am sworne that for to schaw.
(Quod he) quhat said he of the king?
(Quod scho) of gude he spak na thing,
(Quod he) his grace of that sall wit,
And he sall lose his lyfe for it.
Quhen scho in mynd did mair reuolue,
(Quod he) I can nocht ȝow absolue,
Bot to my chalmer cum at euin,
Absoluit for to be and schreuin.
(Quod scho) I will pas till ane vther,
And I met with schir Andro my brother
And he full clenely did me schryue,
Bot he was sumthing talkatyue,
He speirit mony strange cace,
How that my lufe did me imbrace,
Quhat day, how oft quhat sort, & quhare
(Quod he) I wald I had bene thare,
He me absoluit for ane plak,
Thocht he na pryce with me wald mak,
And mekle Latyne he did mummill,
I hard na think bot hummill bummill,

He

He schew me nocht of Goddis word,
Quhilk scharper is than ony sword,
And deip in till our hart dois prent,
Our sin quhare throw we do repent,
He pat me na thing into feir,
Quharethrow I suld my sin forbeir.
He schew me nocht the Maledictioun,
Of God, for sin, nor the afflictioun,
And in this lyfe the greit mischeif,
Ordainit to punische hure and theif,
Nor schew he me of hellis pane,
That I micht feir and vice refrane,
He counsalit me nocht till abstene,
And leid ane holy lyfe and clene.
Of Christis blude na thing he knew,
Nor of his promissis full trew,
That satfis all that will beleue,
That Sathan sall vs neuer greue.
He teichit me nocht for till traist,
The comfort of the haly Gaist,
He bad me nocht to Christ be kynd,
To keip his Law with hart and mynd,
And loue and thank his greit mercie
Fra sin and hell that sauit me.
And lufe my Nichtbour as my sell,
Of this na thing he could me tell.
Bot gaue me pennance ilk ane day,
Ane Aue Marie for to say:
And Frydayis fyue na fische to eit,
Bot butter and eggis ar better meit,
And with ane plak to by ane Messe,
Fra drounkin schir Jhone latyne lesse,

Quod

Quod he)ane plak I will garf ande,
Giue the agane with hand bande,
Syne into Pilgramage to pas,
The verray way to wantounes,
Of all his pennance I was glaid,
I had thame all perqueir, I said.
To mow and steill, I ken the pryce,
I fall it fet on Cirtq and Syce.
Bot he my counfale could nocht keip,
He maid him be the fyre to fleip.
Syne crpit Colleris, berf, and Coillis:
Hois and fchone with dowbill foillis,
Caikis and Candill, Creifche and falt,
Curnis of meill, and luiffillis of Malt,
Wollin and linning, werp and woft,
Dame keip the keis of your woll loft.
Throw drink and fleip maid him to raif,
And fwa with vs thay play the knaif,
Freiris fweiris be thair profeffioun,
Nane can be faif but this confeffioun,
And garris all men vnderftand,
That it is Goddis awin command,
Zit is it nocht bot mennis dreame,
The pepill to confound and fchame.
It is nocht ellis bot mennis Law,
Maid mennis myndis for to knaw,
Quhairthrow thay fyle thame as thay will,
And makis thare law conforme thair till,
Sittand in mennis confcience,
Abone & oddis Magnificence,
And dois the pepill teche and tyfte,
To ferue the Pape the Antechryfte,

                          To the

To the greit God Omnipotent,
Confes thy sin and soir repent:
And traist in Chriſt , as wrytis Paule,
Quhilk ſched his blude to saif thy saule:
For nane can the abſolue bot he,
Nor tak away thy sin from the,
Gif of gude counſaill thow hes neid,
Or hes nocht leirnit weill thy Creid,
Or wickit vicis regne in the,
The quhilk thow can nocht mortifie,
Or be in Deſperatioun,
And wald haue Conſolatioun,
Than till ane preichour trew thow pas.
And ſchaw thy sin, and thy treſpas,
Thow neidis nocht to ſchaw him all,
Nor tell thy sin baith greit and ſmall,
Quhilk is vnpoſſibill to be.
Bot ſchaw the vice that troubillis the:
And he ſall of thy ſaule haue reuth,
And the Inſtruct into the treuth,
And with the word of veritie,
Sall confort, ane ſall counſall the.
The Sacramentis ſchaw the at lenth,
Thy lytill faith to ſtark and ſtrenth.
And how thow ſuld thame richtlie vſe,
And all Hypocriſie refuſe.
Confeſſioun firſt wes ordanit fre,
In this ſort in the Kirk to be,
Swa to confes as I deſcryue,
Was in the gude Kirk primitiue,
Swa was Confeſſioun ordanit firſt,
Thocht Codrus kyte ſuld cleue and birſt

FINIS.

VIII. The Justing betuixt
Iames Watsoun, & Ihone Barbour

Seruitouris to King Iames the Fyft.
Compylit be Schir Dauid Lindesay
of the Mount Knicht &c.

IN Sāctandrois on Witsoun Mon
  nunday,
Twa cāpionȝ yair māheid did assay
Past to the Barres enarmit heid &
  handis,
Was neuer sene sic Justing in na landis,
In presence of the Kingis grace and Quene,
Quhare mony lustie Lady micht be sene.
Mony ane Knicht, Barroun and Baurent,
Came for to se that awfull tornament,
The ane of thame was gentill Iames Watsoun,
And Ihone Barbour the vther Campioun,
Unto the King thay war familiaris,
And of his Chalmer baith Cubicularis,
Iames was ane man of greit intelligence,
Ane Medicinar full of Experience,
And Ihone Barbour, he was ane nobill Leche,
Crukit Carlingis he wald gar thame get speche
¶ From tyme thay enterit war into the feild,
Full womanlie thay weildit speir and scheild,
And wichtlie waiffit in the wynd thare heillis,
Hobland lyke Cadgeris rydand on thair creillis,

Bot

Bot ather ran at vther with ſic haiſt,
That thay could neuer thair ſpeir get in the raiſt
Quhē gētill James trowit beſt w Johne to meit
His ſpeir did fald amang his horſis feit.

I am richt ſure, gude Jamas had bene vndone,
War not that Johne his mark tuke be the Mone
(Quod Johne) howbeit þ thinkȝ my leggis lyke
My ſpeir is gude, now keip þ fra my knokȝ (rokȝ
Tary (quod James) ane quhyle for be my thrift,
The feind ane thing I can ſe bot the liſt,
No more can I (quod Johne) be Goddis breid,
I ſe na thing except the ſteipill heid,
Zit thocht thy braunȝ be lyk twa barrow trāmȝ,
Defend the man, than ran thay to lyke rammis,
At that rude rink James had ben ſtrykin doun,
War not that Johne for feiriſnes fell in ſwoun,
And richt ſa James to Johne had done greit deir
War not amangis his hors feit he brak his ſpeir.
Quod James to Johne, zit for our Ladyis ſaikȝ
Lat vs togidder ſtraik thre market ſtraikis.
I had (quod Johne) that ſall on the be wrokin,
Bot or he ſpurrit his horȝ, his ſpeir was brokin,
Frō tyme w ſpeiris none could his marrow meit
James drew ane ſweird w ane richt awful ſpreit
And ran till Johne, till haue raucht him ane rout
Johnȝ ſweird was rouſtit, & wald na way cū out
Thā James leit dryfe at Johne w baith his fyſtis
He myſt the man, and dang vpon the lyſtis,
And w that ſtraik he trowit þ Johne was ſlane,
His ſweird ſtak faſt and gat it neuer agane,
Be this gude Johne had gottin furth his ſword,
And ran to James with mony awfull word.
                                            My

My furiousnes forsuith now sall thow find,
Straikād at James his sword slew in the wind
Than gentil James began to crak greit wordis
Allace(quod he)this day for falt of swordis:
Than ather ran at vther with new racis,
With gluifis of plait thay dang at vther facis.
Quha wan this feild, na creature could ken,
Till at the last, Jhone cryit fy, red the men,
Ze red (quod James)for that is my desyre,
It is ane hour sen I began to tyre,
Sone be thay had endit that royall rink,
Into the feild micht na man stand for stink.
Than euery man that stude on far, cryit fy,
Sayand adew, for dyrt partis cumpany,
Thair hors, harnes, and all geir was so gude,
Louyng to God, that day was sched na blude.

FINIS
Quod Lindesay at command of
King Iames the Fifte.

Newlie correctit and
Imprintit at Edinburgh be Thomas
Bassandine, dwelland at the Nether Bow.
M. D. LXXIIII.

Date Due

			UML 735